D0487524

CAPTURED
MEMORIES
1900–1918

Dedication

This book is dedicated respectfully to the memory
of all those whose 1914–18 lives are documented
in the Liddle Collection of First World War
Archives Materials in Brotherton Library, the
University of Leeds

CAPTURED MEMORIES 1900–1918

Across the Threshold of War

by

Peter Liddle

Pen & Sword
MILITARY

First published in Great Britain in 2010 by
Pen & Sword Military
an imprint of
Pen & Sword Books Ltd
47 Church Street
Barnsley
South Yorkshire
S70 2AS

ISBN 978 1 84884 234 2

A CIP catalogue record for this book is
available from the British Library

Pen & Sword Books Ltd incorporates the Imprints of Pen & Sword Aviation,
Pen & Sword Maritime, Pen & Sword Military, Wharncliffe Local History, Pen
& Sword Select, Pen & Sword Military Classics and Leo Cooper.

For a complete list of Pen & Sword titles please contact
PEN & SWORD BOOKS LIMITED
47 Church Street, Barnsley, South Yorkshire, S70 2AS, England
E-mail: enquiries@pen-and-sword.co.uk
Website: www.pen-and-sword.co.uk

Contents

Acknowledgements

My appreciation must first be expressed in relation to all the people mentioned in this book and those who namelessly stand with them in being the subject of my interviews over the last forty years. I have clear memories of so many and I recognize the privilege bound up with my work.

That work involved the building of two archives and I must thank those in institutional responsibility at Sunderland Polytechnic (now Sunderland University) for sanctioning my commitment to rescuing 1914–18 personal experience testimony, then those in management responsibility at the University of Leeds for taking on a new 'special collection', and finally the Trustees of the Second World War Experience Centre in Leeds for their faith in creating the second archive. In these respects, HWL Miller at Sunderland, David Dilks and Reg Carr at the University of Leeds, Graham Stow and Hugh Cecil of the Centre in Horsforth were the men to whom I remain personally indebted in the laying of foundation stones.

Each stage in the building was facilitated by young people, as well as those in mid-career or more mature. For this volume, I have in mind of the young people Kevin Kelly in Sunderland, so well informed on the Royal Flying Corps, and in Leeds, Adam Smith and Matthew Richardson, laying down the foundation of their successful museum careers. With similar warmth of recall I remember Nick Gander and Andrew Cheney, also in Leeds.

From what might arguably be called 'middle age', Nobby Clark, Nell Sadler, Maureen Hine, Bill Lawson and Joan Henshaw helped me in the North-East, and of more senior years in Sunderland, Charlie Ward meticulously trawled through *Who's Who* and other reference sources for 1914–18 men and women while nonagenarian, Bill Weatherall, addressed countless envelopes to establish contact with those found by this research. If I were to have had a sense of mission, it was certainly shared by others. I shall not forget too the generosity of Brigadier Maurice Lush who did so much to fuel with encouragement and resources the development of the archive in Sunderland.

At the University of Leeds, I shall always affectionately remember volunteers Albert Smith, Gerry Godfrey, Braham Myers, all Second World War veterans, as I shall the years of selfless dedication to the rescue cause by Keith and Brenda Clifton. Terry Mumford, whose daughter, Carolyn, transcribed almost all of the interviews chosen for this book, was also dedicated to the cause of the archive transferred to Leeds, her husband, Trevor, generous in support of the electronic preparation of this book.

Retired businessman, Robert Carrington, for many years applied a shrewd mind, as indeed was the case with the veterans mentioned above, to recording the significant cross-references thrown up by the original letters, diaries and tape transcripts, thus facilitating student dissertations and the published work of historians researching in Leeds University's Brotherton Library. This recognition is just the place to express my personal appreciation for the unconditional support and benefaction given me by authorities in Brotherton Library. I thank first Chris Sheppard, Head of Special Collections, then Richard Davies and Kasia Drozdziak in particular for her work specifically in dealing with my requests for information and action when by definition she was helping so many others too. When photographs were needed, further members of staff were uniformly helpful. What a service is provided by this research source!

In my search of illustrations outside the resources of The University of Leeds I have come upon staff in a whole range of photographic archives who have been interested, helpful and friendly as well as professionally efficient. I thank the respective authorities for permission to publish photographs from The National Maritime Museum, The National Army Museum, The Imperial War Musuem, The British Library of Political and Economic Science, The Women's Library, the Museum of the City of Lloydminster, Manitoba, Canada, The Museum of Military

Flying, The Guards Museum, The Lancashire Fusiliers Museum, Beamish, The North of England Open Air Museum, and The Tyne and Wear Archive Service (Sunderland).

It is with pleasure that I acknowledge the special helpfulness of the following at their respective institutions: Andrew Choong and Julie Cochrane (NMM), Julian Harrop at Beamish, Andrew Routledge at Sunderland, Keith Male at the Museum of Army Flying, Gail Cameron at the Women's Library, Franklin Foster in Lloydminster, Darren Treadwill at the British Library of Political and Economic Science, Josephine Garnier and Edgar Aromin at the IWM, Colonel C Seymour, Regimental Archivist, The Grenadier Guards, Mike Glover and Tony Sprason at the Lancashire Fusiliers Museum, Emily Peters at The Henry Moore Foundation, and Juliet McConnell, researcher par excellence, at the National Army Museum.

Family archive help came generously from Mrs Margaret Jacob Hyatt (re: Gordon Jacob), from Mrs Mary Stopes-Roe (re: Barnes Wallis), and from The Lady Middleton (re: James Marshall-Cornwall).

This book would have taken so much longer if my beloved wife, Louise, were not to have dragged me to the fringe of modernity by teaching me to use a computer. In this and in so many ways my debt to her is inestimable but unreservedly acknowledged.

There are still more whom I might deservedly mention here and I must select two, begging forgiveness from anyone regrettably omitted. First a truly noble gentleman, Richard Campbell-Begg of Nelson, New Zealand, a Second World War Naval Officer, who tape recorded many 1914–18 and 1939–45 men and women for me in New Zealand. Richard sadly passed away in 2009 but I shall never forget him as an example of how one should live one's life, positively, and with goodwill to all. One element there may be considered within reach of most of us, but what about the other?

The other person who must be mentioned here is my friend, Bill Haygarth, whose companionship, first in work and then more significantly in retirement as I adjusted to it, I have found quite inspiring against any readiness to call it a day in academic activity. Weekly walks and coffee discussions on the progress of this book have kept me up to the mark and as knee and hip replacement operations curtailed the walking, Bolton Abbey tearoom has regularly resonated to animated discussion on both world wars from which I certainly have benefited.

Working with Pen and Sword has again been a delight and I would like to thank Charles Hewitt and all the staff in Barnsley for their professional skill.

The two archives, and by definition this book, would not exist were it not for the help I have outlined above. It remains for me in conclusion to recognize with overdue humility that the sort of work with which I have been concerned tends to become all-consuming. It can require an extraordinary degree of home support. I have been incredibly fortunate in this respect. Unfathomable thanks are due both to my first wife, Sheila, and to my wife, Louise. As adults now, the children from both families have shown interest and understanding in what drove me, sometimes excessively I am sure, to work on what I saw as pre-eminently important at the time. Thank you all for your tolerance.

Peter Liddle, Rawdon, Leeds

List of Illustrations

Bellpool, a foreign-built (1904) three-masted, square-rigged ship, docked in a British port; the sort of vessel in which Jimmy Hooper began his apprenticeship. [The National Maritime Museum]

Like Tom Easton, working at a colliery near Ashington, these are pit lads at Netherton, near Bedlington, Northumberland in 1908. [Beamish, The North of England Open Air Museum, NO30812]

Nellie Elson and her family attended a chapel like this one; Huddlestone Street Mission in Sunderland, 1900. [Tyne & Wear Archives & Museums]

Regents Street, London, at the turn of the century as Howard Marten would have experienced it. [R Wilkinson Archives]

J N Fletcher trained in man-carrying kites, as in this photograph. [Museum of Army Flying, Middle Wallop, Hampshire]

Margery Corbett Ashby (seated second right) campaigning for Women's Suffrage, photographed in New York in 1920. [The Women's Library, London]

Restored Hebridean blackhouse showing some of the features described by Donald Macdonald. [www.photoeverywhere .co.uk]

The sort of life which George Ives would have experienced in his first days in Manitoba: breaking land which had never been touched by a plough, probably from the summer of 1903. [Lloydminster Regional Archives/Barr Colony Heritage and Cultural Centre]

George Ives tried his hand 'On the Trail'. A typical I M Barr Colonist Outfit along the Trail in 1903. Most didn't have the billowing white canvas top now associated with 'prairie schooners'. They were loaded high with 'stuff'. [Lloydminster Regional Archives/Barr Colony Heritage and Cultural Centre]

Victor Goddard became an airship pilot. Here a non-rigid coastal-type is being drawn with some difficulty from its hangar under stormy conditions. [Liddle Collection (Goddard), Brotherton Library, University of Leeds]

Robin Money, on 5 May, 1915, in a communication trench near Houplines, Belgium. Engineers had installed the pump which Money is holding in an unsuccessful attempt at drainage. [Liddle Collection (Money), Brotherton Library, University of Leeds]

A letter written for Charles (Cecil) Hughes Hallett after the explosion and fire which injured the young midshipman. [Liddle Collection (Hughes Hallett), Brotherton Library, University of Leeds]

Manny Shinwell (standing) with his Agent, J Salmon, and a miner's leader, campaigning at a 1918 General Election meeting. [The British Library of Political and Economic Science, London; Ref: Shinwell 6/4]

The handsome fighter pilot ace, Peter Fullard. [Liddle Collection (Fullard), Brotherton Library, University of Leeds]

James Marshall-Cornwall, as a Major-General, c. 1937. [Middleton Family Archives]

Henry Moore in uniform, 1917. [Reproduced by Permission of The Henry Moore Foundation; Ref: 00000009]

Elsie Knocker in Pervyse, 1915. [Imperial War Museum; Neg No: Q105892]

Sub-Lieutenant Barnes Neville Wallis, RNVR, attached to the Royal Naval Air Service in 1915, aged twenty-eight. [Mrs Mary Stopes-Roe, family papers]

Henry Rich in the battledress uniform of the 120th Rajputana Rifles, Belgaum, India, 1914. [Liddle Collection (Rich), Brotherton Library, University of Leeds]

Henry Rich, serving with the Rajputana Rifles, endured the tragic Siege of Kut leading to defeat and capture by the Turks. Here the Norfolk Regiment is in trenches during this long drawn-out engagement. [Liddle Collection (WH Miles), Brotherton Library, University of Leeds]

Introduction

More than forty years ago, when I began interviewing older people about the life experience of their youth, time and again I felt the excitement of being taken, almost by hand, into circumstances which previously I had far less adequately grasped through the flickering, jerkily moving images of silent films. Workers in woollen mills, in coalmines and shipyards, or at harvest time on farms; city trams, eerily deprived of the noise of their straining wheels, power unit headgear, bodywork and peremptory bells; barefoot children playing street games with black-shawled women looking on from the doorways of back to back terraced houses; or perhaps soldiers overseas in South Africa driving horse-drawn gun carriages through rivers and up the muddy climb of the far bank, such scenes were familiar from the cinema but now interviewees were sharing with me the practical realities behind the black and white filmed images and I was seeking still further to explore their life at the time. From an early stage too I was keenly interested in their youthful reaction to whatsoever life had held in store for them.

In due course over the years to follow I was to seek out men and women for interview throughout the British Isles, then in France, Turkey, Australia, New Zealand, Canada, South Africa and the United States. I am fortunate in still being engaged in this work but it is time I think to share some of the fruits of the journeying more widely than just with historians.

My travelling has been in pursuit of the conviction that pre-1914, 1914–18, inter-war and 1939–45 memories, in the voices of the people concerned, must not be lost. We are all the losers, I have long felt, if this were to be the case.

My first recordings were made in 1968 and now, so many years later and with something up to four thousand recordings lodged in two archives, of course I remain convinced that oral history has its part to play in capturing the past for posterity and for the study of human experience in years gone by. However, for me personally, in being engaged upon this work, there has been life enhancement to an almost transforming degree. Yes, I may have tackled the work with sustained passion but again and again I have had the reward of meeting men and women with such individual qualities, such challenging life experience or exceptional achievement, that for their interviewer the encounter has been uplifting, even on occasion, unforgettable.

The recordings themselves provide invaluable vignettes into life long ago. Vividly detailed recall, the re-captured immediacy of an instance, an hour, a day, or longer in time, have been conveyed almost magically, letting the listener or reader of a transcript into events, emotions, periods, far gone. Pre-1914, I have in mind 'life before the mast' in sailing ship deep sea voyages; service with the Yeomanry in the Boer War; travelling with a party of 'colonists' to Canada and breaking new land on the prairie; suffragist activity; reliving conditions of harsh poverty; a collier's lot in the North-East; age-old simple living conditions in the Hebrides. Such has been my privilege to question and listen to the responses of men and women from all walks of life talking of matters of daily familiarity in their youth in years now so long ago.

Some of the memories in these recordings go back well over 120 years from our standpoint today. What a shame it is that my very first recording was made with love but without understanding in about 1951 and so must be discounted. It was made with my grandfather, then alert and seemingly defying his 90 years. Henry Liddle, an early member of the Amalgamated Society of Woodworkers and Joiners, had been a delegate at a meeting to try to resolve a pay dispute. On the tape he tells me of a Scottish industrialist who got up from his chair, closed his attaché case, and declared that even if the grass grew in the shipyards, 'Y'll nae get a penny mair frae me'. I have to admit that he told me the story with a merry twinkle of emotional recall in his eye. He had spoken of the industrialist with respect and the twinkle was not of course on the audiotape. Was something lost thereby, and I think I have to say yes. In any case I have disclaimed the archival utility of the recording but it does remind me of a still more vivid illustration of the limitation built into oral rather than audio-visual recording.

A man in Alderney told me of three years of POW life in Bavaria in 1915–8, adding the detail of compensation in his less than restricted incarceration on a farm. He had enjoyed the charms of the farmer's two young, men-starved daughters for much of the time. When I asked him, as automatically I would any POW: 'Did you make any attempt to escape?' there was nothing but silence on the tape. In my memory still today is a clear picture of his eyes unmistakeably making his mental response: 'What a bloody silly question!'

Returning to my grandfather, where and when did the incident he described so well, take place? Alas I did not ask – an illustration of sins of omission incurring as much regret as those of commission. However, I did begin seriously to record in 1968 and have striven to do better since.

But why is it though that we remember the tragedies in our work so clearly, often better than any perceived triumphs? In 1968, in Sunderland, a Mr Moir made a marvellous tape of the last months of the Boer War ending with an amusing if a little disreputable story of coming upon a newly vacated farm as his Yeomanry troop searched for a Boer commando. Looting a pair of women's long silk drawers, knotting the ends of the legs, pouring down one, oats, and the other, sugar, they placed the well-filled drawers on the back of a mule. Taking and emptying a used chamber pot, they tied this on to the mule too. Next morning, encamped on the Veldt, using the ingredients mentioned, heated in the potty, delicious porridge warmed the start of their day. The tragedy? The week the recording was made, the machine, with the tape on it, was stolen from the student using it for his work. I was insufficiently confident of Mr Moir's reaction to go back to him asking if I might re-do the interview and his story remains only in my head. The loss still grieves me but mercifully it is the only tape that has been lost.

At the time of my contact with Mr Moir, retired Masters of Merchant Navy vessels were beached in goodly numbers in South Shields and in Sunderland where I lived. You may imagine the frisson running up my spine when I found that numbers of them had had an apprenticeship in sail. There was much more excitement to come once I became fixed in fascination upon the First World War. As I widened my recording travels I was to learn that Hampshire held a rich harvest of flag rank Royal Navy officers and of retired airmen with distinguished records. And Wiltshire for example provided 1914–8 Army officers who had risen later to high command. *Who's Who*, meticulously examined, end to end, enabled me to contact men and women of the generation I was after and overwhelmingly I had a generously cooperative response. There were other sources profitably used, most notably the *British Medical Directory* for former Army doctors and surgeons and *Crockford's* which enabled me to establish links to former Army chaplains but marvellously put me in touch with some German soldiers whose Lutheran faith and appointments in post-1933 Germany led to their spiritual and bodily escape to livings in the Church of England through the good offices of the Bishop of Chichester.

Returning to the theme of what I found to be regional hunting grounds for kindred experience, 1916–18 conscientious objectors remained in some number in Buckinghamshire, in Lutterworth and more predictably in the Cadbury and Rowntree chocolate-making areas of Birmingham and York respectively. One thing or person led to another and, searching in the mid 1970s for conscientious objectors, I found eight or nine of the 1916 Death Sentence men still alive and ready to revisit their testing times.

This present book is to be the first of two volumes. Its datal span is 1900 to 1918 with its emphasis on the First World War. (The second volume will be dedicated to the inter-war years and the Second World War.) Coverage of 1914–18 experience will be wide but not comprehensive. The battles of the Somme and of Jutland are represented and so is the Dardanelles/Gallipoli campaign, the siege of Kut, life as a POW, as a fighter pilot, as a conscientious objector and as a nurse, but I want also to take the opportunity of sharing memories from some people who are well known for their achievements in their later years but whose Great War life is seldom envisaged as is the case for example of Victor Silvester, World Ballroom Dancing Champion and more famous still as a dance band leader. It may not be easy to imagine him as an under-age soldier in 1916 charged by lot with the duties of a firing squad and then later, released from the Army on account of his age, enlisting in an

Ambulance Unit and in Italy being awarded a decoration for rescuing wounded under fire.

Selection for inclusion from several thousand recordings has been difficult. The full range of the recordings I have made, and those made by others towards the same end, is available for consultation in the Liddle Collection held in The Brotherton Library, The University of Leeds. If you were to be interested in cricket, you will find Arthur Gilligan there, Hubert and Gilbert Ashton, famous for their part in the victory over Armstrong's all-conquering Australian tour immediately following upon the War. Internationalists will find Philip Noel Baker and Arnold Toynbee, devotees of vintage TV comedy will find Arnold Ridley of *Dad's Army* and Jack Warner from a still earlier favourite series too but here in this book it will not just be the famous you meet. I want to put before the reader some people who are likely to be unknown but whose life-story I found compelling by reason of special qualities they exhibited or exceptional experiences in which they participated.

Perhaps I should offer an explanation of how I came to be involved in this commitment (or obsession) of rescuing early twentieth century oral testimony. In essence and unsurprisingly it grew out of schoolmastering – teaching history, finding the subject thrilling and satisfying, the evidence all around but disappearing so fast. Fires had been lit within me not just to learn more, not just to convey the past more effectively, but to rescue where I could the threatened physical presence of the past in a world too busily preoccupied to see, never mind value, what it was losing.

As a schoolmaster and then as a lecturer in Teacher Training, I had explored avenues of historical enquiry for both an understanding of the past and the inculcation of a life-enhancing interest in times gone by. The examination of original documents, architectural interpretation, dramatic re-construction, field work, an attempt at immersion in the culture of a period, music, song and dance, a way of life and worship, all this was essayed. Then I came to a consideration of the part memory had played and could play in passing on some of the record of what had transpired in years long gone.

Within reach of every schoolchild there lay members of his family perhaps two generations more senior. The historical source material was there but I needed to train myself, and so to teach students, how to 'dig it out'. I began to practise oral history.

Teaching myself how to work to capture the memories of older people; becoming better and better informed on the social scene of their background, learning with surprise that what had happened and how they had felt about it, were not infrequently different from what my 'knowledge' had led me to anticipate; all this became a magnetic attraction. It was made the more so by an awareness that, just as I had tried to save pit pony harness from bonfires at collieries being closed in County Durham, and nineteenth century ledgers from warehouse damp in Sunderland, memory was just as vulnerable, but in this particular case, to increasing frailty and then extinction. It seemed that there was no time to lose.

Like the salmon, I rose to the bait, tempted by the fisherman's fly of historical evidence being lost. The lure which actually hooked me and drew me to the riverbank for gaffing, was the First World War. I met so many men and women who spoke of 'their' war with animation, a gleam in the eye as if nothing in their later life had matched the intensity of the experience of those years. With knowledge that I gained later, two things might be added here; first that many men clearly held to a quiet satisfaction at having proved able to accept the challenges which had faced them and second, that women had relished the opportunities afforded by the war, without in any way losing sight of the suffering and loss which befell so many. If I were ever to seek inner assurance that a lifetime of recording had been worthwhile, I could recall interview after interview relating to 1914–8 which would provide that blessing.

Properly conducted, oral history has for some decades now established a deserved reputation as an additional element worthy of consideration in descriptive evaluation of the past. Its practitioners had to work hard in books, articles, conference lectures and seminars to make their case against opposition, which sometimes seemed entrenched, with no attempt to reconnoitre into the no-man's-land where some were engaged in reasoned debate. The arguments will not be re-marshalled here. It is accepted that oral evidence can both confirm and challenge evidence drawn from a range of other sources and just occasionally there is such a paucity of evidence from other sources that we may breathe sighs of relief that at least we have something to go on whatever may be said about its subjectivity and fallibility.

What was I aiming for in my interviews? Consistently I tried to exclude latter-day judgements, comparisons and contrasts with circumstances and attitudes which have changed. I wanted my interviewee to be taken naturally from a quite detailed account of his childhood and upbringing, into the new circumstances to be described, with the freshness of just having come upon them as a nineteen year old with the influences of his background and personal make-up conditioning his emotional response.

I tried never to take my subject out of what he or she did, saw, felt, experienced, and I strove to explore precise duties, responsibilities fulfilled, so that they were described in detail. In this I believe I have been consistent in all my work but sadly, only for 1939–45 men and women, did I have the wisdom to allow them in every case the opportunity to offer reflective thoughts on the significance of their war years in shaping them into the individuals they were today. The evidence gathered on this alone offers I believe valuable source material for a future social scientist engaged upon research into the legacy of human reaction to the experience of war.

And now for the individuals selected: each one has the central significance of the interview given in the introductory heading. The date and sometimes the circumstance of the recording are noted. From long before I began oral work I kept quite a detailed diary and on occasion here I have found it appropriate to quote from my entries on the day in question. The person's date and place of birth, education and social background are summarized if they were not a part of the interview shown here, then there follows an edited transcript of the most compelling sections of the tape. In this volume all the interviews published here are held in The Liddle Collection, Brotherton Library, the University of Leeds.

When I was planning the book, it is true to state that to some extent I was moved by a sense of obligation to share more widely my privilege in drawing out these stories; as the work developed it became for me a delight affording so much pleasure in my recall of the men and women and the circumstances associated with the interviews. It is my hope that for those who read it, the book will give pleasure as well as an insight into the past.

Section One

Pre-1914

1

CAPTAIN JIMMY HOOPER,
Mercantile Marine

A 1904 Apprenticeship in Sail

There was something especially exciting about tape-recording my first man 'in sail'. In February 1973 in South Shields, in his home overlooking the sea and the estuary of the Tyne, I met Mercantile Marine Captain Jimmy Hooper, born in South Shields in 1889. He had a lifetime of deep-sea service in the Merchant Navy and the Royal Navy and in his retirement still with a sea view from the town of his birth, it was scarcely surprising that Jimmy's recall of days in sail was as convincing as it was fascinating. His father was a captain in the Merchant Navy and Jimmy left school at the age of fourteen to serve an apprenticeship in the same service. His first experience at sea was in a sailing ship in 1904.

My mother took me down to the docks at Barry, buying me my 'donkey's breakfast' – my straw mattress – and of course the belt and sheath knife which was a general utility knife because it was used for everything, for eating as well. Then she left and I was still in the apprentice's uniform and the ship's mate came to where I was standing a bit lost and said: 'You're a new hand are you, what's your name?' Then he said, 'Get those brass buttons off. You won't need them any more until you get to Sydney.' So he gave me the job of sweeping the poop (deck), the cookhouse and the accommodation clear of coal dust. That was the first job I had – sweeping.

The ship was full-rigged, carrying coal to Newcastle in Australia. She had three square-rigged masts. I don't remember the number of men in the crew but there were eight men in the watch and with the master, the mate, the second mate and the bo's'n, there was a carpenter, a sail-maker, a cook, and a steward.

I liked the challenge of climbing the rigging. We boys always thought it was fine to go running up the rigging. We soon learnt to get over and put the shrouds out and away up the top and, of course, you know when you come to think of it, only on a foot rope on the yard going out from the mast – just standing on the foot rope, nothing to hold you, only just when you were working with the sails, making sail or shortening sail. As soon as we got into warmer weather we were barefoot too and never bothered with shoes. Keeping your footing? Well it just came automatically. When I come to think of it I don't know how we used to hold on. You were just leaning against the yard blowing a gale of wind and heavy hailstones hitting you on the back or perhaps snow, numb fingered. Gloves were no use to you.

In bad weather you never got any sleep at all, hardly. You no sooner got turned in when the bo's'n's whistle would go: 'All hands on deck, shorten sail.' Later, back to your bunk, and you would just lie down with your sea boots and waterproofs on and soon you were called out again.

Bullying of apprentices? Well of course there was bullying. When I was a second voyage apprentice I remember the captain swore at me for something and I swore back and he just lifted his foot and he kicked me right off the poop onto the next deck, on to the lower deck. Then he didn't show any concern or apologise, he just said, 'Get out.'

Let me tell you about our living accommodation. There were four apprentices and they lived in what they called the half deck. We all had bunks. The bo's'n, carpenter, sail-maker and cook lived in the fore end of the half deck. The captain was king of the island, king of the ship, everything was under his authority. The captain's law was paramount. He could punish you in whichever way he liked and there was no one to say 'oh you can't do that', you know. If we apprentices did anything wrong, we were sent away up to the top of the mast for a couple of hours, stuck up there, and that was our punishment. But the men, if they did anything wrong it was in the logbook, an official log, and they would lose wages.

Our wages? Well, we apprentices didn't get anything because my father had had to pay forty pounds for my four year apprentice-ship. I can remember when we went to Sydney we used to get I think a pound and that used to have to last us all the time we were in Sydney. This would be from the ship owner who had taken me on as an apprentice.

The voyage to Australia from Barry took, I think, a hundred and five days. An interesting thing is that sometimes we didn't see sight of land till we arrived off Sydney Heads. My first voyage to getting back home took two years. You can well imagine I left Barry a boy and came back a man.

We were usually carrying coal from South Wales and from Australia we brought wheat. We also used to go to Chile to load nitrate for home but we had to work our own cargo you know and our own ballast. If we were going to Durban or Australia then we would go in ballast to Chile, Antofagasta, and there we had to discharge the ballast – sand or scrap-iron.

We had no intermediate stops. It was too dangerous with a sailing ship to be caught on a lee shore, so nearly all the ships used to go mid ocean all the way.

Now the food and its condition very much depended on the captain. My first captain, a Scotsman, hadn't got a good name. He was mean. He had to buy his own fresh water, you know. And then at Antofagasta, Chile, all the water had to come out in a lighter. Well, it was very expensive and he wouldn't part with a lot of money so consequently if we had a longer voyage home we would be short, we would be on water rations. The only thing we depended on was when we got into the tropics and got heavy thunderstorms and that replenished our water. When the water was rationed, the cook was only allowed to give a cup of tea, one cup of tea, and we only had water in the limejuice rations. We had to take limejuice on account of preventing scurvy you see. And the steward used to dish the lime-juice out every meal. Every dinner hour we were all lined up and we used to have the limejuice allocation.

The food? Hard biscuits. Sometimes we had to knock them for the weevils to come out. And that is quite true, not an old seafarer's tale. Little white maggots. This really depended on where you got your stores before you left. Whatever, we still ate them. With the biscuits we had salt pork and salt beef and soup three or four times a week, pea soup. I remember breakfast was a cup of coffee or tea and biscuits, and that's about all we got, I think. We used to soak the biscuits and make cracker hash out of it you know, break the biscuits up and the cook sometimes used to put a bit of salt beef in it.

You have asked me about accidents. We did lose a man overboard once. We were running reef down when a man fell off. If you fell off the yard in bad weather as we were having, there was no hope, because you couldn't heave the ship to. The sea was too big and, of course, he just went. I saw him go. There was nothing that could be done. If we hove to, we got caught broadside on and all of us would go. They threw a lifebuoy, but a lifebuoy wasn't any good there with the seas roaring along. You couldn't do anything. The seas could be sixty and more feet to the crest. When the ship's running, to be caught on the quarter sometimes she used to lie well over, the decks awash, full of water.

If a man died aboard, as far as ceremony was concerned, it all depended on the captain, whether he was a religious man or not. But when a man died I suppose the captain would have to check that he was dead. Then the sail-maker would come and sew him up in a bag, sew the dead man up in a bag. (It was common practice for the last stitch to be put through the man's nose, a grim means of certifying that he was dead!) Then he was put on a plank and the plank was on the bulwark and a couple of sailors at the other end and the captain used to read the burial service and then he would put up his hand and conclude with the well-known phrase: 'Commit you to the deep.' They used to lift the plank and his body would slide down into the water. And a bag of sand or pig iron at the bottom of the sack would ensure it sank.

Jimmy Hooper's four-year apprenticeship was spent entirely in sail. He was now securely launched into a maritime career, serving his tickets as a mate of rising status successfully in a range of vessels, most notably a Royal Mail ship chartered pre-war by a wealthy aristocratic Belgian family for a cruise. He also joined the Royal Naval Reserve which led to warship service in the Dardanelles in 1915: first, 'social', and then, 'active service' extensions of a lifetime's experience at sea.

2

TOM EASTON

A Northumberland Pit Boy

In the early 1970s I met and worked with many County Durham and Northumberland miners and although my particular reason for interviewing them related to their First World War experience I learned so much from them about their work in the area's pits pre-war that it became an especial commitment for me one way or another to play a tiny but very satisfying part in the rescue of the disappearing heritage of their work. My students and I persuaded authorities at the superb Beamish Open Air Museum that every effort must be made to secure an early nineteenth century coal sled which we had been shown in situ at Herrington Drift Mine. While the pit ponies from collieries being closed almost as we visited them were to be well-looked after, we were concerned that pony harnesses, the coal tubs or chauldrons, miner's lamps, a colliery's 'books' and other vestiges of an industry vanishing in the North East should go to some appropriate institution. Many others, some on a professionally grand scale, were engaged in similar rescue work and the museums of the area are the richer for the endeavour.

Accidents in the pits, Trade Union activities, disputes, working conditions and practices, were related to me vividly by many – I remember clearly to my discomfort mentioning to one man in Houghton le Spring the name of the man I was going to see next as I got up to take my leave: alas, in the judgement of the man I was leaving, the next man had been a 'blackleg', a strike-breaker, and visibly I had damaged the good rapport established in the previous two hours. A happier memory of Houghton le Spring is of the ex-miner in his late seventies easily getting to the floor to crawl beneath chairs and table to demonstrate the work of a hewer in a narrow seam.

Tom Easton's story of pre-1914 mining was not filled with the drama of accidents or disputes but it was told with convincing authority. I interviewed him in a mining village near Ashington, Northumberland, in April 1974.

I was born in 1896 near Bedlington. My earliest recollections are of a small colliery village which contained only three streets of houses. There was one coalmine, two Methodist chapels and a parish church. Of course, the pit was the focal centre of the village at most times, not forgetting the village school which was I believe partly owned by the coal-owning authority. In other words it was a colliery school. I remember my early days at school where we had one huge class with a schoolmistress and she looked after the whole of the intake – infants from five to seven I would presume. After that you went out into the various classes upwards in age to Class Seven. This or a year earlier was when you left school. I was happy at school and our teacher in Class Seven was a Mr Harper.

Of the streets in our village, in North Row, the top one, the top door as we called it, contained what we termed our overman and it held the colliery office where all work regarding the colliery was recorded. One room was set apart as a colliery office. They also paid the wages there once every fortnight. Any complaints or any questions or anything that had to be answered would be addressed to the colliery office. The colliery office was open for most parts of the day because one of the four overmen, which were the under managers in that sense, terminated his round of duty about 10 in the morning and during the day he would be available to meet most people who had any complaints or seeking advice concerning the colliery. In the evening, at 5 o'clock, I remember my father having to do this, at 5 o'clock the office would be opened when the night shift workers, or rather their charge men, would report at the colliery office. Also coming from the pit would be the deputy overman on the back shift. Now these people would meet together, compare their notes regarding their various districts and go on their way down the pit or down their way home because there were only baths in the houses in those days. There was no such thing as pithead baths.

The first shift deputy overman, he also had to come back to the office at 6 o'clock every evening when he got the directions from the night shift people and the four overmen to commence the first shift in the morning which would start at 3 o'clock in the morning. That was the whole round of business managed from the colliery office.

I don't remember any pre-war disputes at our pit but the 1911 Coal Mines Regulation Act did produce some very curious attitudes regarding the eight-hour day. You see, I had started at the pit in 1909. My colliery never went on strike but there were collieries which went on strike due to opposition to what we termed then as the three-shift system. I am talking about the Bedlington Coal Company, which owned five pits – A, B, C, D, E, and later F Pit. I worked at E.

Now I do remember the owner's agent coming to inspect the pit, a Mr Weekes was the agent then, and as it happened his son followed him. Mr Weekes would come in a carriage with two horses. A man would be set aside to get those horses and put them in the colliery stable and then the carriage would be put into the colliery yard. Mr Weekes would go down the mine and have a look round. Then the same thing happened. He would just come out and the horses were put in the carriage and he was taken home.

I should say that there were some very benevolent people in the coal companies in which I had to work all my life. I remember the marriage of one of these people and they put on a whole fête day for everybody within, not only my own colliery, but in the collieries all round and there was a whole day off for us for the marriage of this young lady of the coal-owning class. The old coal-owner person whose name I should remember well because it's the same as mine, she dedicated a Trust which is still in existence in my village yet, of what she termed 'The Easton Homes' where ex-miners live to this day free of any rent or anything else. I think there are ten or twelve houses in that group; 'The Easton Homes of Rest' still are maintained today.

Coming back to my own story, I began at the pit when I was thirteen. It was not as a trapper as you might expect (opening and closing the usually leather 'doors' at intervals along the underground 'roads' or 'ways' to regulate the circulation of air) because this wasn't practised in my colliery. I hadn't a great option for the pits. I had two brothers senior to me. My eldest brother was athletic. My next brother went into the mine, and then my parents had relatives who owned a building trade and they offered this type of work to my older, athletic, brother on the condition that the next brother would have to go there too so he would be constant guardian of this one. Well this looked a good idea to me. I didn't fancy the pit at all. I couldn't say I was any more academic than anybody else but I was wondering about what I might do in the future. My birthday was in July and I was still running about in October without any job to do. I used to help Mother. We were a family of six and I used to help all I could. However, I went past the colliery office on this Wednesday and the overman came out. He said, 'Here Tom. Why aren't you at school?' I said, 'I left school Mr Miller.' 'When did you leave school?' I told him I left school at the summer holidays. 'What have you been doing since then?' I said that I had just been helping Mother. He said, 'Get yourself away down here and be at the office tonight at 6 o'clock. I want to see you.'

I went home and I told Mother: 'I have just seen Mr Miller and he says I have got to go to the office tonight.' Well, she said: 'You had better go if he has said that.' I asked what it was all about. She said: 'I don't know but you will have to go.' So, I marched down to the colliery office at 6 o'clock after he was finished with the deputy people, you know. He said: 'Go away to bed and report to Mr Wood on the gate at half past 6 tomorrow morning.' I couldn't say anything. I was dumbstruck. I went home and they asked what the matter was and I told them. My mother said, 'I have got no clothes or nothing for you.' However, I got rigged up and reported the next morning. When I went to work somebody took a picture of me because I had a worn out old coat belonging to my father, I had a cap belonging to somebody else and I had clothes belonging to my older brothers and I had any old shoes that I could get hold of and that was how I presented myself at work that morning.

In the first instance, I had a job which was called 'carrying the pick'. You know miners used to have about ten picks for use in sequence on the one wooden shaft. The picks were brought up to the surface to go to the pick sharpeners for sharpening. Well, new boys were given this work. The picks came off the top of the coal-loaded tubs and they were thrown off on to a steel sheet. We boys had to convey them from there to the pick sharpening shop and you did that for half a day. Then after half a day you would have to return them back and you would have to remember all the 'districts' of the pit. You had to put them into the tubs, mark them for the district where they had to go to and that was your function every day and, oh yes, also all the drills engaged in the work had to be dealt with the same. So that was the first job all the new boys got.

My wage was 10 pence a day for 10 hours. You see, we had to return home for breakfast, which was from 8 to 8.30. You had to return home for dinner or lunch whatever you would call it. We always called it dinner. That would be from 12 o'clock to one o'clock. Those one and a half hours were taken out of your day's work with the consequential result that you had been 10 hours at the pit and you worked through to half past 4.

Then they brought you further up on to the 'heap' stage because all hewers had their own number on the coal tub that they filled. We called these 'tokens' in Northumberland. Well then, on the weighing machine, which is about six yards back from the shafts, there was a weigh-man there who weighed the tubs on behalf of the coal company. There was also a check weigh-man who watched the weighing on behalf of the miner. Then you were trained to call those numbers into the man and each sheet was marked off with all the numbers and whatever weights were on the pointers of those weighing machines, that weight was put in that line. So, at the end of the day, the man weighing the coal brought up from the pit could give the total weight of production half an hour after he was finished. Now he had to complete that weigh sheet, take that to the colliery office and it was telephoned straight up to the central office and they knew the output, within an hour, of the whole group of pits.

After you yourself had completed your 'heap' job, then you went on to your other job, a constant one. You moved down to where they emptied the coal out of the wagons by circular tip loss. Now we had to take the tokens off those tubs. Also the putter had a token. He was the man who had the pony. Well you see his token was not exhibited outside because he was paid by the score and not by weight.

Four tubs came up in the cage and we boys were responsible for two tubs each. We took all the tokens off belonging to the putters and we hadn't to mix them up or we would get into trouble. We put them all through one hole in the token cabin where on hooks up to two or three hundred tokens were hung. If the stone content of a tub was above, I think it was half a stone, that was 'laid out'. If the man who was checking that, found that for a particular tub that was the case, we had to surrender that token. The man checking this had a board on which he would chalk that token number. The master weigh-man would see this board and there was a deduction made of so much per ton for every tub that was 'laid out'.

The next move up for us as boys was as each cage was unloaded and the empty tubs loaded, we would let these other tubs away for the next cycle. My company was good this way. Unless you showed you wanted to go down the pit, they didn't put you straight down. You got used to working with tubs without injuring yourself. You had a sort of two-year probation till you were fifteen. If you were a bright lad, you could migrate into the token cabin to help keep the records in there.

At fifteen, they would say we want you down the pit next week. Down at the pit bottom it was usually a weigh-man who supervised your introduction to working below ground. After a week of becoming familiar with what went on, in some collieries, you were given a trapping job; that is opening the doors regulating the airflow to let a pony through and then shutting them. You are there for your shift with just your oil-fuelled 'midgey' lamp, for illumination, and you had to buy your own oil for your lamp.

You would then be told to get a pony and would have a driving course to learn management of the pony. We were responsible for the ponies hauling the coal tubs from the workings to the shaft bottom. We used to love those ponies and anyone mis-treating them was soon admonished. Then I had to become familiar with 'endless rope' haulage, steam-driven from the surface. And, by a system of wheels, bringing haulage power throughout the pit workings – very cheap and very good.

Ventilation in my time was no longer by furnace power but by electric fan, and, in our pit, conditions were good concerning both the atmosphere and the fact that it was not wet. Mind you, the hewers were working in very narrow seams, as small as two foot three. My parents would not allow me to be trained as a hewer, actually digging out the coal, nor as a putter, shovelling it from where the hewer was working, into a tub. I was still working on haulage and getting bored with it when I joined up, under-age in November, 1914.

3

NELLIE ELSDON

Working-Class Life in Sunderland

In December 1968, in one of my earliest recordings, as I was gaining confidence, Nellie Elsdon brought home to me the worthwhile nature of what I was doing. A rapport was established, she sensed my keen interest, she had a good memory and the capacity to convey a picture of a long-gone time. Nellie was part of my education and I remember her with appreciation today.

I was born in Monkwearmouth, Sunderland, in 1884. We lived in Mulgrave Street just behind Thompson's shipyard. My father, Hugh Hardie, was a builder's labourer. I had five brothers and one sister, but one brother died when he was twelve and one when he was twenty-one. My mother came from the Shetland Isles. She was very skilled at knitting; she used to knit Shetland Island shawls. My mother also used to make ginger beer – thirty bottles at a penny a time.

I went to Stansfield Street School when I was four in 1887 but you may be surprised to know that already I could read. I was always interested in reading and when I was at school I always had to read out loud to the other children, while they sewed, and my mother gave me a pillowcase to make and it took me a year to make it because I never did any sewing. I always read to them and we used to read this *Daisy in the Field* by Elizabeth Wetherell and some of the books of Katherine Mansfield.

Now I remember another reason I could read so early; my uncle, who came from the Shetland Isles but lived in South Shields, promised me a blue velvet bonnet when I could read.

We learned to write and do our tables copying from the board and we had a counting frame for our numbers too. At seven I went from the infants to the Girls' School at Stansfield Street. Here for example in geography we learned the capitals of the other European countries and I remember St Petersburg for Russia. We had to draw all the maps, and Italy was drawn like a shoe – all copied free-hand from the board. We learned about volcanoes and Mount Etna and then Vesuvius where so many were buried alive.

For scripture, every morning when we went to school, we had to read the Bible. We had to learn parts of the Bible and also sing, and there's things that I learnt in those days I still remember. We all learned the 23rd Psalm, 'The Lord Is My Shepherd' and I think it was the twelfth chapter of Romans and it started with, 'I beseech you therefore brethren by the mercies of God that you present your body'. I think that was it. As it happened we in our family were Presbyterians but nothing in school was taught in what might be called a denominational way.

Oh yes, I remember on washing day I could take my youngest brother – really too young for school – with me to school and the teacher used to give him a sweet when he came. That was just my youngest brother, I don't know if she did it with the rest of them. Mind you we had a Mr Young, Frosty Knuckles we used to call him because he always caned the boys on a frosty morning. He was tall, lived at Roker, and smacked my brother very hard.

A deep, but I have to say 'received memory' I have, is of our next-door neighbour being taken to the workhouse on Hylton Road. All her furniture was put outside her house in the street and a large horse-drawn sort of van took her and her goods to the workhouse. She died not long after.

Now another thing that was within my own experience was this. There was an old man and he was neglected by all his friends. My mother used to make broth every day for us and she always took a pot into this old man. And he died and after he'd died all his friends and relations came to see him and then they came and asked my mother if she would go and see him. She didn't want to go and they said that they would be very much annoyed if she didn't go because she had done so much for him. And when she opened the door and went in, he was in the corner of the entrance hall passage dressed up in his usual things and an empty bottle of whiskey tied in his hand. My mother told me he was held up straight by a long broom-shank up the back of his jacket. He was fastened to the wall. This was a Catholic Wake but my mother just screamed and fled, leaving them to carry on their singing, dancing, drinking and eating . . .

Now I remember one year when the men were all out of work. The Salvation Army in Roker Avenue opened their doors and the children went there for dinners every day. Everyone thought well of The Salvation Army, but my father had strong views about the Catholics. He came from New Luce near Stranraer and there was a lot of Irish labourers came over and he said they used to drink a terrible lot. They used to work on the harvest and he said there were some very bad characters among them. In Sunderland we never seemed to have much to do with them. Me father never had any use for Catholics.

To return to schooling and what we wore to go to school: boots and knitted stockings with garters to keep them up. My mother used to make us knitted petticoats and for school it was grey with a red border round. For Sundays it was white with a pink border. We had a knitted vest and we always had frocks. My mother made us frocks except for Sunday, and there was a dressmaker who made us a Sunday dress and we wore it one year for Sunday and the next year it was let down and if we were going to any concerts or anything like that we wore it and then for the next year it was ready for school. We had to change on a Sunday morning when we came from church into our ordinary things and take all our Sunday things off.

On Sunday morning my father would never have any newspapers read and the boys couldn't read Saturday's *Football Echo*. Of course when I was old enough I went to Sunday school too, at St George's, walking there and back across Wearmouth Bridge. It was a very old bridge built by Robert Stephenson.

You could also cross the river by ferry. We had the Ettrick's ferry from Thompson's, and every Friday night I had to go to an old aunt that lived down at the east end of the town. She was alone and my mother baked bread and I took two loaves and a teacake over the river by ferry to her every Friday night after tea. That was when I was about eight or nine. And every Saturday night my mother and father came over for me. I had stayed the night with my auntie and on Saturday we always came back through the old market and they were always selling things cheaply late on. One man would shout out 'a joint of beef'. And he would say it was so much and add, 'Oh I'll give you some chops with this,' and then, 'You don't want chops? Well, I'll put a piece of steak on and there's a pound of sausage, now there's some dripping. Nobody wants it?' And then it went on until you got a great bargain. And another man was selling plates and if nobody wanted them every one was smashed in the ground afterwards. 'A penny this plate, a penny this plate. Nobody wants it?' Over it went, drowning out the shouts of others selling their wares like that of the fishmonger's, 'Oily kippers. Oily kippers.'

Things were also exhibited in the market and I had an uncle – not a very good man but a clever man, he could paint and make models. He made a beautiful model of Durham Cathedral, charging a penny to see it then he raffled it twice and disappeared with the money and the model.

Another thing we did on Saturday evenings was to sharpen the knives on a board with a bath-brick and we knitted for so long and then my father used to make 'clippy' mats and we had to cut all the clippings up the size of a matchbox. We always had a new one for Christmas.

Every winter, every year when the herrings were in, a man used to come up the back street with cartloads of fresh herring and my mother used to get a hundred fresh herring. She cleaned them and she folded them in a wooden pail and in the winter nights when it was cold she used to boil a big iron pot full of potatoes, which were fourpence a stone, and we had to have a little brush and scrub all the potatoes before they went in the pan. And my father was very fond of these and at night there was a big dish put on the table and we all had our plates and we used to have the boiled potatoes and the fresh herring. She used to steep the herring, you know, during the day. We were well fed. And she used to get sheep heads and make brawn, and brain puddings, little dumplings with the brains inside. They were lovely and very good for you. She'd get a sheep's head for a penny. We enjoyed pan haggerty too – potatoes, meat, gravy, carrots and probably scrapings or leftovers. A very cheap dish my mother used to do was a cod's head with onions round it in the oven. When we bought cod at three pence a pound we always got cod liver too and so we had cod liver oil.

And every morning when I had to go to school I used to run and get a penny for the pot stuff at the shop at the end of the street. And we got celery and leeks and carrots, and turnip for a penny, and if everything wasn't just right my mother sent us straight back so the man got to know me and he said, 'It's no use you giving Nellie Hardie that, because her mother will send her back.'

I always liked to go messages. I would have gone anybody's messages or taken any child out that was going, and my sister didn't like to go messaging.

Coal was ten shilling a ton. We always had a good fire in the winter but you must remember we had to be careful in our use or consumption of everything because my father was only on, at most, twenty-four shillings a week. Yes, and there was one day my mother sent me for some cod and I just went to the shop in Roker Avenue and I said: 'A pound of cod and my mother wants it fresh?' He says: 'Go back and tell your mother we've just got stinking cod and I'm not selling it to you.' My mother really had a good sense of humour as well but everything had to be right.

Now for a treat my mother and father would take us to Whitburn, a mile or so up the coast. We sat on the rocks and we used to paddle in the pools left by the tide. My mother always read a book. But there was sports in Whitburn cricket field and my father always took the boys there and my sister and I used to sit and read or paddle in the sea. We took our teas with us. I think this was the only easy day my mother had apart from having a lie-down on a Sunday afternoon.

In the evening of course we went back to Enon Baptist Church in Barclay Street for the evening service, our name, Hardie, in front of us on the pew. After church it was to bed; we never stayed up late.

You asked about how our house was lit, well it was with oil lamps. I should think I'd be about eight years old before we had gas in the house, and it was just a gas mantle. The streetlights were lit by oil lamps, with a man with a ladder seeing to them. I don't remember when the streets got gas lamps.

Our doctor was a Dr Mitchell, medical surgeon to the town. He always came on horseback and he used to fasten the horse's reins to the handle of the door, and I always stood beside it and put me hand on the reins and I thought I was looking after the horse. Of course I was very small then.

When I was about eighteen I went and saw Harry Lauder in the Avenue Theatre and we used to go before I was married to the Harrison concerts in the Victoria Hall and then there was Madam Clara Butt and the last time we were there she sang *I Will Give You The Keys of Heaven* and *To Have and To Hold* and so on, and she was lovely.

Now as for football, I think I went to my first match at Roker Park when I was fourteen and it was soon after the ground opened. Would that be in 1898? We didn't pay, we used to sneak in. When my husband took me later and we went to a match at Newcastle, he paid a shilling and as ladies got in free I got in and had a seat. Of Sunderland footballers I remember the goalkeeper, Doig, who wore a skullcap to cover his bald head, and Arthur Bridgett, McCombie, Watson and then later the famous Charlie Buchan. The Buchan family lived in the same street as us and we were all great friends. After a match at home Charlie used to come and have tea at our house. This was in Horatio Street or Forster Street when we moved there. But how sad it was when they lost that Cup Final at Crystal Palace to Aston Villa just a year before the outbreak of the war I think it was.

Now I haven't told you of a vivid memory I have concerning the Boer War. Leaving school at fifteen I had gone to work in Auld's Bookshop in Union Street, but I had got a seriously bad cold and the doctor, for some reason, said I must not go back there to work. His wife asked my mother if she would allow me to go to them as a nursemaid. They had a baby a month old and a son six. Well I did and the family took me on their holiday to Ilkley. We stayed in a boarding house and were there when news came in of the relief of Mafeking. We went out with Mrs Campbell at night and we saw bonfires lit up in celebration all over the place and cheering, singing and dancing.

My father was a Liberal and at election times we used to go round the streets, with our little blue rosettes, singing to support their candidate:

'Vote, vote, vote for Sammy Storey.
Storey's sure to win the day.
With my little penny gun,
We'll make the Tories run'
And so on.

I forget the final line but in any case Sammy Storey finished up as a Tory!

Leaving politics to one side, you may not know that near the mouth of the river, at Hendon, the town held a popular regatta. The churches all entered boats and there were other boating clubs I suppose. My brother was in St George's boating club and my husband to be was in Enon Boating Club and we used to go up the river every other Saturday and have tea at Cox Green and have lovely times there at Girdle Cake Cottage. This would be in about 1908. We used to play cricket and other games on the riverbank. Then it was back to the Wheatsheaf, near where we lived, for ice cream for a penny or 'dreamers', that is ice cream and lemonade.

I should add that public transport in the town was horse-drawn trams running on lines. It's scarcely surprising that there was a blacksmiths at the Wheatsheaf which was quite a traffic hub in the town. The fare was a penny from Roker Terrace to the Wheatsheaf and a penny across the river into town from there. I think they got electric trams in about 1900.

Nellie got married just before the war broke out and in the continuation of this interview she related her memories of the war.

4

HOWARD CRUTTENDEN MARTEN

Middle-Class Life and Work in London

In 1973 I managed to trace a man with a wholly exceptional experience – the first conscientious objector to be sentenced to death in the First World War. His experience in that respect appears later in this volume but from my initial meeting a friendship grew and I came to visit him regularly on my travels south within the region of Chorleywood. He was born in 1884. His conversations ranged, most illuminatingly for me, on his memories of middle-class business life in London before the outbreak of the Great War. In May 1974 I persuaded him to talk more formally of those years.

I think the disappearance of the horse is probably the thing that would strike anyone returning to London today and by definition the increase or the appearance rather of mechanized transport. You see, London at that time was entirely given up, as far as transport was concerned, to the railway train which was more of a novelty than you might at first think; because steam trains for passengers were only some forty or so years old when I was born in the early 1880s and one of the most appreciated toys among boys were railway trains. But then the special novelty in London of course was the underground railway, a very smoky dirty contraption. It is amazing to me how people managed to keep clean under the circumstances because the railway window ledges were smothered with black grease and curtains had to be washed two or three times in winter to keep them clean. Men's shirts at the end of a week, cuffs and the separate collars particularly, would be filthy. Even under the most satisfactory conditions it was a job to keep clean.

As for the fog in London, I remember arriving at Victoria Station and I wanted to walk up towards Hyde Park Corner and I found myself walking round Grosvenor Gardens in a complete circle arriving back at the point at which I had started. The fog was so dense that I had completely lost myself. You could ask directions of a policeman or a postman and they would tell you, "I am very sorry Sir, I don't know where I am myself." A fog could last off and on for two or three days. It was a more regular feature of the November scene. Fogs were quite common. Every chimney in London was belching out smoke. All the domestic heating was all done by the open fire. Radiators were practically unknown. There was no central heating as we understand it. I think a few public buildings were heated by central stoves which fed some sort of boiler but it was a very primitive sort of contraption and many public buildings wouldn't have any heating at all.

Now as for public lighting, there was no electric light. Electric light was a rarity. It was just coming in but I only remember one public highway in London that was lit electrically and that was at Holborn Viaduct where they had a sort of bright, white carbonized light but otherwise all the shops in Oxford Street and Regent Street were all gas lit and that was even before the mantle came in. Shops like the drapers, Lewis and Evans, Peter Robinson's, were all gas lit and some with even open gas jets. Just the old fashioned spread, the leaf gas jet.

Of course, many private houses had no electric light, just ordinary gas jets that you have to light a match when you got in the room to light the gas. Anybody who will have seen that picture *Gaslight* will appreciate the conditions of having to light a gas light in the sitting room before you sat down to have a meal or read or have a conversation.

Now you might think that this lack of general lighting would have meant a great aid to the criminal but I should say there was far less widespread crime when I was a boy than there is now: far less crime in the streets. It was confined to certain areas and people avoided those areas. The back of King's Cross and parts of the East End were notoriously rough where, in the latter case, sailors docked at Wapping and so on but there was not the open crime that there is now.

For instance, I was engaged in banking for something like fifteen years and I don't remember a single instance of a hold-up as we get them now. Banks were not robbed openly as they are today. The bank that I was in was close to Piccadilly Circus and the only incident we had was some poor, starved, fellow throwing a brick through just before Christmas to get locked up. Not with the intention of robbing the bank but to get a week's lodging over Christmas. There was petty pilfering. Pickpockets and thieves and that sort of thing but there wasn't the big time crime that we get now.

What crime there was in the world of banking and finance was largely the handy work of the forger and the fraud: the man who cooked the books. There was a famous case in Liverpool where The Bank of Liverpool I think, was involved, called The Goody Case. It was a classic for many years and that was largely the result of ledger counter clerks forging the books. That was the common form of crime. A fraudulent cashier or a ledger keeper would keep a duplicate set of books. One for the bank and one for the customer so that his falsifications were hidden up from both sides. The bank would see one version and the customer would see another version until of course, eventually it was bound to be exploded. When I first went to banking, the old grills were fast disappearing. The cashier at that time had been protected by a brass grill in front of his till. Well, those gradually disappeared and the open till was the customary thing. Until, it is only recently they have had to invent these unbreakable glass shields.

You have asked me about the evidence of poverty, that is, from my perspective. It was very marked. You saw children without boots and shoes. That was quite common in some of the areas of London and I remember, I was at one time in my life associated with Quinton Hogg, the grandfather of the present Lord Chancellor, and he was a young man in comfortable circumstances and he was so concerned with the unhappy lot of the shoeblacks working round Piccadilly Circus and The Strand and so on, that he spent a week or so working as a shoeblack to investigate the conditions of their life and from that arose The Regent Street Polytechnic. He opened a club for these shoeblacks in one street and then that grew out of all knowledge until the institution which became known as The Regent Street Polytechnic was the ultimate outcome.

He was a man of great stature. I think one of his activities was in the West Indies. He had interests there but primarily he was the Chairman of the North British and Mercantile Insurance and he still, with all his commercial interests, maintained a very close interest in the work of The Polytechnic itself. There was one rather quaint touch. When they formed the Day School which operated in connection with The Young Men's Institute, he used to stand on the steps of the main entrance of The Polytechnic and insist on shaking hands with all the various boys who entered the building and he wouldn't, as it were, take no for an answer. A boy had to go through the ritual of shaking hands or he was called back. He was a wonderful man.

I have no direct personal knowledge of the so-called 'sweated industries' but by the interest of my parents in what was known as The West London Mission, operated by the Wesleyan Methodists in west London. The Wesleyans maintained, in addition to their resident chaplains, a sisterhood – somewhat on the lines of The Salvation Army – and it still survives in its modern form in The Kingsway Hall. I think Donald Soper is their presiding man but one interesting sidelight of that sisterhood was that most of the sisters were known by their Christian names. Sister Gertrude, Sister Emily and so on and one of them, Sister Emily, was the original Emily Lawrence who was prominent in the women's suffrage agitation. I think her husband too was also very active in the women suffrage movement.

Moving on to another subject, entertainment. The first thing I would stress is that with the middle classes there was much more entertainment in the home. The music hall wasn't looked on as a respectable place for the middle classes and the theatre was very largely, as far as what were then known as the expensive seats, were occupied by the elite and the aristocracy. The class distinctions were much more marked in those days than they are now.

Of course if you went to the music hall you could get a seat for a few pence. I remember for a time the old Lyceum Theatre was turned into a sort of popular music hall and you could get a very respectable seat for about three pence or six pence at the early house.

I was brought up in a fairly strict circle where the music hall was rather taboo. I did go later on but when I wasn't really able to go I saw the bills outside The London Pavilion. We had friends living in a private house at Piccadilly Circus, which is a thing one can hardly visualize today. The husband kept a surgical instrument business. He had a shop and consulting room and then the rest of the private house in which they lived. They occupied the whole building and I believe in the basement they actually had a forge which seems incredible in these days but that was necessary because they were working in metals for building up some of their surgical instruments. I suppose they would be necessary in the case of false limbs and so on. There were certain metallic parts that had to be forged.

There were very distinct forms of entertainment which have gone out now. There was of course, the concert hall which was very much in vogue. Wigmore Street where I lived for a number of years had two or three famous small concert halls. Then, among musical circles, The Queen's Hall was almost paramount in those days. It held a unique position. It was a very fine building for its acoustic properties, which are far better than the bigger Albert Hall. They have a lot of trouble with the Albert Hall and they had to string certain wires across the roof to overcome it. I think it was an echo that was giving a lot of trouble. Then there was St James's Hall, Piccadilly, which was famous for its ballad concerts.

Moving more specifically to my family, my father was a chemist, an unorthodox form of pharmacist, a homoeopathic chemist. Homeopathy came in with the Prince Consort. It was a special form of pharmacy based on a principle of what is known as like curing like. For instance if a person had a high temperature you gave a modified form of a drug which produced a feverish condition and the whole basis of homoeopathy was framed on that principle of like curing like in minute doses. You gave it in a dose of almost tiny proportions. It was very interesting. I was talking to somebody a few years ago at The Healing Association and he mentioned to me that it is rather curious the number of homeopaths I met in the Indian Army when I was in India. I said, that can be easily explained by the fact that Lord Roberts and particularly his good wife Lady Roberts were very keen and I think the principle was almost laid down as a military order in India and that accounts for the fact that so many members of the old Indian Army were versed in its principles.

Returning to the subject of transport: there were three grades of railway carriage and I think that rather settled the principle of life, First, Second and Third. I believe in France at that time there were Fourth Class carriages but I only knew that from later when I went on my fateful journey to France in 1916. Of course, it is difficult for us in these days of electricity to visualize the smoke of these trains. All trains were steam driven, there were a few electric lines but they were very few and far between. I remember up Brixton Hill they had a sort of cable car but I think that cable may have been on a hydraulic principle but it wasn't electrically driven.

In London now, the first line of importance, and I remember its opening quite well, was just the time I left school; the Central London Railway, from Shepherds Bush to the Bank. It was known as the 'tuppenny tube'. You paid one fare of two pence whatever distance you travelled.

You have asked about newspapers and libraries: well the public library had this strange system of indicators right across the serving hatches or wherever they distributed their books. There were big indicators with all the numbers of the books in stock and if the book was in the library it was left in a blue. Then when it was taken out the indicator was altered so that the number then appeared in red and you didn't take the books. The shelves were not open as they are now. You handed your book to the librarian with a list of what you wanted. She returned the old book to its proper place and altered the number. Then she looked to see whether your numbers were in. That was a help to her but the indicator was the method by which it was known whether books were in circulation or not.

You couldn't look at books off hand. You had to know the book you wanted or you had to look through the catalogue. The catalogues were open to the public but I don't remember any opportunity for examining books as you do today on the shelves. You had to know the book you wanted.

Concerning newspapers, the strange thing is that newspapers were much cheaper than they are today and I should think managed to exist on smaller circulations than is necessary now to keep a big national daily going. I remember the *Daily Mail*, which came out as the first halfpenny paper. That was about 1897 when the *Daily Mail* came out. That was a morning paper and that created quite a flutter to bring out a halfpenny paper. Then it was quickly followed by several other morning dailies and they remained at a halfpenny for some years.

My family supported The Liberal Party and our papers were *The Daily News*, always associated with Charles Dickens, *The Daily Chronicle* and *The Morning Leader*. I should say that *The Morning Leader* would be the most left of that lot and then *The Daily Chronicle* more to the right and *The Daily News* about midway. Then *The Telegraph* was very much what it is today the hallmark of solid respectability, which would to some extent apply to the *Liberal News Chronicle*. One of the most respected Liberal papers, as it is regarded now, was *The Westminster Gazette*, famous for the cartoons of F C Gee. There were several very fine cartoonists at that period and then there were the other Conservative and Liberal evening papers, *The Pall Mall Gazette* and *The St James's Gazette*, and *The Globe*, which was very much a financial paper.

Quite an unusual thing; *The Globe* published a whole page of Stock Exchange quotations for that day. Well, you get no evening papers now that publish the whole range of Stock Exchange quotations the same evening. I don't think in some respects, we have progressed as far as time and promptness are concerned. You take the postal arrangements. You could post a letter in London and it would be delivered the same day. In fact, in time for you to reply that evening and then of course, there were collections at the pillar boxes every hour and deliveries every hour up to about 9 o'clock at night. The postal service was far superior to anything we know now. I remember as a boy when my father was in business that it was quite common for us to hear the postman knock at 9 o'clock at night. We knew there was a 9 o'clock delivery. I don't want to exaggerate but certainly ten times during the day.

How much did letters cost? A penny. That was the famous Rowland Hill Penny Post and it went on for years unaltered; and unsealed letters, receipts and so on, a halfpenny. We didn't have the violent fluctuations in postal rates that we get now. That went on year in, year out.

Now as for public transport other than the railways, the

omnibuses were much more used, the horse omnibus, and then types of hackney carriage; the four-wheeled hackney carriage, the one horse, a very broken down looking affair known as a growler, and then the hansom cab with the two people sitting side by side and the driver perched up at the back. They were looked on as the more superior type of conveyance to the growler, and then of course private horse vehicles were much more common and the aristocracy, so called, often used their own two horse vehicles, grooms and carriages, and I have seen more than one case of coachmen and footmen with powdered wigs. That wasn't at all uncommon in the area around Mayfair and Belgravia and it wasn't remarked on as anything unusual. You could see them round Rotten Row and the East Carriage Drive, which in those days was strictly limited to private conveyances. In fact, they didn't even allow hackney carriages so that the only form of horse vehicle allowed in the Park, except in one road, was private carriages, no buses or any form of public transport were permitted.

Again moving to another subject I must stress one thing, political meetings were far more frequent and evident than today. A general election would last for a week. We didn't have one day for voting as we do today. The election might start on the Monday and go right through until the Friday and it was rather interesting to follow the results through because it was quite evident that the sway of voting in one direction would influence the voting the following day and it was a great feature for Londoners to go out and see the results being placarded up in prominent places – Trafalgar Square and Fleet Street, Oxford Circus; screens would be there and crowds would watch the results.

I remember well the 1906 election when the Liberals returned with an enormous majority and that I think was one that went on for a long period.

As for the advent of socialism and whether it set up apprehension among the middle classes: no, it came in more like a tide, unobtrusively and quietly. At first the socialists weren't known as socialists except for one paper, they were known as The Labour Party and most journals referred to them as Labour. It was only I think the *Daily Mail* that insisted on labelling them as socialists. They didn't encourage the idea of socialism themselves and it wasn't at all in the minds of many of the original founders of The Labour Party that they were necessarily adherents of socialism. The Labour Party was formed, as I understood it, to advocate the interests of the labouring classes of the country. Socialism was a political theory and did not form part of the political system of this country in those days. It was a one-man band almost at one time and Keir Hardie was the only Labour Member of Parliament. John Burns, who espoused the Labour cause, was a Liberal. He sat in the Liberal interest and the 1906 Parliament was made up of something like 300 odd Liberals and round about 100 Labour members with the Conservatives making up a very small minority.

Mind you, I have always had the feeling myself that the political differences are very much exaggerated for public consumption and among themselves. It is unquestionable there were certain men who put up for Parliament purely as a matter of self-interest and they would adopt the party that they thought was going to suit their own interest but had no great, deep political convictions of their own. It is not to say that there weren't many others who held principled views.

If we consider for a moment the issue of women's suffrage: I think most middle class people were strongly opposed to the movement. They weren't against women's suffrage but I think in the early days the militant methods of the Women's Social and Political Union, to put it bluntly, disgusted them and many people who were sympathetically inclined to the idea. I myself never, although I was a youngster at the time, but I could never go with the militant methods of the breaking of shop windows and things like that, I felt their methods were completely inconsistent with their honourable aim. It may have achieved results in the end but it is not a method which I personally liked. I always considered if one disagreed with a political movement, well, you just came out and said so. As you know from my later experiences, I didn't mince matters. You couldn't hedge on certain things that were matters of principle.

Returning to education, I went to the kindergarten school attached to the polytechnic. There was a girls' school with a kinder-garten branch and I had the advantage of going right through from that and then when we passed into what was known as the transition form, we had to choose which branch of education we would adopt at about eleven years of age. We could either go to the Commercial School or the Technical School or the Professional School. There was no examination for it but a boy or his parents selected which branch he would go to and to my mind that was a pretty advanced method of arrangement which the parents chose. I don't know looking back whether I might have fared better if I had gone into the professional side but with the commercial side we took bookkeeping, shorthand and typing. I think now it would have been very much better if they had included economics because I think most schools suffer from children not being taught some elementary form of political economy.

Some other youthful memories? I remember the Serpentine being frozen over and that was a pretty drastic winter. For about a week or two they had in the evenings men with torches and chairs hiring out skates and my recollection is that the winters in London at that time were much more severe than they seem to be now. Whether it is imagination or not, I put it down to the fact that there is far more heating. For the horse omnibuses in the winter, they would lay straw on the floor to keep the passengers' feet warm and another curious custom in the London streets, if there was an illness in the neighbourhood, it was the custom to lay straw in the street. It was particularly noticeable in the West End of London – streets like Grosvenor Street and Mount Street and Brooke Street and the area round Mayfair.

The laying of straw was very common to silence the traffic. The only noisy traffic was the tingling of the bells of the hansom cabs. When we lived in Wigmore Street, that was on the main mail route from Paddington to the General Post Office, you had a continual run of traffic all night long but it wasn't the same sort of rumble that you get from the motor car. It was a much more modified sort of noise.

In my boyhood the old street cries were still heard but were falling into disuse. I do remember the Muffin Man, the Hot Potato Man, the Hot Chestnut Man. I remember an old chap going round with shrimps. In fact, he used to get the nickname of 'old shrimp'. Nice fresh shrimps and bananas were very common. You could get bananas at half penny a piece.

Just round the corner from where we lived, at 55 Maddock Street, in Bond Street was a famous violin shop, Hills. They were quite well known makers of violins and then along the other way, Chattles, the piano people, and then the perfumery business. One firm I became connected with, when I joined Unilever later, was Atkinsons. At that time, long before they joined the Lever concern, I believe they used to compound their perfumes in the basement of their Bond Street shop. Of course, the business of perfume compounding is a very complex one. Many of the ladies of that period, it was quite common for them to order their own distinctive perfumes and these perfumes might contain as many as a hundred different ingredients. So Lady X would have a special blend of perfume. It wasn't a case of going to Woolworths and buying a bottle of Californian Poppy. It was all specially compounded.

It was the same with most businesses. For example the bootmaker – each customer had his or her own particular last. I am speaking of the more well-to-do, but I don't think you would find many people now having their own particular boot and shoe lasts and then another thing, the silk hat was much more common. An office boy could wear a silk hat without its being exceptional, I did as a junior in the bank. I often wore a silk hat and never attracted any special attention and it was quite common if you wanted to get the silk hat ironed, that ironing process was carried out at almost any hat shop free of charge and many hairdressing establishments did silk hat ironing. It was quite a feature of business at that time.

Then of course, eating out has altered considerably. There were very humble establishments for the less well-to-do, the sort of sausage and mash type of place. You saw the stuff being cooked in the window and then there were restaurants of not the most famous. Not like the The Strand Palace, but places where the middle-class man could take his wife for an evening out. You could get a very substantial, satisfactory meal for about half a crown. Steak and chips would cost something under 2 shillings. Drinks were in proportion to that. The Lowther Arcade was another famous place in The Strand. It was made immortal by a song about the little tin soldier.

Preceding or coinciding with the beginning of the moving

picture, a lot of places were opened for roller skating. It was a very short-lived craze. I think it must have been just before the growth of the picture palace. I remember the earliest moving pictures I saw. That was at the Polytechnic strangely enough. They hired the great hall of the Polytechnic and the one I saw was a picture of men leaving or moving into Portsmouth dockyard. Then, of course, another thing that arose at that time was the picture postcard and the earliest ones that I recollect were 1897 when they brought out a special pictorial card of the Diamond Jubilee and I don't remember many picture postcards prior to that. There were a very few issued at the seaside, the comic cards and the pictorial cards, but by the beginning of the century cards as such had begun to establish themselves and the picture card has kept its popularity ever since.

Yes, I remember something you might be interested in; it was very usual in those days for people of all classes to stand outside the mansions of the well-to-do in Grosvenor Street and the adjacent thoroughfares to watch the opulent aristocracy going into their dinner parties and so on and I remember Lord Randolph Churchill, the father of Winston Churchill. He had a mansion at the corner of Grosvenor Square and I remember we were walking back from the Park one evening and I think I was with my mother and one or two others and they said, 'let's see who is going in there,' and we stood at the entrance and watched everyone going in and a young swell turned up and I was standing there, and he tipped me half a crown. It could well have been Winston as a young man. It would have been a fellow of about his age but I have to say that I am not sure. It might have been any other guest going into the house.

All of central London was a mixture of residential property and business accommodation; the loss of this mix I deplore, tradesmen living above their business premises. Can you imagine a better combination of business life and private life? I think we have lost an enormous amount in the life of the city by this separation of the two. You see, all the streets of central London were designed in that way. It is true that Edgware Road, for instance, the private houses where there were front gardens, the gardens were turned into shops and they lost their gardens and now they have mostly gone but they have been turned into big blocks of flats and other premises but the old shops of Edgware Road were very long. By using up their own gardens they had converted them into long narrow shops.

It was in that area that Marks & Spencer had their first penny bazaar. I think it was one of the Marks who opened the penny bazaar there and Lyons teashops. I don't think I remember them before the turn of the century. Before that, about the 1890s, their first tea shops were at Piccadilly Circus and Oxford Street.

Of course lots of customary practices have now gone like that of people going shopping in their private vehicles and the proprietor or manager of a business was called out to attend them at the kerbside. He would have to wait on the lady sitting in her carriage and attend to her requirements in that way. I remember my father often having to go out of his shop to attend to the requirements of a customer.

The coachman would come in and say, 'Mrs So and So,' or 'The Honourable Mrs So and So,' or 'Lady So and So. Would somebody please attend to her?' and that was quite customary and also in the shops there were rows and rows of seats, chairs. It would have been unthinkable for a customer to be allowed to stand in the shop and wait for attention. A shop walker would be waiting at the door and as soon as the lady appeared, 'Oh this way Madam. Madam, please be seated' and Madam did take a seat.

You have asked about my memories of the immigrant communities of London. Well, the earliest form came to my own knowledge because I came of Huguenot stock and some of my forebears actually settled in Spitalfields in connection with the silk industry. I had on my maternal side some generations back an old lady came over with her daughters, was smuggled over by a Dutch trader and they settled in Spitalfields and in the family's possession we had a sort of certificate of an enemy alien. The family of that time had to register as enemy aliens during the times of the Napoleonic Wars. So that the registering of enemy aliens is nothing new. It was operating as long ago as 200 years back nearly.

Then there were definite pockets of aliens in various parts of London. For instance, there was the Italian quarter round Hatton Garden and then round Goode Street off Tottenham Court Road there was a large German and Dutch colony. The Germans had a very close hold on the hairdressing business. Nearly every hairdresser of note in London at that time had a German name. That was before the First World War.

I remember the German band playing in the street; about eight or nine men playing different brass instruments. They were a very crude sort of music but they gave the streets some life. The streets were so comparatively quiet that a woman could walk down the middle of a road singing a mournful ballad in a dreadful voice for the benefit of such audience as she could attract and this could be in the middle of the West End. In the streets, I don't know whether in Bond Street or Oxford Street, it would have been practical even then but certainly in the side streets. The street we lived in, Maddock Street, or in Grosvenor Street, it was nothing for a wandering singer to walk the whole length of the street signing as she or he went and then there were vendors of all sorts of descriptions. We had a chap who used to come round, we knew him as 'old beard', a venerable old bearded man and he dealt in old prints and pictures. They were all very cheap reproductions and then fruit sellers were very common. I think we were fairly tight on the vendors. He didn't have such a free run as he gets today. They got moved on much more quickly by the police.

The police had comparatively no traffic problem as we understand it. That has added immensely to the duties of the police and the fire brigade of course, that was a primitive affair to what we know. They were all horse-drawn vehicles. The fire engine had no form of signalling its approach so the men had to stand on the fire engine and shout and that was their signal for clearing the way.

You won't be surprised that prostitutes were very evident in Piccadilly where I worked. In the daytime it wasn't much in evidence but a prostitute there was known as a Piccadilly girl. That was a common expression of the time and the whole of that area between Bond Street and Regent Street and further, was very much confined to the activities of prostitutes at night. Their trade was blatantly and openly advertised. You could almost tell a prostitute by her walk and attitude and posture. A person who was well versed in the life of London could be pretty well clear on picking out a prostitute by her calling.

I must not forget demonstrations and strikes. They have always been with us but they were much more heavily repressed then. I think the police had a much tighter control of industrial troubles than they do today. Obviously the power of the trade unions has advanced to an extent that would have been unheard of in Victorian times.

It is interesting to note that areas of London very largely hold on to their trade links. Tottenham Court Road to this day is very largely restricted in the larger businesses to the furniture trade but in my young days there were several very well-known furniture businesses. There was in addition to Maples, which is still there, a firm called Shulbreads and another firm on Hampstead Road. Just as drapers did in Oxford Street. One feature that has dropped out of London was the number of cloth warehouses and drapery establishments, wholesale drapers in the City. In my young days there were several very large wholesale drapers situated in the centre of London. I think one could have picked out a dozen very large wholesalers, which have mostly gone to the West End now.

Of the big department stores, it is a strange thing that I believe from all one heard at the time, Selfridges in its infancy was in a very precarious state. It was very much of a toss-up whether Selfridges would succeed or not. It wasn't so much that people had doubts about them. I think really they had a difficulty in establishing themselves. Now I remember Harrods when they had two little shops in Brompton Road. One was devoted to meat and the other to groceries and that is how Harrods began and I remember entering in those two shops and they were very high-class shops but they were confined to the two small shops whereas in Knightsbridge their great block stands today.

I should mention that there were a few hotels still left in the City as such. Of course, at one time the City was the recognized centre for hotels. Then it gradually shifted to the West End. Northumberland Avenue had several large hotels, which I think would be the centre for the more lavish display and there were very few middle-class hotels.

If a middle-class woman wanted to get a meal in London it was very difficult for her to find a suitable place. She wouldn't care to go to the more fashionable establishments in The Strand. You would be rather marked out as a woman alone going to a place of that character and then of course, the coffee house type of place, was a little bit dubious too. There again a woman wouldn't care to go into those. They were very rough.

Let me mention the telephone. In my day the whole London telephone directory was the quarter of the size of one volume today and people were very slow in taking it up. The banks wouldn't go on the telephone for a long time and many businesses refused to have their numbers put in the directory. The banks were wary of the phone because they were afraid it would be used improperly. People would be ringing up for other customers' balances and trying to make transactions over the phone and although my father was a chemist, and the phone became necessary, it was a long time before he went on the telephone. I think it was the turn of the century before we went on the telephone and of course, the telephone was a very primitive kind of instrument. You wound the handle at the side to make your connection.

Oh yes, then there was a service, the District Messenger Service, and you could hire a messenger to do almost any job for you. If you wanted a child seen across London you could hire a district messenger to take an infant across the road. There were all kinds of services available. The business community in my opinion had a much greater sense of service than we have today. You could get anything done. The customer was the first consideration of the tradesman. The tradesman wasn't so concerned, now this seems a strange thing to say, but he wasn't so much concerned with his profit. He was concerned that the customer got what he wanted and nothing roused his indignation more than to see a customer disappear without being satisfied.

As for the sending out of bills in my father's business, he only sent bills out twice a year though there were one or two larger accounts that I think he made more frequently. He had one boy to help him in the shop but I should add that convention and need decreed that my mother could not have managed without a maid, but then a London house of our type with a basement, a shop in between and then three floors above had no water laid on except one cold water tap. No hot water system. The only way of heating water was a gas ring apart from the boiler at the side of the open fire. Everything was done on an open fire. There was a boiler at the side of the fire. There were no bathrooms. If you wanted a bath you had to have a hip bath in the bedroom and all the water, hot and cold, had to be carried up.

There was a toilet usually at the top of the house and there was water laid on to the toilet but they were rather primitive, smelly sort of places but they were usable and if they were kept decently they were alright but of course, in crowded, congested areas shared toilets are appalling. I think we have improved sanitation in London beyond all knowledge.

5

WING-COMMANDER J N FLETCHER

The Air Battalion in The Regular Army

In March 1983 in Guildford I keenly anticipated listening to recall of a type of service experience which had hitherto lain outside my imagination – observation from a man-lifting kite. I was not to be disappointed but there was to be much more than just this to excite my interest. My diary noted Wing-Commander Fletcher's physical frailty but that he had been 'quite remarkably good to interview'.

I was born in Bedford in 1889. My father was the senior minister of the Methodist Church, and a Senior Wrangler in Mathematics, at St John's College, Cambridge. I was educated at Berkhamsted School and from there went to The Royal Military Academy, Woolwich. My intention from the first was to be a sapper, that is in the engineers, and not a gunner, in the Artillery. At the end of my course at the School of Military Engineering, the head of the Air Battalion, Royal Engineers, came to Chatham and asked for volunteers to join the Air Battalion as he had just lost two officers in a balloon accident.

As I was the senior under-officer of my batch, I volunteered in order to set an example. And one other man also volunteered but he was rejected because of eyesight and joined the Royal Corps of Signals. I was accepted and was sent to Farnborough where the Air Battalion was based. Though the Air Battalion had airships and balloons, we dealt only with dirigible airships which were built for us in the Academy of Aviation which was alongside the station at Farnborough.

There was a major in command and an adjutant, a captain, and

38

he alone of the two went into the air. He got a team of horses and galloped round Laffan's plain, in a man-carrying kite. Those two were the only senior officers of the Air Battalion. For my own part I have to say that I was too heavy, I never got more than twenty or thirty feet off the ground.

How was it done? Two enormous kites, perhaps fifteen feet across, lifted a wire into the air to which was attached another man-lifting kite on a pulley, and, little by little, kites were added until enough were on the wire to pull a man into the air. The man was harnessed to the man-lifting kite itself but there might be four to six kites on the line to assist in the lifting and then he just floated off the ground. It was rather like sailing a boat. I had done a lot of sailing at Chatham.

It wasn't dangerous but as soon as two of the kites started to circle that was dangerous and we had to come straight down before we were involved in a dive to destruction.

The senior officer had the responsibility of teaching me to fly an airship, a dirigible, but first I had to pass in ballooning by day and ballooning by night and then I had to learn to fly a dirigible by day and by night. As for the dirigible itself, the first one made in England had been made by the man who had come to recruit us in Chatham. He had piloted it from Farnborough, round London and back to Farnborough, and by the time I got to Farnborough the second dirigible was almost ready, well, just about ready to fly.

Imagine a very well-proportioned pear. The fabric used was the skin of animal bladders, and from that pear-shaped balloon hung enough wires to hold a car or suspended compartment with the pilot, engine and engineer. That was the smallest airship we made. The 'pear' or envelope was filled with hydrogen and the car was made of wood and canvas. Just imagine you built a small boat, twenty feet long, in which you could put an engine and an engineer and a driver.

The dirigible was constantly, always, filled with its gas. The gas was contained in steel cylinders twelve feet long and about eight or nine inches in diameter with hydrogen gas at huge pressure inside. And you had to use goodness knows how many, perhaps a hundred of these, to fill this embryonic airship. Once it was filled it stayed filled and when not brought out for use it stayed in a shed or hangar. Sometimes you had enough space to have two dirigibles in side by side.

Now security against fire and explosion of the hydrogen: it was tricky. You could start the engine on the dirigible quite safely, but if you let it run for very long the exhaust pipes grew red hot. I had on one occasion the experience of having both the handling guys at the side of the airship torn off as soon as the ship came down. And I had a pupil in the airship learning to fly it and I had no means of holding him when he landed so I had to signal to him by flash lamp in Morse. Luckily he or the engineer could read my instructions. I had to instruct him to fly over the horizon and come in slowly backwards and as low as he dare fly, and when he reached the landing party use the fire extinguishers which we carried to reduce the temperature of the exhaust pipes, and then rip the balloon to let out the gas and so fall to the ground. He managed everything as I had instructed and it all passed off safely. He came in backwards, very slowly, used the fire extinguishers, ripped and fell, but I have to say that that was during the war.

I took part in Army manoeuvres in two successive years before the war and it became obvious to me and to my CO and instructor that airships would be no use in military action but might be of use in naval action. At that point, 1914 on the eve of war, the Royal Naval Air Service was formed and Army officers, two of us, Waterlow (my CO) and I, joined. Winston Churchill made the Admiralty promise that we should have exactly the same treatment as Naval personnel.

One thing I should add is that whilst I was training in lighter than air work, Cody was flying an aeroplane there and one day I went to his shed on the other side of Laffan's Plain and asked him if he would train me to fly an aeroplane. If I got my certificate the War Office would reward me with 75 pounds and I would give that sum to Cody. Cody said he would and so for a few days I flew Cody's aeroplane. And Cody always sat behind me and the time came when I was ready to pass the Aeronautical Society's test and I was doing a gliding flight, stopped the engine, figures of eight, to come down and land within a specified area. And at the last minute Cody leant over on my shoulder and pushed the elevator hard down. I fell out backwards and head first and landed luckily and safely on both shoulders and sat up and to my horror the engine started up and the aeroplane flew away towards Farnham, five minutes petrol in the tank, and I was on the ground watching it!

Cody had fallen out beside me and had switched on the engine with his foot as he fell. He wasn't seriously hurt and I wasn't hurt at all. By the grace of God a tip of the wing hit a tree on the canal bank and the aeroplane crashed. Cody telegraphed the Aeronautical Society that there would be no test next day. And a few days later he built another aeroplane and, I flew it and passed my test. Let me tell you Cody could neither read nor write and his carpenter one day brought him a twelve-foot length of hickory, about four by two and twelve foot long. 'Where should I cut the . . . ,' the carpenter began. Cody just took the thing in his hand and balanced it like that and he said 'there' and 'there'. Oh I'd forgotten to say that in his shed had been for some time four beautiful kite-shaped things. I said, 'What, are those Cody?' 'Those are the rudders and elevators of my new monoplane but I can't think how to fit them to the fuselage.' And I said, 'Give me a piece of paper.' I folded it into four and cut the tip and opened it out so that I had a piece of paper like that. 'Oh,' said Cody, 'Thank you. That's going to be my fuselage.' And so he got rudders and elevators working like that within the thing I'd shaped for him.

So that was my link to Cody. Well, in 1913 Mr Churchill purchased for the Royal Naval Air Service the German airship *Parseval* and I was given command of her. I was sent to Kingsnorth on the left bank of the Medway just below Chatham dockyard. By now I was Lieutenant Fletcher RNAS, a Flight-Commander, in command of Airship Four. It was Thursday July 23rd 1914.

Wing-Commander Fletcher's wartime service was in airships and his account of his experiences during the war continues in this interview but is not being published here.

6

DAME MARGERY CORBETT ASHBY
DBE

Political Activist and Suffragist

Thirty years on from interviewing Dame Margery, my diary comment that, 'She was excellent,' does not seem to do her justice. I was invited to stay at her home in Horsted Keynes, Sussex, in September 1979 for the interview to take place. It stretched over two sessions, after supper and after breakfast. To say that she held my attention throughout would be no less than the truth. Intuitively alert to my hope of recreating in her words the intellectual, social, political, family, and individual milieu in which she was so active, she captured it thematically and perceptively. She did not tire; anecdotal recall supporting point after point. I make the issue of her interview performance and her age – ninety-seven – simply with admiration; astonishment not being appropriate for this special lady.

I was born in Inverness Terrace in London in 1882 but stayed there only for a few months until my grandfather's death put my father at the head of the family and he brought me down to the shooting estate in Sussex where I spent my childhood and indeed lived there until I was married. We were the Corbett family and I am proud that it was an enterprising family for my father came with little or no money from the North of England as a more or less poor architect. He made friends with another architect and between them, but chiefly my father, they built the first business blocks in the City of London. That is to say he built the first offices which were not also the residence of the owner of the business, Seventeen Gracechurch Street, now alas demolished to make room for a bank.

My father's brother, Julian Corbett, was to become pre-eminent as a naval historian, having developed quite young as the author of novels chiefly concerned with Drake but also touching on such alien subject as a brilliant book on Norwegian mysticism. He became reporter in foreign wars for *The Times*. I remember especially Egypt, and he always said it helped him to be a successful reporter that he gained so much facility by writing novels. His books on naval history and tactics attracted so much attention that though he was not officially connected with the Navy, he was asked to give lectures on the substance of his books, that is to say lectures on strategy and tactics, to the Flag Officers and other senior officers. By this means and through the success of this work he became responsible to the Committee of Imperial Defence for the writing of the *Official History of the War at Sea* during the 1914–18 war.

My childhood was for the most part spent in Sussex but was broken in the very early years by twice a year going to stay for a couple of months at least with my father's mother, Granny Corbett, at a village across the Thames from Hampton Court and there we had the extra fun of a small tributary to the Thames running through the garden, which gave us much fun bathing, boating, canoeing and in the winter a mile of rough skating.

My parents had a tremendous influence on me because they were both ahead of their time. They were extraordinarily generous and both had an immense sense of responsibility towards their neighbours so that I was used to hearing and knowing that if anything went wrong or there was any disaster in the village, the men would come up as a matter of course to my father in his study, or, for any family difficulty, the women would go to seek help from my mother. This was at Danehill in Sussex.

My mother became one of the very first female Poor Law Guardians elected in the country and her great work was to empty not only Uckfield Workhouse of its children whom she boarded out happily in neighbouring villages but her work was so appreciated at the headquarters that she also emptied the workhouse in Eastbourne and took some children from London. So that at one moment I remember she was personally responsible for 40 children in the neighbouring villages, happily housed with village families.

When we went to Danehill and my father was asked if he would stand as candidate for a parliamentary election as a Liberal, there was only one other family able to keep a horse and carriage who were Liberal. He was boycotted by the neighbourhood because of being the only, shall we say, man of substance, who was a declared Liberal.

My first involvement in politics was in proudly folding pamphlets, all kinds of literature for distribution from the first election he fought in 1906. My brother and I were enthusiastic, energetic canvassers distributing literature. As the constituency was geographically large, we used to go out in the high dog cart in the morning with the leaflets announcing the meeting and the speaker that evening and we were so involved that I remember one bitter night when snow prevented my father getting to a meeting on time, first I and then my brother, took it in turns to make the political speech and my father arrived thank goodness before we had both exhausted all our ideas. (I was twenty-four at the time.) Anyway my father won this East Grinstead Division of Sussex seat.

My father was keen on our learning languages and we had the luck of having a very distinguished German woman as a friend. She lectured at the Crystal Palace and other centres teaching German and she came to teach us German because she found that teaching in the spring and summer allowed her to collect enough money to go out and help Flinders Petrie as a personal assistant in his archaeological work in Egypt. Through that my father became treasurer to Flinders Petrie and drew me into interest in that side of her life. It also gave me complete facility in German, which of course has been, or was in the early days, an enormous asset in international work.

For the university stage of my education there were four colleges to choose from, the two at Cambridge and two at Oxford but I was told, I don't know how, that certainly the two senior colleges at Cambridge were much more integrated into university work than were the younger colleges in Oxford. The Cambridge colleges were Girton and Newnham. So I chose, of course, the more mature university with regard to women, and decided that it would be far preferable to enter Newnham on the edge of the town rather than Girton which required a bicycle or a cab to get into the city. I passed the entrance examination without difficulty and then had to select the subject of my studies and I chose Classics. Very ill-equipped I was for this choice!

We had our own lecturers from among the staff. We had men lecturers coming in from various colleges and we ourselves under chaperonage went to attend the leading lecturers of the day in whatever college they were working. I had reasoned that as I had had no school discipline but had only been educated at home, I needed something tough to tackle. I was bi-lingual in French, quite fluent in German, so Modern Languages didn't appeal to me. I can't do more than 2 and 2 make 4, so Mathematics was out and the most strict discipline I could envisage was Classics. So I chose Classics to the horror of the dons who sent me up to London to consult my father. I went to him in his city offices and said the dons want to know what I am to study at Cambridge. 'What do you want to study?' 'Classics,' I replied, and he said, 'Well, study Classics and come out to lunch at Pimm's on oysters.' (**Pimm's was the nineteenth century oyster bar in London where the drink was invented by the owner, James Pimm.**)

Of course, I did badly but under cover of measles and doing my finals in the sick room I scraped through and they have given me enormous pleasure all through my life. I might add here that Cambridge was years after Oxford in granting a degree. All we had was a certificate from the Chancellor or Vice Chancellor and that of course, though recognized in England, was useless if one wanted to take a post abroad. So when my sister was in the same position, we both went over to Dublin and took our degrees there.

Dublin University was short of funds to increase the accommodation for women students and the brilliant head got the University to decide that they would give degrees (to women) and the fees would go to the fund on which the women's buildings were erected. No studying was required, they gave the degree on your Cambridge certificate.

I was at Newnham between 1901 and 1903 and I remember that I was introduced to 'fives' which I played with enormous pleasure especially as my grandmother's house had its private fives court in the garden and so I had some practice and I enjoyed fives very much. I enjoyed hockey too, though I was never very good at sport.

We had two first rate debating societies. One, 'General' on which any subject could be chosen and the other, which particularly interested me, was a debating society where we alternated. We were a complete copy of Parliament with parliamentary orders and a party set-up. There were only two parties in those days and we took it in turns to be government and opposition and I was there with some outstanding members of well-known political parties; the Buxton's, for example. I had close connection with the Rowntree's, and the Clark's, and the Fry's mostly, but because of my father's position in the party, if any Liberal speakers came to lecture to the University, I was invited to be there. So I heard Buckmaster and all the brilliant men of the day came.

There was the connection that if you joined and were elected an officer, there must be another woman besides you on the committee or whatever, or list of officers. That is to say, we were not supposed to go to anything by ourselves. We had to have someone of our own sex with us and that, not because the college really was much interested, but because it was to free us from the constant adverse criticism of rank and file in Cambridge. That is to say, I don't think I am exaggerating, if an undergraduate was seen speaking to a pretty girl, there was at once you know, 'Look at him flirting with one of those awful Newnham girls,' whereas probably she was either a cousin or somebody from a shop.

I won't say that Newnham girls had a bad reputation but there was the constant sniping of the anti-feminists. Remember that by the time I went to college, we were the second generation and my close friends, who were a little bunch of four, and two of them were daughters of extremely respected professors, one at Cambridge and the other at Glasgow. But there again birds of a feather flock together and of our little group, we had all come to Cambridge straight from a man's world and not from a girls' school and so our interests were instinctively wider.

As far as the development of my political convictions is concerned; it was through listening to people a year, or even two years, older than me who were ardent Liberals concerning suffrage and feminism, that goes so far back I really hardly know where to begin. You see if my mother was one of the earliest of the women elected guardians, she was clearly a feminist and I naturally was a feminist. My father brought up my brother, sister and me on a basis of complete equality. There was no question of one being more interested in anything than another. We were treated completely equally from the intellectual standpoint and I suppose we never thought of moral equality. We took that for granted. So I started out with this tremendously solid foundation for feminism and my mother was a keen supporter.

My position on this was challenged at Newnham and so was fortified. I was horrified to find that many of the dons were not only indifferent but strongly against women's political work and this infuriated me. To think that women who were taking advantage of the progress in women's education should be blocking the way to other women attempting to play a role in political responsibility!

There were exceptions but on the whole, under Mrs Sedgwick, I think they felt that their main responsibility – this is being generous to them – was to ensure the reputation of the college as a very serious place for women students. To become involved in feminist activity would undermine that reputation.

For my career I had thought of teaching and so went for a year to the training college at Cambridge after trying Statistics at University College my first year after Newnham, and I don't know why, I can't remember what drove me. I suppose I had some instinct or feeling for teaching, but I went to the training college at Cambridge and I was bitterly disappointed. It seemed to me such a poor intellectual level after Newnham. I had great fun because I had a lot of friends but I remember my last interview was saying goodbye to the Principal and she said to me, 'I hope you have enjoyed your time here.' She was an enthusiast but not at a very high intellectual level and I was just saying, 'Yes,' to order as it were, and then it suddenly struck me, why should I say yes. So I said, 'Well, the only thing it's done for me is to tell me I can't teach.' I hadn't been happy. However, I got a glowing testimonial.

Well, if not teaching, what then? Of course, in those days, no girl whose family had above a certain income level would ever consider working for money. So I threw myself into unpaid social work of various kinds. I helped with the girls' clubs in London. I took relief work in the village school if the teacher were ill or away on a course.

I went round for one of the northern boroughs visiting newborn babies and putting in reports as to whether the family needed further help. And then of course there was work to further the cause of women's suffrage.

The first title of the cause was The International Suffrage Alliance of Women. Well, we dropped suffrage and called ourselves The International Alliance of Women and it was started in New York in 1902. It got its constitution and framework in 1904 and has grown from the number of countries affiliated from the first seven to the latest forty-seven and we hope for five more in September this year.

In 1904 I joined as a British member of the British affiliate and worked with Mrs Fawcett and at The International Alliance office in London, and have just continued to work with it ever since. Mrs Fawcett was a charming, quiet, extremely dignified, person, not in the least pompous, very quiet but carrying somehow a great prestige with her. I mean you felt here is a first rate woman and she was very generous. When she found I could speak, and she was invited to speak, on several occasions she sent me because she thought I would suit the audience by my age and so on and I remember she sent me to one of the men's colleges at Oxford but most of all the things she trusted me with, was sending me to the Paris Peace Congress. But that, of course, is very much later.

In 1904 I was going up and down the country speaking on suffrage. It was a very popular subject for girls' prize giving. I told the girls when they were asked to do anything, not to think it was beautifully modest to say no when it was simply they were too lazy to tackle it. My advice was if other people think you can do it, have a go.

My father thoroughly approved of my political activities. Mrs Fawcett described him as 'the best friend of woman's suffrage in the House of Commons' and that I think was because he never deceived her as to the strength of suffrage or anti-suffrage feeling in the House and could always give an exact picture of where she had better not believe the word of such and such a man who always failed at the last minute.

I don't think I was ever shouted down at meetings. I had every kind of missile thrown at me but I have always been rather good at answering objections and the audience would be more interested in the dialogue and repartee than they would be in just shouting down. So, although I have had eggs and tomatoes and dried haddock and various other things, stones, thrown at me. I have not been shouted down I think except on one occasion. Yes, I suppose when there was a big meeting in Nottingham and our innocent organizers had arranged the demonstration for the last day of the local races. So when the toffs had finished with the races, they came and broke up our three platforms.

Of course, I met all the leading Liberals and spoke with them on the different platforms. Lloyd George was an entrancing person to watch at work. Over and over again I saw him face a really hostile audience and by the time he had finished his speech, he was given a standing ovation. I consider that Churchill was the finest orator we produced but I would put Lady Violet Bonham-Carter a very close second. She had her father's magnificent vocabulary, great eloquence and really to hear her on any subject was pure joy. It was so beautifully done. Grey was some speaker. I suppose one is more enthusiastic about people who are superbly outlining one's own convictions but I think the standard of oratory then was really very high indeed. Naturally I didn't hear the Conservative speakers because I didn't go to their meetings.

While my father was in the House, having a very unselfish mother, I went with him to the big Foreign Office parties. I went with my brother and danced in all the Liberal aristocratic houses when a London season was certainly a wonderfully amusing and interesting period but I don't think, I don't remember any outstanding Conservative except Lord Cecil for whom I had the greatest admiration and I also enjoyed very much, but that of course, was much later, working with Austin Chamberlain on League of Nations work.

You ask me about awareness of the challenge of the new party, The Independent Labour Party. I think we were not fully aware of the danger because it began by Liberals and Labour working together and I think we rather expected to continue being the senior partner and as the Independent Labour Party people were new to politics and came from a different class or a set of people – we didn't think in classes but they were representing a different set of life experiences but there didn't seem to be anything that would occasion differences between Liberal and Labour attitude.

Returning to suffrage, I began real work in London when my father became MP for East Grinstead in 1906 and having a base in London I became national secretary to The National Union of Women's Suffrage Societies because their office was almost next door to our flat in Artillery Mansions, Victoria Street. I went in and had an office with a typist: of course, in those days a secretary was not supposed to type. You had a typist. You dictated or wrote your letters and then we had a Treasurer who did the finance work with the help of a second secretary in the office and I not only had to run the office but if no one else would do it, edit the monthly magazine, called I think *National Women's News*.

Yes we were known as suffragists and when you ask me about the split in our movement which gave rise to the suffragettes, that stage occurred extremely late and was a very small break-off of determined, frustrated women, a small pressure group, quite late in the movement after we had had suffrage bills thrown out year by year. And when our leader, Mrs Fawcett, was faced with the charge that was she not disgusted or embarrassed by the activities of this small group, her reply in effect was: 'It's entirely your fault. We have asked like ladies for fifty years and you have not paid any attention to us. Don't blame me.'

Our attitude was, we prefer constitutional measures in the way in which men's franchise has been advanced. We do not believe in violent agitation but we respect the convictions of women who are working for the same goal as we are and we will not criticize them. Mrs Fawcett's response was our laid down official policy.

We also differed from the suffragettes in the way in which we supported or did not support a candidate standing for Parliament. Their theory was that only a government could change the franchise laws. No party or all-party movement would have any effect and therefore they opposed any government candidate however favourable he was personally to the cause. They fought the government of the day if it was not ready to grant suffrage.

We, on the other hand, being a very much all-party society, supported candidates who were favourable to our cause. When suffragette activities first occurred and when they first began their policy, I was tremendously impressed by their enthusiasm and I spoke on the same platform as Mrs Pankhurst and her daughters as long as their violent action recoiled only on themselves. I admired them as martyrs. When they started violence which hurt other people, like burning the contents of pillar boxes or destroying other people's property, I had to make a choice and I decided that I would stick to constitutional non-violent methods. It was impossible, however much one admired their courage, to serve the two camps at once. However, I think we accepted that there were two concepts of how to get the vote and we left each other alone.

The Pankhursts were extremely able. Fanatical in their faith and brilliant in their organization but they were extreme dictators. I think that Mrs Pankhurst and especially Christabel simply laid down the law and you had to follow it or leave the society. There was no discussion of policy. I think there were get-together groups to agree on the special action of violence but I think there was no real get-together to decide on policy. That was laid down by the Pankhursts and there was very little financial control of the very large sums of money which they collected. Their treasurer, whose name I have forgotten, resigned. There were no accounts kept and I believe that every penny of the money they collected was spent on their work. I have not the slightest reason to believe that it was diverted but it was not publicly accounted for.

7

DONALD MACDONALD

A Crofter's Boyhood in the Hebrides

I went to the Isle of Uist in August 1978 on a family camper van holiday which gave me the opportunity of meeting a former Cameron Highlander who had served in the First World War on the Western Front and been thrice wounded. His pre-1914 memories of life in a crofting family considerably widened my vision of the life experience of people living on those then remote islands before the outbreak of war and at the same time enabled Donald to document a vanished way of life . Donald was born in South Uist in 1892, the son of a crofter and fisherman.

There were plenty of fish but the price of the fish was low. The crofts were small and on them we kept cattle and sheep. We cultivated a patch of land with 'lazy beds' and a plough. You would carefully choose your most cultivable piece of land, and you then cut it with parallel lines about three or four inches apart. When you had finished, that was your 'lazy bed'. When it came time to put fertilizer on it that of course was seaweed as a manure. You put it between the lines leaving a foot of space on each side. When this was done you turned it over in small divots, turning the divots onto the seaweed. Then you had to start digging it all in, digging the seaweed in. There was now soil on top. With this done you started planting your potatoes and that was your 'lazy bed' cultivation.

Our staple diet was fish and potatoes. For breakfast, eggs and fish and maybe porridge, for lunch, fish and potatoes and for tea, porridge and milk.

We lived in what were called 'black houses'. A real black house was not made of stone but of spade-cuts of soil, one upon another.

The triangle top was made of timber, sods of turf put on that, and then thatch on top of that. We had a timber doorway and a space left for a window, a window with a wooden frame to open or close. I remember when there was hardly any glass. As it happened our black house had the distinction of having the first glass window in the village. A black house had two rooms or compartments and lighting was from an oil lamp. The oil was made from fish liver and the wick from rushes. For toilet needs we had a pit outside.

Yes it was simple and it was hard but pretty nearly every night we youngsters gathered round or in certain houses and the oldest people would tell us stories, and among the elderly there would be some who had been sailors, who had sailed the world, and their stories would be listened to more attentively than children listening to any schoolmaster.

I remember as a boy trying to follow what was an age-old common practice in putting down a sick dog or a dog turned vicious when all customary remedies had been tried and had failed. There was no vet within reach and one would hate to use a shotgun – I certainly could never have used a shotgun for this purpose. The method was by drowning it. My friend and I had this sad task but we had insufficient experience. I was tying some string round a stone and he was putting a loop round the dog's neck. I have to say that my friend was just out of an asylum but I was not frightened of him. The dog was ours. He was too vicious and was a danger to the sheep. We went to a small cliff over the sea. We tried to throw dog and stone together. Down they went. The stone hit the fairly shallow bottom and the twine came off – the dog surfaced. My partner in the affair was sure the dog would come after him. He started to run away, slipped and fell into the sea himself. When he was climbing back up to me I had some anxiety I would be next for a throw! In fact the experience may have cured the dog because he lost his viciousness and lived on for many years.

Donald then moved on to tell me of his soldiering. I remember the beauty of his island: a beauty which I understand endures, though his way of life did not. As it happens, that evening, in August 1978, I got a reminder that with the beauty there could still be, even in the summer, a harsh challenge from the elements. Such a gale blew

up with fearful gusts that I thought our camper van would make its own aerial tour of the Outer Hebrides. Donald Macdonald remains in my mind as a quietly spoken, humorous man who graciously led his listener into what was for him an unimagined way of life.

8

GEORGE IVES

Boer War Trooper and Colonist to Canada

In 1992 I was teaching at a summer school in Vancouver at the University of British Columbia when I read in a local newspaper of a man of one hundred and ten living close by in Aldergrove. I rang up the 'sheltered accommodation' where George Ives was resident, learned that Mr Ives would be pleased to see me and I bussed out to Aldergrove. At that stage there was only the remarkable age to give me any indication that I was near to recording memories which took me into life experiences which had been hitherto but scantily recorded. When George Ives swung his legs off his daybed to stand, shake hands and greet me, clear-eyed and soon with evidence of being alert, quick on the uptake, and without problems of defective hearing, I was sensing the excitement of what was to follow.

My diary reports that Mr Ives 'answered everything well'. It does not record that if I were to have been more familiar with campaigning details of the Boer War, I had an awareness at the time, and reaffirm today, that George's tape would have moved still higher up the scale of excellence.

Mr Ives was born in Brighton, Sussex, in November 1881, the son of a coachman. His father's responsibility with horses led to George himself becoming involved even while still at a National or Church of England school in Cheltenham where his father was then engaged in work. Through an acquaintance with a chimney sweep who worked for gentry folk in and around Cheltenham, the Ives family had come to the notice of wealthy people named Morrison who had two daughters.

My mother was employed as a sort of children's maid to look after them. Now both my parents conversed in French. They had done more work in France than they had done in England and they preferred to converse even together always in the French language but they understood English perfectly too.

Through the Morrisons, I became a jockey for a man racing his horses in the West Country and in France. I rode for him more in France than in England. An Englishman was in charge of six young riders and I was regularly given some of the best horses winning numbers of races in the St Malo area. On occasion I was instructed not to bring the best out of a good horse because of betting considerations. Unfortunately I began to put on weight and could not keep this weight down, rising from 97 to 128 pounds despite being put on a diet of lettuce and vinegar. This particular losing battle coincided with the outbreak of the Boer War in 1899 and I decided to enlist. Of course I had to go back to England to do this and I enlisted as a trooper in the 1st Wiltshire Imperial Yeomanry whose colonel was Sir Thomas Fowler whom we were soon all to call Tommy.

So, I suppose I must have felt I wanted to fight for my country. The war had been on for some time. Such training as we did was carried out at Aldershot where we were all gathered. They had goodness knows how many thousands of new troops all picked out. They were able to ride and in most cases to shoot but they had to ride a horse, that was the main thing. Now I didn't know anything about marksmanship but before this was put right off we went to South Africa and we did a bit of training with our carbines on the boat. Our transport was a Canadian cattle boat. We looked after our own horses and I remembered what I had learned from my father when I was only ten, rubbing a bottle of lubrication on the fetlocks of any which seemed to have injured themselves.

As for my first time in action after we got to South Africa, I couldn't tell you where this took place but I know we were on a railroad and we were going from Durban to the fighting area and while we were on the train we could hear rifle shots somewhere and sometimes a small gun. Every four companies had a 2-pounder, they used to call it. That was when they were catching Boers. A very poor way of going about it but I suppose that was all there was.

The first task we had to undertake was to take all the Boer wives and children – they were mostly country people – and put them in wired compounds. We would search for a farm and any men, but they had always gone, find the women and children and take them to a camp.

We would take everything useful to us and perhaps have to make a second trip for the cattle. Some of them had a lot of sheep and these sheep were taken from them of course. On one particular occasion when it was estimated that there were about 3,000 of them, they were in the charge of native people and they drove them up into a coil of a wire fence one night and light rain came along. All the sheep used to like keeping very close together actually touching each other when they were asleep. After the initial light rain, a great big storm came along and lightning striking the wire killed them all. You couldn't go near the place for three months on account of the smell.

Our job was to shoot Boers and they were to do the same with us. That was our job. If they captured any of us, they had no place to keep us and nothing to feed us with. So they used to take all your clothes off in the morning when the sun was up and send you off to your camp bare-footed and stripped, and the sun would burn you to pieces. Exactly that happened to one of my mates.

You have to appreciate it is a pretty big country and there was the room for men from the opposing sides to plan ambushes to capture the unwary. On one occasion we were ambushed by forty-four Boers for whom we were searching. In the action which followed I was wounded by a ricochet but we captured them. That is a long time ago and I have been carrying a Queen Victoria Medal for eighty-eight years. One thing I remember is that we went out there with helmets on our head but it soon changed from a helmet to what was called a slouch hat. It came from South Australia. Good hats, nice to fan your breakfast fire up with in the morning to make your tea. Never any coffee, it was always tea. I remember too that when the war was nearly ended our Commanding officer, Sir Thomas Fowler, was shot in the head and it killed him at once. We rather missed him. He used to treat us as if we were all his equals. He was always 'Tommy' and he had an estate in Wiltshire and he promised that when the war was over, we could go out there and he would put us in tents for two weeks and of course, it never happened.

With the war over I returned to England and left the Army. A year later I was in Canada. I read in a weekly paper, I think printed in Sheffield by a clergyman, that he was going to take out to Canada fifty men and put them to work with farmers. I read it and wrote to him. He agreed to take me out and the conditions I had to agree to. I had to have fifty sovereigns and good clothes.

We were to leave Liverpool for Nova Scotia and were to join up with some other colonists. We were the I M Barr Colony. I M Barr had made a big thing out of the whole enterprise. Altogether he brought out to Canada 1,700 people and he took over anything he could steal. He promised us that that we were going to have a co-operative store to supply us with all our needs. I put 50 Canadian dollars into it and my father put 100 Canadian dollars in. He took it all away. He robbed everybody and went to Australia. However, with this money lost, my father and I were still in favour of the venture. We sold to the other colonists what my father had accumulated for the running of a grocery store and I myself was set on a new life in Canada.

(The transatlantic crossing, perhaps surprisingly, did not give rise to special memories. From Halifax, Nova Scotia, the Canadian Pacific Railroad took the adventurers west – five trains in all, one, with 'settlers effects'. They went up via Winnipeg to Saskatoon but George and his father went on further west with some of the party towards, but not as far as, Edmonton.)

I found some people we could stay with and the Reverend Royd sent a tent down to a lot of the freighters. Some had horses and some had oxen. It was a very good place to feed the cattle and there was a nice stream there for the water which they all thought was a better place to drink fresh water than what they called slew water because the slew water was full of mosquitoes. There wasn't anything in the way of a settlement there. There were a few bushes in some places and a few trees. South of us there were hardly any trees at all but the north side was pretty good. There was a lot of wood there to build log shacks with sod roofs. You put poles on the roof and put slew grass on top of the poles and then cut piles of sod and put it on the top.

Of course there was no church. We had to wait for a church to be built but that was a peculiar thing, pretty well every nationality wanted to start their own district up with a small church. It is rather strange anyway because some people pay no attention to religion but here nearly every nationality wanted a church before they wanted a school.

Well, my father kept the store and I was on the freighting. First of all I went to Saskatoon to get groceries from The Hudson Bay Company and I took them up to where we were beginning to build. Then I began to think about it, no more Saskatoon trips for me. The reason was I had the load behind the horses twice as long as I needed it to be because half of it was for another settlement further along the road. I could make twenty-five miles a day and I was on the road four days at a stretch, sleeping and eating on my own. I liked to be with people and this was no life for me. I became a carpenter, helped to build schools.

The settlement which George Ives helped to build is today the big city of Lloydminster with well over a hundred thousand citizens. It can be given to few men to see in their lifetime such urban development from playing a part in its earliest days. But George had another more personal distinction too – seventy-six happy years of marriage to the girl he met at a dance on board the ship which took him to Canada, something which wasn't mentioned until the end of the interview.

Section Two
The First World War

1

AIR MARSHAL SIR VICTOR GODDARD
KCB CBE

Training in Balloons

In March 1974 I went to see Sir Victor Goddard at his home in Brasted near Westerham in Kent. It may well be thirty-six years since the interview but I knew what I would find in my diary record of the occasion and there it was 'told me two marvellously funny stories of his balloon training experiences, one simply hilarious'.

Sir Victor was born in 1897, the son of a country doctor in a place with no rural associations today, Wembley. At the age of twelve and a half he went to the Royal Naval College, Osborne, on the Isle of Wight, with his having no choice in the matter. Two years at Osborne were followed by two at the senior college establishment, Dartmouth, in South Devon and then a six months' training cruise in HMS *Cornwall*.

My memories of life at the College are on the whole happy but there was a great deal of bullying. Fortunately we had the stamina to stick it out. We were beastly to our juniors and rather cocky when we were seniors and thoroughly nasty little boys in some respects and yet I think that the young naval officer turned out to be a very fine fellow. It was essentially a scientific and technical education; one third of our time was spent in engineering and everything was slanted towards understanding 'what it was all about' in the Navy – how ships worked and how engines work and how guns work and all this sort of thing and also we had the smatterings of strategy and tactics and Naval History. We were imbued with the past and we were supposed to be able to look forward to the future with understanding but in fact, it was a godsend for the Navy that the system was changed or at least was supplemented towards the end of my time at Dartmouth, let us say round about 1913 when the Public School entry was started to supplement the flow of officers into the Navy and there they drew young men who had been trained towards leadership in the public schools system. This was a great thing for the Navy. We thought it was a bad thing at the time but I was young and all very conservative, rather died in the wool against this idea but in retrospect I was wrong.

One thing I must tell you about was that it was a very remarkable and delightful experience for a young fellow that the petty officers helped to train the midshipmen more than the senior officers did. They really had a compassionate attitude towards these very young types who were aspiring to be officers. They were brought up to a tradition in the Navy just like we in the officer branch were. They wished well for the Navy. They wanted to see their young officers turning out into being good officers and they were also brought up on what was called the catechism. Most people went to church or had dealings with the religious side and I think that the greater proportion of the lower deck felt that it was, as it were, God's will that they should be happy to serve in the station to which they had been called.

Well, as war loomed, Winston Churchill, the First Lord of The Admiralty, had commissioned every ship in the Navy that could be of use including those that were lying waiting to be broken up. I was just about to become a midshipman and in the natural order of things I would have been going on holiday but in fact I was sent rather secretly by night from Plymouth directly to Grimsby. We weren't supposed to know where we were but of course, we couldn't help seeing the name of Grimsby on the railway station and I joined an old battleship called *Victorious* with two funnels abreast which was lying at anchor with three other old battleships in the Humber. They were members of The Third Fleet and they had paint about a quarter of an inch thick all over them. They had been white at some time when serving on the China station and we spent the first week or so of war in chipping the paint off and getting the guns to work and getting the ship to work. We had reservist crews and so forth but I joined her only two days before with another group of my term as very junior midshipmen, in fact as naval cadets. We hadn't been given the rank of midshipmen.

Although no officer below the rank of lieutenant was supposed to handle secret ciphers, the cipher message which was sent out to The Fleet to order the commencement of hostilities against Germany, was decoded by me and I took it up to the Bridge. The Captain happened to be on the bridge. I suppose he had been sleeping in his sea cabin and we had been already alerted and at our guns in case of submarine attack or something of the sort and I took him this message decoded which was to commence hostilities against Germany at once. This was at 11pm our time, 12 o'clock German time. So that was the start of the war. It was very foggy in the Humber on that particular night and as I was descending the ladder and going on to the fore and aft bridge as it was called, back to where the coding room was, I was startled and nearly knocked over by a shattering noise of a 12-pounder gun going off on the fore shelter deck. After a loud cry, I had heard, 'Destroyer coming up harbour,' so I turned round and went back. The searchlights hadn't come on then. This gun had blazed out before the searchlights came on and finally the searchlights came on and peered through the fog. No destroyer was to be seen. In fact, you couldn't see the bow of the ship but what had been seen, glimpsed by the gun layer, was the anchor buoy in the tideway and that was what he had opened fire at and this was only a few moments after 12 o'clock. So, it was certainly the first shot fired in anger. This became a great joke.

Well, I was posted away from *Victorious* to the Third Battle Squadron in the Grand Fleet at Scapa Flow, to a battleship called *Britannia* of King Edward VII class. She was pre-dreadnought in design. I found to my horror that the entire Gunroom, all the junior officers and sub lieutenants, who should have left the ship to do their courses on shore, they were all bearded. Every man jack of them was wearing a beard. At that time this was very unusual and I discovered that they had taken a vow that none of them would shave until the war was over and of course in the Navy you weren't allowed to grow unless you grew the whole beard as well as the moustache and they looked a very piratical lot of chaps. Well, the Captain knew that he, having allowed them to grow at the start, he couldn't withdraw the permission to have beards and moustaches, but he did say that he expected to see his young officers clean and this was taken to mean that they had better be clean shaven I think. Gradually beards disappeared.

As for the role we fulfilled at sea, well the Grand Fleet 'kept the seas'. It was a fleet 'in being' and there was always about half the fleet out at sea, with the others at some state of readiness at anchor in Scapa Flow. We used to go out for about three or four days and do what was called a 'sweep' down the North Sea and it was pretty exhausting work because we used to steam at fairly high speeds, zigzagging most of the time but it was very good training for manoeuvres and practising observation but as there was no sign of the German fleet to be seen, and no real prospect of this it seemed after a bit, I was glad that I didn't have to continue doing that arduous work.

Before I left the ship we did have one calamity in fog, running ashore near the mouth of the Tyne. It was one of the occasions when an Admiral interfered rather disastrously. The Admiral really was responsible for the whole happening because he was in the leading ship. The *Dominion* was acting as flagship and we were the second ship of the line and suddenly, I was on the bridge at the time as midshipman of the watch, when we could suddenly see, although we were 'darkened' ships, almost straight ahead of us, broadside on, the *Dominion* and we were actually aiming at her midship and she had seen this island at the top of the Tyne and had sheered away but had not sounded her siren and so we didn't know that she had sheered away and we very nearly had a collision with her and the officer of the watch had the helm put hard over and we ran ashore.

By our own efforts we had just about got the ship off when the Admiral came on board and gave an order and we went on the rocks again. We had already been holed in our double bottom and then we got all our coal out and ammunition out and everything else out of the ship working for three days and nights.

Now, about my transfer to the Royal Naval Air Service: we were at sea in *Britannia*. We had just gone to sea that morning. We were in calm waters and the crew was mustering for divisions (inspection parade and prayers). We always had prayers at 9 o'clock every morning and we would all march off to aft on the quarter-deck. Sunday mornings were rather special. We had rather more church services at that time but every morning we had divisions and prayers. The ship's company was inspected by its officers and then we were assembled for prayers and the Captain would always read a portion of scripture and the Chaplain would take the service. While I was doing the roll call to see that my foretop men were all present, a messenger came and said that the Captain wished to see me in his cabin. So I had to report to the officer of my division and then go to the Captain. This was an extraordinary happening for a midshipman to be sent for by a Captain of a ship who was a bit of a tin god and nobody really spoke to him unless he was spoken to.

So down I went. I found the Captain with the Commander, that is the second in command, and the Captain's clerk. When I arrived the Captain said to the Commander: 'Will you take Divisions for me, I want to see this young officer?' He then sent his clerk away and I was left alone with the Captain. This was very, very unusual. The Commander went off but he came back a few minutes later to report that the ship's company was mustered aft and would the Captain come up and he was sent away again and the Captain then put his hand on my shoulder and said, ' Young man, I have a very grave question to ask you.' I then thought I was in some sort of trouble. I couldn't think what crime I had committed. Then he said, 'Are you prepared to volunteer for special temporary service of a secret and dangerous nature?' I really wanted to say that I didn't but I hadn't the nerve to say that. I said, 'Yes Sir,' and he told me that he had a letter from the Commander in Chief which had arrived just before we put to sea asking for the names of volunteers from the battleships, perhaps one midshipman might be taken from each ship as there was a small number of midshipmen required for this special job. So, I asked if he could you tell me what it was all about but he said he knew nothing about it. So I then left after a talk and of course, made myself scarce because divisions was not over at that time.

So I went down in the ship and wasn't seen until lunch time. When of course, there was a demand in the gunroom that I should tell them why I went down to the Captain, why the Captain wasn't attending divisions and all this, but I had been sworn to secrecy. I had to tell them that I was sorry but it was a secret matter and of course, much suspicion was aroused about all this. However, it all died away and nothing more was heard for about three weeks. We were then playing deck hockey and again I was sent for by the Captain. We were in harbour at Rosyth and down I went in my sweaty condition in shorts and so forth and he said, 'You are to leave the ship at nightfall with sealed orders.' I can't remember at how many bells it was but it was about 7 o'clock. I asked if I could tell the gunroom now and also tell them what I was going to be doing but he said he still didn't know but I need only take a seaman's bag: 'I think it is something in the open air and you won't be there long.'

So I packed a seaman's bag with a few things and the gunroom bar was opened and we drank some beer and then the wardroom sent for me and I had a glass of sherry with them and then off to the Captain to get my sealed orders. On deck I found that the wardroom were all up there, the senior officers, to see me off but none of the gunroom. I thought, well they must still be drinking beer. So I went down into the picket boat and waved goodbye and that was how I left the ship. When we were out of sight of the ship, hidden by other ships because there were many ships in Rosyth, the hatchway opened up and the entire gunroom came out and came down to the after part of the picket boat that I was in and demanded to see my sealed orders. I showed them that they weren't to be opened until I got ashore. In effect they said they knew that but were coming ashore with me. Then a frightful melee took place when we got ashore and my sealed orders were grabbed and they opened them. All they found inside was another sealed envelope plus one railway warrant to London and I went off to the station. All they knew was that I was going to London and they didn't open the other sealed orders.

The other sealed orders were marked not to be opened until a hundred miles on the journey. So there they were and that was at about Newcastle and I thought well perhaps this London thing is a blind. Perhaps I am going to get off at Newcastle because that was the nearest point to Germany and all that. Well, I got out and walked up and down the platform. All the sealed orders said was report to the Second Sea Lord, the following morning at The Admiralty at 10.30. There was no need for all that secrecy but still there it was but there was another sealed envelope inside addressed to Admiral Hamilton. So I put that in my pocket and I walked up and down the platform for a bit while the train was waiting at Newcastle and I saw another midshipman, a Midshipman Drew, who was one term senior to me. I didn't speak to him. I waited for him to speak to me and he called me up and asked where I was going. I told him I am on this train. He said: 'Well don't be so cagey about it. Are you going to The Admiralty tomorrow morning?' I said I was and so he asked if I were going to see the Second Sea Lord. When I had to reply that that was so, he of course told me that we were both in for the same enterprise which was, he said, to sink some cement boats in the Kiel Canal and this seemed to me to be a very alarming prospect which I didn't like at all and I could quite see why I didn't really need very much kit.

Anyway we appeared the next morning at The Admiralty and there turned out to be twelve of us and I was the junior of the lot. So I stood in the background. Several of them were acting sub lieutenants and several of us were midshipmen and we went up to the Second Sea Lord's office and the senior spokesman knocked at the door and he was admitted but presently he came out again and was followed by a very tall, splendid looking Commander who said to us in the passage, 'Second Sea Lord is not in the habit of seeing any officer below the rank of post captain and then only by appointment. You may rejoin your ships.' So at that point we were rather disconcerted and didn't know what to do next because we didn't think we could go all the way back to Rosyth and Scapa Flow. I then announced that I had a letter for Admiral Hamilton and then the Senior Sub Lieutenant said, 'Well for Christ sake he is The Second Sea Lord, for goodness sake take it in.' So, I took it in and the Commander took the letter into the Admiral inside and presently I was admitted and he sat at his big desk and looked at me over the top of his spectacles and holding the letter in his right hand he looked at me pretty hard and said, 'So you are in for this enterprise are you?' I said, 'Yes Sir' and he said: 'Well, I don't approve of it, good morning.' And so I then began to say could you tell me what we are going to do Sir when the Commander clapped a hand on my shoulder and wheeled me out of the office and I was pushed out into the passage again.

Well this was no good so there was a discussion about where we should get a warrant to get back to our ships. Then a door banged down the passage and a figure came out wearing a monkey jacket with brass buttons. We recognized that it was the First Sea Lord, the famous 'Jackie' Fisher and what a scowling face he had!

The date was 12 May 1915 at the height of the quarrel between Fisher and Churchill over the deployment of Naval units to the Dardanelles.

The great man said, 'What are you young officers cluttering up the gangway for?' The senior acting sub lieutenant said that we were ordered to see the Second Sea Lord and that we have come from the Grand Fleet. The Second Sea Lord doesn't want to see us and we don't quite know what to do. Admiral Fisher said that we must be his midshipmen and to come in. We went into his office and stood round his big table. He was obviously furious. He was speechless for a minute or two and then he looked up at us and looked at each one of us in turn standing in a sort of a semi circle round his table and said: 'If any of you young officers ever rise to high positions and have to deal with politicians, don't trust them.' This was his opening remark, which rather shocked us. Nothing more was said for a moment or two and then he went on to say, 'If I have difficult work to be done and I often do, I prefer to have junior officers to do it. They do what they are told.' This wasn't a very promising start. He went on to talk about 'derring-do' and he talked about Admiral Nelson with great respect – how brave and splendid he was in many circumstances. This didn't really hearten us very much indeed because we knew that we were in for some dangerous enterprise, the nature of which we weren't at all clear about.

So, after he had talked for a good long time he then began to talk, much to my surprise, about Lady Hamilton. He said nobody knew how much was owed to Lady Hamilton whose influence on Nelson was all to the good and had buoyed him up when he needed support and so forth. Then he walked away from his desk and he parted this rank of young officers. He walked across his room. We all continued to look to our front being very disciplined young men. We didn't look to see what he was doing. I heard him unhook what I thought was a picture off the wall and he walked back carrying what seemed to me to be a picture and he said, I am going to read to you the finest piece of prose in the English language and I didn't know what it was but it was Nelson's last prayer. At that moment one of the midshipmen blurted out: 'Please can you tell us what we are going to do Sir?' and Fisher said, 'Don't you know, you are going to fly airships?' That is really the story of how I became an airship pilot, not really as a volunteer for flying but as one who was 'selected' to be a volunteer.

Admiral Fisher, seething with rage over his political subordination and hence defeat by Churchill in their Dardanelles disagreement, was in fact on that very day to vanish from the Admiralty and be uncontactable for some time.

Our training was at Roehampton, living in a splendid house that had been donated or lent to The Admiralty. As preparation for airship pilot training, we did our balloon work at Hurlingham, which was rather a rich man's sports club. Ballooning was quite a thing that used to be done before the war in gas balloons and we learned how the balloons were inflated and the nets put over them. Then we drifted away in our balloons carrying our lunch on board, with maps and so forth wherever the wind would take us. We would try to look for a nice big country house that was marked on our map, which would be on our line of flight, and we would try to come down in their park. In the training balloons we could carry as many as six, that is five under instruction and one instructor and there were only twelve of us. No, we used to carry seven because we used to use two rather big balloons.

The first time up of course we were nervous but determined not to show it. Later I would say that it was not exciting but it was delightful. You would test the balloon for its buoyancy by saying: 'Hands off and ease the guys' and that sort of thing and then if the balloon continued to sit on the floor you would just put a sandbag out and may be two sandbags and then when you were balanced, you would put out one more and that would be sufficient lift for you to rise up gracefully into the air. You are all in the basket with your few instruments and your lunch. The fellows who have rigged the balloon and inflated it with coal gas, some of them would be manning the guys which are just ropes going sideways from the net which goes over the balloon. The balloon is above you full of gas, with the net coming down into the basket.

The balloon is not fully filled but nearly filled. It probably allows you to rise to perhaps 2,000 or 3,000 feet before you lose any gas depending on how many people have got to be lifted. We didn't wear any special clothing. I think it was springtime or summertime. We may have had a sweater to wear underneath our uniform jackets. I don't think we had overcoats. Lunch was put up in luncheon baskets from The Hurlingham Club and you can imagine they were done rather well. Rather above our normal standard of Gunroom fare.

There were disasters every time pretty well but they were amusing disasters. You see, it wasn't so much as you rise, the ground would fall away from you, but that you would see the ground disappearing downstairs so to speak while you remained more or less stationary. You didn't feel any acceleration as you rose and gradually the perspective of the countryside or town or whatever it was and the noises of the town all came up to you and you just silently drifted over without any sound at all of your own making and went with the wind.

The gas expands as you go up and it begins to leak and consequently you lose buoyancy after a bit. So you start off with a balloon not fully inflated so that you can go to a couple of thousand feet anyway but if you haven't got such a big load of people you can go much higher. When I went on my solo I went up to 13,000 feet straight away quite easily without losing any gas at all. Blue skies and rather delightful and I did that from Wormwood Scrubs.

The wind being fairly steady and you would say well by tea time I ought to be at a certain place and the big country houses are marked on the map you see and although you didn't know who lived in them, you would accidentally on purpose land in their Park and they would surely have the provisions to give you tea even though it was wartime. The first time we did this the wind wasn't strong. We hadn't got very far. We had only just got out of London to the north east in Essex. To a splendid house and we decided to come down in the Park. Our instructor, a man by the name of Pollock, a delightful old character — he always used to put on his galoshes which was wise because we used to come down on wet grass – ordered the letting out of some gas. One by the name of Montague pulled on the gas valve and this Pollock stooped down to put on his galoshes and they didn't want to go on. This took time and Montague let out too much gas too and by the time Pollock looked up to say: 'Stop, shut off the gas,' we were coming down pretty fast and we hit the ground and bounced like a tennis ball. Well, then this wasn't as planned at all.

We had been trailing a rope which is quite a heavy bit of rope and about 200 feet long and that acts rather as elastic. It puts its weight on the ground and relieves you of some of the load on the balloon and so that acts as it were as a brake but that wasn't enough. Well, if you don't stop, if the wind is too strong, you slip a grapnel down the line which we promptly did when we bounced and we slipped our grapnel down and that slipped down the rope to the bottom and we could see it trailing through the grass and I looked to see where we were going and we were going straight towards this big house. We didn't actually hit the big house itself. We rose above it but the rope trailed over the high wall with no windows in it and I could see as we got over the top of this thing that it was the high wall of a conservatory and it had in the middle of it a chimney and this grapnel grabbed the chimney and pulled it off and dropped it through the conservatory with a hell of a crash and then the grapnel itself fell in. There was a tennis match going on at the time. A tennis party, men and women you know playing tennis all intent on this. No one had heard anything coming until this dreadful explosion. So they assumed it was a Zeppelin raid I learned afterwards.

Immediately they left the tennis court and went under the trees which were alongside the tennis court and they took cover. By this time we had pulled out of the side of the conservatory with a great crash and breaking glass. The grapnel went through the gooseberry bushes and other things in the soft fruit garden. Trailed across, believe it or not, this is actually true, grabbed the tennis net across the tennis court. Was too strong for the tennis posts altogether which gave way and the net. By this time old Captain Pollock had lost his nerve and he pulled the rip cord and that means that it tears out a whole sort of orange peel out of the fabric and lets the gas all go suddenly. So we came down very fast then having dragged the tennis net over the top of the trees where these people were taking shelter underneath and we came crashing down, not knowing until we pretty well arrived that we were falling into a duck pond and the balloon fell into this duck pond and we had to wade ashore and we got absolutely black doing so, covered with mud. Nobody was hurt. It was all quite amusing in its way except that the tennis party were concerned to find that we weren't a Zeppelin, that we were English.

We all went in covered in mud and the owner of the house had a big dressing room with large wardrobes and lots of clothes. So, the six of us were rigged out in the clothes made available, came down and had this splendid strawberry cream tea which was arranged for the tennis party. In the meantime the farm hands and others had packed up the balloon and old Pollock had been supervising all this and had put it on a hay wagon and taken it to the station. The owner's spare Rolls Royce was trotted out. We didn't know that he was an admiral. He wasn't there because just as we departed Lady M, who owned this house or at least the admiral who owned this house, said, 'My husband will be so sorry to have missed meeting you.' So, one of us said that we didn't know who her husband was. So she said, 'He is Admiral M , the Commander in Chief at Portsmouth now.' So, we thought how lucky it was that he wasn't there to examine us on how it came about that we ever landed at that place. They had said how fortunate that you had happened to land here where we can take care of you, little knowing that we designed to land there anyway.

I should have told you that in our training Pollock had instructed us to bend our knees on landing so we got our knees bent and when we hit we all sat down suddenly in the bottom of the basket but nobody was hurt. If we had kept our knees straight and our back straight and tried to have stood to attention we would probably have hurt ourselves. You do a colossal bounce in a balloon if you do land fast. That was the way we learned how an airship would perform when it became a balloon because after all an airship is only a balloon elongated and with an engine which makes it a 'dirigible' balloon and that is what they used to be called.

I think we spent a month in balloons. We did about twelve trips and a couple of night trips and it was on one of those night trips that I saw my first Zeppelin raid because Zeppelins were then beginning to attack. I had previously to that seen a Zeppelin attack because I had been at the receiving end of it. We were the first military targets that the Zeppelins ever attacked and that was after we ran on the rocks in the *Britannia*. We went into dry dock on the Tyne and we were illuminated up to the sky by flares in the dry docks because they were working on us day and night to repair the double bottom of the ship. When a Zeppelin came over we didn't know that it had come over because it came over silently. It was broken clouds, a moonlit night and we the midshipmen were doing a signals exercise on the bridge at about 7 o'clock in the evening before dinner. During this exercise with a concealed beam light practising Morse, we suddenly heard a whizzing sound, immediately followed by three loud plops as three incendiary bombs, dropped into this dry dock – a very close near miss.

They were immediately followed by three loud detonations in the water on the other side of the dock gates, about 100 yards away. The nearest one was near enough to buckle the dock gates a little bit so that it leaked. That would have been about January 1915. It was soon after the Dogger Bank action.

Now as for seeing a Zeppelin from a balloon, we didn't know that we were seeing it. London was supposed to be blacked out but it wasn't very efficient. It was supposed to be defended with anti-aircraft guns and there were several searchlights which had been taken out of ships and we saw them operating vaguely in various directions but it was a starlit night and I was really looking at the stars. Successively stars would go out completely. It wasn't a twinkling. They would completely disappear and then light up again and it was clear that something had been concealing those stars and this was the track of a Zeppelin which we couldn't actually see against the stars except that the stars were extinguished by its passage. We were up over London I suppose a few miles distant from an unseen Zeppelin which hadn't been picked up by the searchlights. They hadn't got sound locaters then and, as it was more or less calm, we simply stayed over London all night and then in the morning we came down not far from Barking.

All this ballooning was free ballooning but there was no wind. You see, it was just calm. We were just loitering over London and we hoped to get out to the country and land in the open country but, as we knew, it was difficult to land a balloon just where you wanted. Anyway that night we finally found ourselves sitting over an area that was fairly open. Three sides of a square and a road and cottages and I suppose it was 150 yards across and we landed on this green. It was about half past six in the morning and it was daylight and all the cottage doors were open and a man was standing at each of the cottage doors and people were looking out of the windows at this strange object which had landed and they had been experiencing a Zeppelin raid during the night. They had heard the guns and we heard the guns too.

When we landed there, we ripped. We didn't want to have any delay. So we pulled the ripcord and the balloon deflated quickly. Obviously to the onlookers this was a wrecked Zeppelin and there was a rush from the house of all the men and they were carrying carving knives and all sorts of things because they had seen us coming down for some time and stood spellbound there. When they saw that we were wrecked and helpless, they came out to capture the lot of us and perhaps slit our throats because there was a great animosity towards the Zeppelins. They were called 'baby killers' and so forth. So, one of us said, 'We are English.' The villagers then reined in their vengeful intent and we became heroes. Their conclusion was that we had been up chasing the Zeppelins and therefore we were really rather brave chaps. The women brought us out cups of tea and they all helped to load up the basket and the balloon. The balloon was rather shredded by the carving knives that had been brought because they all wanted souvenirs of this thing because they thought she was wrecked and there was no harm in hacking a bit off. So that balloon wasn't serviceable for some time but anyway we went in a triumphal procession to the railway station and away we went.

Victor Goddard's training in airships and then active service experience as an airship pilot were full of interest too but his meeting with Sir John Fisher and his balloon training incidents I thought demanded re-telling here.

2

MAJOR-GENERAL R C MONEY CB MC

The Western Front, August 1914–1918

The keen intelligence, outstanding memory, kindliness and the classically handsome profile of General Money, combine to make him one of the most impressive men I have met. To add to the absorbing account of his service in the first weeks of the war, there was clear recall of 1915 in France, and then of the Battle of The Somme. I met him in July 1977, my diary reminding me that I had the pleasure of staying with him at his home in Cholesbury, Hertfordshire. The diary reports: 'Cameronian, very fine man, outstanding tape, simply exceptional for his age.' I rather wish I had put something warmer which is as I remember him.

Robin Money was born at Alverstoke, Gosport in Hampshire in 1888, the son of a Regular Army officer. Prep school in North Wales was followed by Wellington College and from there to the Royal Military College, Sandhurst. He was commissioned into the Cameronians and joined its 2nd Battalion, then at Aldershot, in 1909 but was in fact posted to the 1st Battalion in South Africa. The role of the battalion was internal security in the aftermath of the second Boer War and a recent Zulu rebellion.

It may be of some interest that our Commander at Bloemfontein in South Africa was General Townshend, later associated with the siege and surrender of Kut, and he was the first senior officer that I had ever met who was keenly interested in training for war. There was the ordinary open warfare of which there was any amount of country available. You could go anywhere, of course, and to an extent in certain areas it laid itself open for quite good mountain warfare training of which the battalion happened to be rather expert because they had just come from India. Anyway we came home from Africa in 1911/12 and we trained for two seasons in Scotland based in Glasgow and it was in Glasgow that we mobilized in 1914. I think we did that mobilized readiness for war on the Continent in five days flat.

There was a lot to do. There was the calling up of Reservists who had to come from here, there and everywhere. There was a lot of work to be done, particularly in connection with harnessing the great number of horses because all the stuff was in the store. And needless to say new stiff leather is pretty difficult to handle and people got sore hands by the time it was done. And there was spare equipment for machine guns which had to be sorted out and got together, spare uniform, all sorts of things of that sort that one was hardly aware of, was there to be seen to, but they all seemed to appear rather miraculously.

Our send-off from Glasgow was singularly quiet because it took place in the middle of the night and we just slipped quietly out of the gates of Maryhill Barracks; and very few of us ever saw them again. We got down to Southampton, I think it must have been pretty early in the morning, and we set off from Southampton having embarked in the *Caledonia* I think her name was. Anyway, she had been recently victualled for a passage to Canada so there was any amount of grub, which we were very glad to see, and we went off from Southampton at night, just as the light went. Got into Le Havre in the early morning and it was very early. I saw a familiar figure on the quay and I looked at it twice and, yes, it was definitely my father. He had been called up and was a base commandant. His job was to meet all the incoming ships. The French were very kind, very enthusiastic and as soon as we got off the ship we marched about four miles up to the camp which was on the top of the hill.

I was a lieutenant in command of the battalion's rather compact number of machine-gunners and it was easy to keep an eye on them. I know buttons and badges were given or were solicited by welcoming French civilians but I don't think my men were involved. The pipers went down very well of course but in our 'trews' we may not have quite held the attraction of the regiments in kilts.

Later there was an immense train waiting for us, miles long. Took all the battalion, all the horses, all the wagons, everything, and we trundled up through Northern France, arriving at a place just short of the Belgian frontier. Detraining there we were billeted in the local convent, which I think had been vacated. We were at this place for a day and then we moved up to the canal, the Mons Canal.

We would have been a little east of Mons itself and we were told to take up an outpost position. Well, there was the canal and there was one bridge across it and the commanding officer decided to put two companies on the far side of the canal and the headquarters and the remainder on the near side, on the 'French' side, and there was nothing to indicate that war was on. There were no sounds or anything of that sort and some of the young officers were unwise enough to take their bedding to the far side of the canal and then at 2am we were told that if we weren't out of that position in about an hour we would probably remain there for life. So, that created quite a stir and I remember the commanding officer getting progressively more anxious as the last of the chaps got across the single bridge. How we got across complete and moved off to a destination unknown, I think that is one of the characteristics of the whole of this operation. You never really quite knew where you were going or where you were going to pitch up or in fact why. We had heard some small arms shooting by the time we moved off of course.

We were in column of route but very ready to deploy for action, machine guns to the rear so you could wheel about and form up very quickly in extended order across the road, taking up firing positions. In fact the only time that we really did this was a slightly humorous instance. It was a rather nice warm morning. It must have been about 5 o'clock in the morning and we were sitting down for ten minutes and everything was more peaceful than it is possible to say. And over the skyline about 1,000 yards away there came a single French cavalryman and he had his sword drawn and he was cantering along pretty briskly and in a matter of moments five *Uhlans* (**German cavalrymen**) popped over the same skyline. So, I said to my machine-gunners – of course, we were ready to fire instantly, 'Give them half a belt,' which apparently landed all round them because they turned round and disappeared over the skyline. Whereupon, the little Frenchman, turned round in his saddle, waved his sword, turned his horse round and belted off after them. What happened to him I really don't know but he was a very gallant chap.

We never really got into action throughout the retreat. We lined up to take action any number of times. Even at Le Cateau, we never really got into action because our brigade, 19th Infantry Brigade, was the Reserve Brigade and so one spent a very great deal of time moving from the right flank to the left flank and never really coming into action; because the moment you thought you were going to do something you were switched away somewhere else and it wasn't until we were rearguard leaving Le Cateau towards dusk that we lined up and had to fire, and even then there was more of our own cavalry in the line of fire than the enemy cavalry.

In these early stages, unless you came fully into action, it was all taken, you know, as part of the game and I don't think any of us realized that there was a very unpleasant side to war until we got into the first trenches and then a lot of one's friends got killed. This was further south at La Bassée. We had been up to Ypres and then we had done what was for us our first ever move by bus, south to this place, La Bassée, and we came into action very promptly. In fact, we were beginning to dig in when it was apparent that the Germans were there, and there in very considerable numbers, and two of our companies went forward into the village and they came in for a rather heavy mauling. With my machine-gunners I had been sent forward in support of battalions of the brigade further forward.

We were on a very slight ridge, and the village which they had been sent down to defend must have been 1,000 yards to our front and I suppose 200 feet below us. One couldn't see what was going on because of the houses but it was quite evident that a great deal was going on. One could see Germans further away. There was a lot of firing in the village and then, platoon by platoon, our people were coming back. I had my machine guns lined up there but of course, we had never been taught anything about indirect fire and I just didn't dare do anything about it because I just hadn't enough knowledge to fire over our men at their pursuers. With hindsight of course one might have done quite a bit of damage. The Germans were firing over the heads of their own people but we hadn't learnt that and it was then that we really started to dig in seriously and that position remained I think pretty well as we had dug it until the end of the war.

We remained there for quite a while, perhaps five or six weeks and Major Oakley and I were still in the area when orders came to us on 17 March 1915 that the 2nd Battalion had had a baddish knock and that somebody was required to go and take command, and somebody else was required to go and be adjutant. Major Oakley and I set off at once that day and a few miles down the line we found the 2nd Battalion consisted of a regimental sergeant major and 187 other ranks; all that remained from thirty-six officers and nearly 1,000 men who had gone into the Battle of Neuve Chapelle. So, I then became the 2nd Battalion adjutant.

We were taken out of the line and Richard Oakley, the acting CO, who was a notable personality, had, within three weeks, a battalion fit to go to war again which they did. Another man took command and we were ready for the next battle, the Battle of Aubers Ridge in May, particularly pointless really from our point of view. We were the reserve battalion of the brigade and as far as I recall two battalions went into the German line after certain mines had been exploded and then we were required to follow up. The country was quite open. There were a number of entirely un-silenced German machine guns firing from our flank at a range of about 300 yards. Fortunately the firing hadn't quite settled down to a degree of perfect accuracy or I shouldn't be here now but a great number of us were knocked out having achieved exactly nothing.

I think it is only fair to say, without naming him, that the commanding officer, an extremely gallant man but a bit unbalanced, had again let his enthusiasm run away with his common sense. Better leadership I think would have got the battalion a bit of ground with less loss. He wasn't prepared to take advice and he felt that if you waved your sword and said, 'On, On,' all would be well but unfortunately it was not. I took a bullet through the arm and through the hip. As I say, fortunately the Germans hadn't got the range exactly right or otherwise it would have done more damage. It did quite enough and I nestled down comfortably behind fourteen inches of hardwood, muttering to myself that it ought to be bullet proof. However, some fellows who had survived Neuve Chapelle, most gallantly came and pulled me out and in due course I got home.

Convalescence took a good long time because the wounds went wrong and I didn't really appear in France again until the following year, just in time for the opening of the Battle of the Somme. I was sent as a sort of reserve second in command of a battalion I didn't know, the 15th Battalion the Durham Light Infantry, and I found myself without a job or employment of any sort or kind of description, merely to attend the battle in order to take over when the commanding officer became a casualty, if he did. The actual second in command was to remain in the wagon line for the battle, so I found myself wandering across no-man's-land. We were opposite Fricourt, the DLI was the third battalion to go over really without anything to do. It was about 600 yards and in neat rows were the people who had gone ahead of us. They were lying there dead. A few had got into the German trenches and we followed up, and as far as I was concerned I 'collected' a piece of bomb just after I got to the German trenches and then there was a most annoying thing.

There was a German dugout and there was a German at the bottom of it. Every time I tried to walk past the door, he took a shot at me. So, I thought, well, the obvious thing to do is to shoot back at him but I found that with a broken left wrist you can't cock an automatic pistol. So, one wonders what to do. Fortunately a soldier came along with a bomb and settled the question for me and then in due course I found myself walking back again and I passed the second in command and wished him the best of luck. And he was walking up to take over because by that time the Commanding Officer had in fact become a casualty.

It was a beautiful morning, which made it worse, and there were all these poor fellows lying there in rows and there was a lot of machine-gunning going on and I think that on the whole one was more interested in not taking too long in crossing this area. One walked of course, and getting into some sort of cover and really trying to find something useful to do.

I don't think it was realized that if you employ a very great deal of heavy artillery in chalk land, you throw up great masses of chalk and you so disfigure the countryside that it becomes almost impossible to advance over. Great mounds of chalk, boulders of 20 feet, sticking up 10 or 12 feet into the air; it was not just the question of the wire.

My wound had broken the wrist, that was all, and I suppose if I had been very gallant I would have put a handkerchief round it and carried on but I thought really there didn't seem to be an awful lot of point because I was scared that I would lose the arm if I didn't do something about it fairly soon, so somebody told me. So, I wandered back and in due course was carted home.

In due course I got back to France, with a staff job in the 15th Scottish Division. This was after the Battle of Arras in April 1917. Later in the year I was made brigade major and as such was involved in two spells of the 3rd Battle of Ypres. This was a dreadful experience.

I should explain what a brigade major does. It is chiefly to make certain that the brigadier's orders get to the proper authority and get there as quickly as possible. Sometimes he goes himself, sometimes he can send a messenger. You have got to translate things into 'orders' first, then go to see that they are issued, and then help to see that they are carried out. I suppose at regimental level it is very like the joining of the role of adjutant and quartermaster.

Our brigade headquarters in our two stints in the Ypres offensive was in Ypres itself, near the Menin Gate: of course under shell fire but rejoicing in the fact that a noted trench engineer had built good solid fortifications because the Germans had a nasty habit of using armour-piercing shells on us and you heard this infernal thing boring its way through it seemed towards us. It always came to a stop fortunately before it got to us, but it was very noisy.

After Ypres, we went again, as far as I was concerned, to being in front of Arras to the left of the huge German thrust on 21 March 1918. We had pulled out of our most advanced positions so the Germans attacked the air. Our rear positions were very sketchy indeed. However, that was just in front of Arras. We stopped them alright and I must tell you about what I thought was one of the most impressive sights I saw on that particular day. We had begun to run a bit short of machine-gunners and things like that and we sent an SOS back to get some machine-gunners from the Reserve and we were told that the machine-gunners were from the Life Guards. I heard that they were on their way so I scuttled up from my cellar and the street was extremely lively. I mean you could see bits of Arras falling down all round and then suddenly up the middle of the road, paying not the slightest attention to anything, marched some thirty-six braves followed by a wagon with their machine guns. The pace was a nice, slow Guards step and I met the man in charge, whom I happened to know, and told him where he had to go, and they marched on and, I am told, they never had any casualties at all. Other people were scuttling down the street from door to door. They paid absolutely no attention to anything at all and they did great work when they got up into the line. It was that occasion when the infantry and the gunners fought in the same line. Our infantry came back to fight on the gun line in other words.

As for myself, I popped in and out of my cellar really. It was my job. Well, then things got quieter again after a bit and I was told I was to go on a staff course to Cambridge with a view to becoming a 2nd grade staff officer in my own division which I thought was going to be marvellous. However, at the end of the course the Commandant said, 'Oh you have been in France some time haven't you?' I said I had and I was then told that I was to be sent to Salonika. In fact it was too late for me to take part in the Macedonian Campaign (**but other adventures lay ahead**).

3

VICE-ADMIRAL
SIR CHARLES HUGHES-HALLETT CBE

The Dardanelles and Jutland

I first met and recorded Sir Charles in November 1977. My diary entry of that visit to Odstock is brief, 'Very good tape and documents,' but I was to be the beneficiary of much more help in due course, most notably in my being introduced to numerous senior naval officers whose service either commenced with that of Sir Charles or later coincided. Without exception they contributed interviews and documents. From the Admiral's social kindnesses, I remember, in particular, later staying in his beautiful old house in Salisbury Cathedral Close.

Sir Charles was born in 1898 in the County of Suffolk. He entered The Royal Naval College, Osborne in 1911 and was in his fifth term at its senior establishment, Dartmouth, when war broke out in August 1914.

Though we had not completed our course we had experienced a test mobilization and we were now in the real mobilization and were immediately shot off to wartime appointments in older ships of the Third Fleet. I was to go to the *Vengeance* which was an elderly battleship but rather a freak one as it turned out in that the Third Fleet to which she belonged was mainly manned by Reservists but *Vengeance* herself was not because she had been the gunnery firing ship at Chatham and had an active service crew and was put down into the Third Fleet where she belonged from her own category but with an active service crew instead of a reserve crew.

When we joined her she was at Portland having come round from Chatham just after the war had been declared and we remained at Portland or in the western Channel for the first two or three months. One of the jobs we did in the Channel was to patrol the western end. Four old British battleships spaced apart, to the south of us French ships of a sort, stopping all ships coming up Channel and boarding them to find out who they were and what they were doing. I remember going on board a French ship, which was coming back from Chile with nitrate, and they were quite unaware that there was a war on. She had been a great number of days at sea.

Well, just before Christmas 1914 we were ordered to Gibraltar where we sat for some weeks doing nothing, as far as I know, in harbour. We then at short notice were sent down to the Cape Verde islands off north-west Africa to relieve a ship which was there. There were eight German merchant ships in the harbour having anchored themselves there when the war broke out. It was a Portuguese colony. Portugal was not at war and there was a fear that they might break out, aided by the *Karlsruhe* I think it was which was in the Atlantic. All this meant that we lay at anchor there for forty days and trained our guns at night in case the *Karlsruhe* made a shot at getting into the harbour. Then, after days of doing very little, our destiny called us east towards the Dardanelles.

We returned to Gibraltar where we hoisted the flag of Admiral de Robeck who was to go out to the eastern Mediterranean. This was done because we were the first ship that was available for him. As a relevant detail, and it is quite interesting how things happened in those days, de Robeck had been working in Atlantic patrol cruisers and he had changed ships thirty-one times when he came to us. I remember this because his most junior secretary in his entourage, who was a young paymaster midshipman or rather assistant clerk in those days, had run out of clean clothes and we had to outfit him. We then went on to Malta with de Robeck where we stayed a few days and then were ordered up to Mudros which was becoming the base from which operations were to be launched against the outer forts of the Dardanelles (**with the ultimate aim of forcing a way through to the Sea of Marmora and so to Constantinople to threaten bombardment of the city and so force**

the Turks out of the war). We varied our base position between the two islands of Mudros and Tenedos.

Of the preliminary bombardment of the outer forts in February 1915, I remember chiefly sitting in the fore turret, which I was a midshipman of, looking at the back end of the guns when they fired; but what they were firing at didn't reach such a low life as myself.

Our Marines were landed on the Asiatic shore at Kum Kale to destroy what they could there and they achieved a good deal and they lost one sergeant who was killed but otherwise I think no casualties. At the beginning of March we were much less successful on the Gallipoli Peninsula itself, attempting at its tip to destroy the defences. We were not involved in this because of problems with our boilers. Three men had been very badly scalded – I think one killed – by a build-up of steam pressure exploding through the housing of the steam-pressure pipes leading from the boiler and of course, the contents of the boiler just cascaded into the boiler room. We had in varying degrees a very large number of boiler explosions. This was the only really bad one but I think there were fifty-eight in the time I was in her and she was getting very shaky.

On March 18, the great day of the assault on the Narrows of the Dardanelles to bombard the forts from close range, *Vengeance* was on the wing so to speak, on the left flank, the European shore, and we spent the time firing pretty steadily at targets which I suppose were clearly marked. I don't know but of course, the trouble with those old ships at that stage was that you could only indicate a target by voice. By telling a chap that you wanted to aim his gun at whatever it was. There was no form of direction sight. I should add that I am an ex-gunnery officer and therefore rather up in this subject later but at the time there was nothing easy or sure about it. It used to be one of the jokes in the ship when somebody described a target as, a 'bushy bush' on the Asiatic shore, which doesn't get you very far. In addition, the trajectory of our shelling was all against the accurate and effective hitting of a low-profile target.

I did see one very dramatic incident on this day even though I was in the turret most of the time – the loss of the old French battleship *Bouvet* – not exactly as it happened but shortly afterwards because the officer of my turret who saw it happening by putting his head out of the hole in the top merely called me up so that I could see. It was all over in three minutes, six hundred or so drowned.

We were hit several times but only by small stuff – nothing that did any serious damage. Mark you, *Vengeance* had a very unusual captain in the sense of a man who had been one of the very earliest people to go through what later became the staff course, but in those days was a senior officers' course at Portsmouth; and therefore he was a person who was picked for intelligence. He had taken the precautions in *Vengeance* of having all possible spare anchor cable dragged up from the cable lockers and arranged on top of the 6-inch casemate and anywhere else where he thought there was a danger of damage, in order to give sufficient protection and that undoubtedly had an effect, apart from a moral effect, because one or two of these light shells did in fact fail to penetrate the top of a 6-inch casemate.

For the actual landings on 25 April 1915, *Vengeance* was earmarked for a major bombarding job: I think the answer was our gunnery was rather better than other people's. I am putting it at that level, not good, and therefore we were going to be on the left flank inside the Dardanelles bombarding positions inshore where the landings at Morto Bay were going to take place. Ironically what I remember most about that day was not what I was in position to see, which was not much, but the rumours circulating in the most amazing way as to what was happening ashore, but when one thinks of it in retrospect there was absolutely no basis in them because there was no communication between the two.

Diverging for a second and in relation to the torpedoing of the two old British battleships subsequent to the April landings, another of my captain's precautions in the *Vengeance*, the same class of ship, was that he wouldn't allow anybody down below the level of the main deck. All watertight doors below that were shut. The result was the Gunroom was shut and we were turned out and lived in the Wardroom. Now I doubt if any other captain took that precaution but it certainly would have had a good effect had there been underwater damage below that. As it happens, the *Vengeance*, was the first ship fired at by the submarine before the *Triumph* was hit. We were coming up from Mudros and we were coming into Gaba Tepe on the north shore of the Gallipoli Peninsula and were fired at. There was a comic episode on the bridge when the torpedo track was sighted. The captain and the navigator saw it simultaneously, one said: 'Hard to port' and the other said: 'Hard to starboard'. The quartermaster did neither and the torpedo missed. However, that having happened I don't know what we did but we circled about I suppose. Meanwhile, the next thing we saw was the *Triumph* hit. I didn't see the actual explosion but I saw her as she was going down.

Vengeance was ordered home in late summer but I remember at periods of about 24-hour stretches we were running *Vengeance*'s picket boat off the Australian beaches and we were employed to do anything the beach masters required which in practice meant that as destroyers were bringing up reinforcements you took out horse boats to collect a cargo of troops and to take them inshore and land them. That was the most usual thing. Occasionally you were detailed to take wounded off to one of the hospital ships. These were usually very badly wounded indeed. I don't quite know what happened to the lightly wounded but my memory stands very strongly of taking out badly wounded men two or three times and one other minor detail was that on one occasion I was instructed to take out a dead Indian Army soldier, a Sikh I think, with some of his live compatriots and bury him at sea. The background to that I don't know but it caused me at the time considerable thought as to what we should do to honour the occasion. Whether you took your shoes off, or stood to attention or what you did. However, it all passed off very well.

I must mention one more thing. There was a bit of a blow one night and one of the horse boats which were not numerous had broken adrift and gone ashore and I was told by the beach master, or the deputy beach master, actually to go and salvage it. Well, I had probably a better idea of the bit of coast than he had and I pointed out that it wasn't actually in the English lines. It was in the Turkish lines. I was told off and told to mind my own business and go and get it. Luckily at that moment the chief beach master turned up who countermanded the order very graphically. Otherwise presumably I should have been shot up or else been captured.

Another thing that happened while we were off the beach was that some general, I have forgotten who, came up from Mudros in the Admiral's yacht, the *Triad*, and I was sent off to bring him ashore. He arrived after dark. It was a moonlight night actually and I went out and picked him up and he was extremely nice to me and we had left the *Triad* about a couple of hundred yards and he got hold of me and said: 'Look I am not in a great hurry to go ashore but I am desperately hungry, can you give me something to eat?' This struck me as a very peculiar episode when we had just left the *Triad*. So we lashed him up to a cup of cocoa and that sort of thing and I had a stoker who had a trick of frying eggs on the slice which is the huge steel thing that you poke the coal with in the boiler. The general was frightfully intrigued over this. It is one of those silly episodes that sticks in your mind.

I would like to express my admiration for our torpedo officer who stands out in my mind in comparison with some of the others. His name was Eric Robinson and he earned a Victoria Cross for leading an attempt to destroy one of our submarines which had run aground behind Turkish lines, but he was also seconded to the trawlers to stiffen the leadership of the North Sea fishermen engaged in the dangerous task of sweeping for mines fully under the guns on the enemy shore. He was a very gallant officer.

Now when we left the Dardanelles we went down to Mytilene as a guard ship and became a sort of cross between a guard ship and a hospital ship because there were various wounded people collected there; some from stupid episodes of trying to cut out Turkish merchant ships which were lying near their harbour. This was attempted by boats' crews under oars but not from our ship: most futile arrangement and they got shot up badly. There were also a few aviators wounded or injured in their ditching on one side or the other of the Gallipoli Peninsula. It maybe that there were some injured in crash landings.

We were not in the main harbour on the island and there was a rock on the way, which they decided they would use to mount a gun on in case a German submarine tried to get in. I was running one of the steam picket boats and I took a party down in order to blow up some bit of the rock which was in the way of mounting the gun and, due to an error shall we say, a gun cotton hose lying in the stern cabin went off and every officer sitting in the stern including myself, who was conducting the affairs of the boat, was burned. One man died. We got back to the ship but we added to the general collection of invalids.

Concerning our return home; *Vengeance* was getting slower and slower owing to the boiler troubles and we proceeded up Channel going flat out at about 12 knots in great fear that we might get into trouble, but they sent out a destroyer escort from Plymouth and we got there safely and paid off and I was appointed to a much newer ship, one of the earlier dreadnoughts, HMS *St Vincent* in The Grand Fleet at Scapa Flow. She was in the Fourth Battle Squadron and of course we were at the Battle of Jutland.

The daytime action as regards to *St Vincent* I know very little about because I was in my turret the whole time. We fired a considerable number of rounds but I don't know what at, because one doesn't see it when one is down there and I hoped with some result but I just did not know. The *St Vincent* class had five turrets. A up in front, P and Q one each side mid ships, X and Y not above each other, both flat on the quarterdeck. My turret, X, was the one between the back end of the main superstructure and a small superstructure between X and Y on the quarterdeck. I was still a midshipman.

We were used to doing sweeps down the North Sea at irregular intervals, or even exercises, and there was always a sense of excitement in any of those, because being young there was always the prospect that it might lead to something, but I don't know there was anything special on that occasion until actually flag signals began showing which made one realize that there was something might be in the wind.

When darkness fell and we went to night action stations, it was one of the rather curious episodes because I was told that I was to take charge of the starboard quarter, secondary armament battery, 4-inch guns, and control it from the stern sheets of a picket boat which was up on the booms. Now why I say this was curious is because I had never done it before. Obviously I knew from instruction that the 4-inch guns were divided into four groups but I had never been put in command of it before and we had never seemed to have practised it for night action. From hindsight I think the

91

reason was because nobody really at that time had visualised night action stations involved keeping the turrets manned and consequently the turret officers had duplicate jobs for night purposes and couldn't fulfil both at the same time.

As they were keeping them manned there were no officers to take charge of the groups. So I retired to my stern sheet picket boat with voice-talking equipment and could talk to the guns quite happily but God knows what would have happened if we had to have fired them because I don't know whether my competence was adequate to do much about it. I am not sure whether I should have let them off and whether I could have ensured that it was in the right direction but I didn't see anything at night so that was that. The German Fleet of course was passing astern of the Battle Fleet and vaguely there were one or two flashes during the course of the night but a hell of a long way away apparently. I suppose they weren't really all that far away but they seemed to be.

Of course in Rosyth we did get the newspapers for reading in the Gunroom almost immediately after the battle had been fought and were aware that the heavy British losses had been reported but we were beginning to learn of the considerable German losses too. The fact remains that we went to sea quite happily shortly afterwards with no let or hindrance, which didn't make it look very much like a German victory.

I left *St Vincent* roughly at the end of 1916 and was sent down South and went as sub lieutenant to HMS *Hardy* operating from Plymouth in the 4th Destroyer Flotilla out on patrol off Stark Point and off the Lizard and round the corner in the entrance to the bottom end of the Bristol Channel. The idea being that you had these destroyer patrols and such shipping as there was kept close inshore inside the patrolling destroyers.

The only thing which was exciting from my point of view was that one of the days we were patrolling off Stark Point we sighted further out at sea a ship which surprised us a little bit and we went out to investigate. I should add that my captain was a senior commander in the flotilla. The ship turned out to be an abandoned Dutch oiler, very much down by the stern but not in any danger of sinking. So my captain decided we better try and get her back to Plymouth. There were two other destroyers either with us or near us who were called in and I was put on board the oiler to get her ready for towing which turned out not to be a very easy job because she was very down, her engine room was flooded and she was down by the stern and with the obvious consequence that her bow was miles in the air and to get a line paid out from her to the destroyer miles below was tricky. Anyhow, we succeeded. We didn't ourselves tow her. One of the other destroyers with better towing arrangements did.

I should have mentioned that in the destroyer as a sub lieutenant you were the third officer and my first lieutenant was a regular lieutenant and a very good one and there was an excellent captain. One realised that you were expected to take charge and act on your own initiative and not be nursemaided the whole time and after a very short time you did, because there was nothing else you could do.

People talk about it being less comfortable in a small ship but I was perfectly comfortable in the *Hardy*. The only thing that used to annoy me in *Hardy* was the fact that when she was moving, as she always was, (I don't mean steaming, I mean due to the sea) there were irritating noises which prevented you sleeping easily. And of course she rolled a good deal in a big sea.

Another thing: in a small ship you get to know your ship's company and they get to know you and you are much more of a body.

As it happened we were not to lose a ship in the convoying we were engaged in but we did have one damaged by torpedo, a White Star cargo boat. We got her into port, and you asked me about airship convoy escort, well it may not be what you want but we picked up an airship crew safely out of the sea on one occasion! The airships working with us were based somewhere in Cornwall and they used to appear rather irregularly over convoys and were obviously a very useful deterrent when there. But you had no means of communicating with them except by flashing lamp, which is a tedious game with an airship or an aeroplane. And I haven't got a lot of views on how valuable they were or not but apart from that one or two destroyers in the flotilla had kite balloons which they used to sail about with and towards the end of the war of course, all sorts of things began happening. We began to get hydrophone destroyers – groups of three who were out for hunting U-boats, also

American, what would now be called, fast motor boats and I suppose they also had hydrophones. They were rather a nuisance because they used to lie about in the Channel with no lights and you never knew they were there until you nearly ran one down.

Also I should add another point on this convoy work. By the time we got going – and my captain had a very good record from the point of view of successes – we started getting put on to the American and Canadian troop convoys. Now those were a different story. You met them further west a bit allowing for your fuel arrangements and you took them without change of escort right up to Dover and you then took the empties, similar ones to the one before, right out again to the next one. It was a hell of a long trip, in days I mean, and we did this oh, half a dozen times. More perhaps. The whole business one way and another took you about three weeks.

4

GENERAL SIR JAMES H MARSHALL-CORNWALL KCB CBE DSO MC

An Intelligence Officer on the Western Front

Several exciting possibilities came together when I was able to arrange for this interview to take place in May 1974. By definition of his senior rank, Sir James had had a distinguished military career, one that was grounded in intellectual attainment; then he had been on Sir Douglas Haig's GHQ and, for my own part, as a student of the war, I was increasingly coming to feel that time and certain historians were dealing less than fairly with Haig's stewardship of the BEF. Then third, Sir James himself had a respected position as a military historian with a new biography out on Haig. Looking today at my questioning in the interview in relation to Haig I see some irony in my persistence in pursuing negative judgements whereas I have, myself, come to an increasingly favourable assessment. The balance of a general verdict in such matters seems to some extent subject to generational change.

In May 1974 I wrote in my diary: 'Delightful man – excellent tape – both recollections and reflections.' My view today on this interview itself is that its information and thought-provoking sparkle certainly pass the test of time.

Sir James was born in 1887 in Karachi, his father being Postmaster General in India. Prep school in India was followed by the army class at Rugby where the language master, Robert Prior, inculcated in his pupil a deep interest in, and almost an affection for, studying foreign languages.

We were destined for either the Royal Military College, Sandhurst, as then it was, or the Royal Military Academy, Woolwich, which took cadets for the Royal Artillery and the Royal Engineers. Now the education provided for boys in the army class differed from the general rule at Rugby. For instance I had to give up the study of Latin and Greek at both of which I had been rather better than Mathematics or Science and we specialized in Modern Languages and subjects like Geography and Military History.

There was an officer cadet force at the school but strange to say the army class was not allowed to join the cadet corps because the cadet corps was allowed off certain hours of study, which the army class was not.

As it happened, the later celebrated Rupert Brooke and I were exact contemporaries at the school. In fact his father was my house-master but by no means a popular one. Rupert Brooke, however, survived this drawback and was extremely popular. He played rugby football for the house and was a charming personality and I remember reading with admiration the first two poems for which, two years running, he won the school poetry prize. He was tall, handsome, in fact, when he went to Cambridge afterwards, he got rather spoilt I think particularly by ladies.

I was in a position of comparative responsibility at Rugby. I gained my football cap and I was a prefect and a member of the sixth form but some of the masters struck me as being rather hard and unsympathetic and I was not particularly fond of my headmaster, the Reverend Dr James. My recollections of life in the house were very pleasant. We were all very good friends. Another of my contemporaries was Geoffrey Keynes who afterwards became well known as a scholar and surgical consultant to the Royal Air Force.

My father had always wanted me to join the army although I had no original inclination that way. As a boy I was anxious to follow in the footsteps of an uncle of mine who was in the Indian Woods and Forests because I thought I would get plenty of tiger shooting, but my father rather wisely advised me not to because he said: 'By the time you are in a position of responsibility you will find that the Indian Woods and Forests Service has been completely Indian-ized. You will have an Indian boss,' so I fell in with his wishes and applied to join the Royal Artillery.

Woolwich was a natural transition from the army class at Rugby with regard to boarding school life at this time except that the curriculum was completely different and entirely concentrated on military subjects, of which I at once became very fond. And we were only allowed to take up one foreign language and I took German, which was my better language rather than French, and I finished up by taking the first prize in German on passing out.

The teaching I thought at Woolwich was of a very high standard. For instance my chief instructor in fortifications and military engineering was Colonel E D Swinton who was afterwards the originator and developer of the tank. He was highly intelligent and so were most of the instructors there for whom I had great admiration and they certainly fostered my interest in military history and all military subjects. I thought the technical training was of a very high standard too.

When I joined as a young officer I found that there was an intense keenness among my fellow subalterns who, of course, like me had been educated at Woolwich. I think the British army at that time had worked up to a very high standard. The year I joined the service was 1907 when we had just digested the lessons of the South African War and I think we all took our duties very seriously and were very anxious to acquire proficiency. In the battery which I joined, the senior subaltern had fought through the South African War and all the captains and majors had also served in the South African War and we felt that our training was being carried out under the most realistic circumstances with recent war experience, which added to our keenness.

I think we all realized that the British army as it went to the South African War at the end of 1899 was very badly trained for any overseas campaign except against savage tribes; and we realized that enormous lessons had been learnt during the war and that we were now on the upgrade and had an advantage over other European nations, which had not had such recent war experience.

We had no antipathy against the French but on the other hand no very high admiration of them but we felt that the next war would be a European war and that the French would be our allies and the Germans would be our enemies. In July 1911 the Agadir incident took place when the Germans tried to pull a fast one over the French in Morocco and I gather we were so near to going to war at that time that I, as a subaltern, but having qualified as an interpreter in German and French, was summoned to headquarters of the Scottish Command at Edinburgh and put through a course as a learner in staff duties under the Chief of Staff, Colonel Hunter-Weston, who later commanded the 29th Division in Gallipoli. That gave me an early inkling into staff duties.

You have asked whether in my view there was any accurate appraisal of what sort of war this anticipated European war might be, given that there were recent indicators in the Far East and more time-distant ones in the United States that it might well not be a swiftly concluded affair. I think most of us in the junior ranks anyway entered the First World War in rather a light-hearted spirit thinking like many senior officers did that it would be all over by Christmas and I think there were very few even in the higher ranks who shared Kitchener's view that it would be a war of long duration. I think that our military teaching before the war had not taken sufficient notice of the Russo-Japanese War where trench warfare really came into being and it was a comparatively recent occurrence. Perhaps Ian Hamilton's *Staff Officers' Scrap Book* gave one an inkling of what might happen but we thought, 'Oh well it is in the Far Eastern theatre and it wouldn't happen in Europe.' On the other hand I think more attention should have been paid to the lessons of the American Civil War.

At Woolwich we were certainly taught the American Civil War and it was also taught at Staff College, Camberley, but with much more emphasis on the strategic manoeuvres of 'Stonewall' Jackson for instance than on the more protracted trench operations which took place round Richmond in 1864. I think certainly we thought that in Europe trench warfare would not stagnate to the extent which it rapidly did but that warfare would be more something like the 1870 Franco-Prussian War.

As to the dominance of the cavalry ethic in general army professionalism pre-war; looking back to those days I have the impression that we in other arms of the service rather looked on the cavalry as a joke and that their officers did not take their profession very seriously but spent most of their time in playing polo and what we used to call 'poodle faking', that is, playing around with ladies. But my experience at the beginning of the First World War rather made me change my opinion because it happened to be at the beginning of the Battle of the Marne I was given command of a squadron of the 15th Hussars as all the officers had been killed or wounded at Le Cateau, and I was surprised at the extraordinary efficiency of the non-commissioned officers who had been highly trained by their officers and to my mind were of a higher professional standard than the non-commissioned officers that we had in the infantry and in the artillery.

However I think that one of the greatest mistakes that the higher command made in the First World War was this persistent theory that the cavalry were bound to give the coup de grâce in any campaign once the enemy's front line had been broken through. This pernicious doctrine certainly permeated the mind of Sir Douglas Haig and I think that was his greatest fault in his leadership. It is a fact that he had entrusted the command of three of his armies to cavalry officers who were perhaps not of the right calibre to command armies in trench warfare and I think that we suffered from this drawback.

Returning to my own career as a subaltern of six years' service, I played a very junior part naturally in the manoeuvres of 1912 but I recollect them very well from a worm's eye point of view. My chief recollection is watching the infantry, the 1st Division, crossing the River Thames by pontoon bridge erected by the sappers and the 3rd Infantry Brigade was halfway across the pontoon bridge when it collapsed and the whole of the transport and the brigade commander fell into the river. As regards the higher command and leadership of the manoeuvres, of course, we were completely ignorant. I did not attend the conference at Cambridge and we knew nothing about who had won the battle and who had not, but this unfortunate incident took place to my memory in front of General Foch, as he then was, and the Grand Duke Nicholas of Russia who were looking on with their missions from their respective countries, which I am afraid did not give them a very high opinion of the efficiency of the British Army.

Yes I know that it should be mentioned that the British Army in these exercises were using aircraft for the first time – for reconnaissance purposes – and I do remember seeing a few aeroplanes flying about but even as a subaltern in a field battery we never had any attempt at cooperation with the air. I think they were not used for artillery spotting in those days purely for general observation and the location of enemy forces.

Coming to the war, as an instructor in map reading at the Royal Military Academy at Woolwich, I happened to be on leave in Spain and Portugal at the time when war broke out. I was firmly convinced that the Asquith government would never be persuaded to take Britain into any war whatever. And although my friends told me and warned me that the war was coming. I said, 'No, I am going to have my holiday in the Iberian Peninsula.' As things happened, when the die was cast, I was lunching with the British Consul General in Oporto and I was where Wellington's troops had crossed the river in May 1809. I then made my way as quickly as I could across Portugal, Spain and France to England and on arriving at the War Office I was told to join a new formation to be called the Intelligence Corps owing no doubt to the fact that I had qualified as a first class interpreter in French and German.

In fact the young officer had Norwegian, Swedish, Dutch, Italian and Spanish in his language quiver too!

When I joined the Intelligence Corps at Southampton in the middle of August 1914 I was told that my main object in life was to interrogate German prisoners, and with that object in view I was to be attached to GHQ of the British Expeditionary Force and then, after a short interlude of doing staff work as a military landing officer, I went to Le Cateau where I arrived on August 22. There were, of course, by that time no German prisoners to interrogate so I kicked my heels about for 24 hours until news of the Battle of Le Cateau came in, and the news was so bad that the Commander in Chief, Sir John French, decided to pack up and retreat on Paris as quickly as he could. We did so and I was given responsibility for 70 chargers of Sir John French's staff. I got these horses to the neighbourhood of Compiègne in two days. I was then informed that I was to join the headquarters of the 3rd Division in the 2nd Corps as Divisional Intelligence Officer officially known as an Agent First Class, and so my fellow officers in the divisional headquarters always addressed me as 'agent'.

Well, during the battles of the Marne, I had a great stroke of luck because Sir Frederick Maurice, Brigadier-General Maurice as he then was, put me in charge of 'A' Squadron of the 15th Hussars (within the divisional cavalry) although the Battle of the Marne was a complete farce as far as the British Expeditionary Force was concerned. All we had to do was to march north-eastwards as fast as we could into the gap between the 1st and 2nd German armies. We had practically no fighting at all except for a little skirmishing where the Germans were blowing up a bridge in front of us but it gave me an enormous opportunity because of interrogating all the German rear guards who had fallen asleep, worn out, in ditches and barns. Also from collecting the requisition notices which they had left for the French farmers for requisitioning their forage, I re-constructed the whole Order of Battle of the German 2nd Cavalry Corps because here it formed the German rearguard.

As to our tiredness of which you will have read a lot, the troops of the 3rd Division had not been quite so heavily engaged at Le Cateau as those of the 5th Division which suffered very severely but the men were extremely exhausted. They had marched 200 miles with their backs to the enemy in very hot weather and on dusty roads and they were really physically worn out when they had to advance again and they were rather lethargic and liable to panic if a bridge blew up. I saw people panicking and rushing to the rear, but by the end of the retreat they were in pretty good fighting form when they reached the Aisne and there of course the Germans stood north of the Aisne and dug themselves in and put out barbed wire from the middle of September onwards and trench warfare started. By that time the casualties at Mons and Le Cateau had been made up. Reservists had come out and the troops were in pretty good form to face the very arduous autumn fighting that we had later on.

Immediately after the Battle of the Aisne, the scope of a divisional intelligence officer was very limited because we were no longer pursuing the retreating Germans and being able to pick up stragglers to interrogate and there was a double row of barbed wire inter-vening between us and the enemy. Matters soon changed however, because in early October we were switched from the Aisne up to the neighbourhood of Ypres and there General Foch and General French both thought they would be able to sweep round the enemy's right flank and advance through Flanders and push the Germans out of France and Belgium.

Unfortunately the Germans then produced five new Army Reserve corps to fill up the gap between their right flank and the sea and we were all stuck so that trench warfare extended from the Swiss frontier to the English Channel. When we got into our new sector of the front just south of Ypres, 3rd Divisional Headquarters was near Mount Kemmel which had a wonderful view over the sector immediately south of Ypres and then as intelligence officer, of course I had to go round the trenches and find out from the battalion commanders whether they could capture any prisoners (which was a rare thing in those days) and if so interrogate them.

We did have a few Alsatian deserters who came over of their own accord and then we had a great field day getting first hand information, but of course it was at their own level and they couldn't tell us much about the intentions of the higher command. Trench warfare really became fixed and I felt that apart from the odd deserter coming over I must do something about getting in touch with the enemy officers. I found there was a cottage in our front line which had not yet been destroyed and which I could get into during the hours of darkness and there, with a powerful telescope, I could survey a sector of the German trenches and even read the numbers on the soldiers' shoulder straps telling me which regiment they belonged to. However that was only on a very limited sector.

I also used to crawl out between the lines of barbed wire, armed with a revolver and a wire cutter and find stray Germans lying dead from which I took their shoulder straps and any papers on them. From time to time the unfortunate battalions in the front line were ordered by higher command to carry out a trench raid, which was a very unpopular form of warfare, and it generally involved very unpleasant things – getting through the barbed wire and raiding the enemy's trench in front under machine-gun fire. Occasionally we did have luck and some prisoners were brought back whom I could interrogate. But later on we had to depend on other methods such as dropping by parachute carrier pigeons behind the line. At first they were very successful. We got a tremendous lot of information from the local peasants, both Belgian and French, who wrote out the identity of the troops in their neighbourhood and put it back into the aluminium capsule on the pigeon's leg until the Germans found out the trick and started sending us back wrong information.

That went on until January 1915 when I was appointed to the General Staff as a General Staff Officer Third Class and made Intelligence Officer to the 2nd Corps (commanded by General Sir Charles Fergusson) which was still holding the same bit of country south of Ypres. There, of course, we were covering a wider front and we had more deserters and prisoners captured in raids to interrogate.

In January 1916 I was promoted to the rank of Major and appointed General Staff Officer Second Class at GHQ, British Expeditionary Force. My immediate chief was Brigadier-General John Charteris, a Royal Engineer officer. He was extremely clever and quick-witted but without in my opinion any real moral appreciation for the truth because he had a theory that he must not discourage his General Officer Commander in Chief in any way and must always prime him with the most optimistic view of the strategic situation. Charteris happened to have been serving on Douglas Haig's personal staff for the last six years having first encountered him in India, and Douglas Haig was fascinated by Charteris' conversational brilliance, whereas he himself was a rather inept speaker and took for gospel truth everything that Charteris told him, thus excluding any advice that he got from his own Chief of Staff.

Charteris was extremely pleasant to work with until your personal opinions differed from his and then he just overrode you saying that you were giving him information based on, shall we say, false information put out by the enemy. He was a big, bluff, hearty person – very pleasant to live with in the mess, very jovial and conversational. He was rather an empire builder. He gradually acquired everything in the way of censorship and conduct of distinguished visitors and press relations and everything else under his wing.

Charteris' point of view was, as I say, that he must only present the bright side of things to his Commander in Chief for fear of upsetting his offensive morale and he tended to disregard any information that was not optimistic. In fact he went this far: when he took the Commander in Chief around a prisoner of war camp he would eliminate all the most healthy looking Prussian guardsmen out of the camp before Douglas Haig saw it, and so he was only presented with the weediest specimens of the German army. Charteris would then say, 'See how their physique has deteriorated.'

Charteris at the time, of course, was in control of the press and press relations so the truth of the matter never got out. However on one occasion during the Battle of Arras when the Canadians captured Vimy Ridge, we captured all the papers of the German army opposing us. Among the papers describing the different units under the German Army Corps Headquarters, there was mention of a carcass-collecting factory and when I showed this to Charters he said, 'This confirms my opinion that the Germans are now boiling down their dead soldiers for fats.' And I said, 'No, I don't think you are right. I think in German it means an animal carcass and not a human body,' and Charteris said, 'My German is just as good as yours and I know this word can equally mean a human body and I am going to have a press conference and inform them all about this deterioration of the German economy.' Well, this happened and it was put in the newspapers except for some of the more respectable papers. I happened to get hold of *The Times* correspondent and told him my version of the thing and he very kindly did not reproduce this rather malicious bit of propaganda.

I think throughout the First World War there was a rather natural and continuing sense of hostility between the front line fighting soldiers, officers and men, and the staffs who lived in comparative luxury in chateaux three or four miles beyond the range of the German shellfire. This hostility was very marked I think at the beginning of the war in the first battle of Ypres but I think it was somewhat exaggerated. After all some people had to live in the mud and be blood-spattered but you couldn't really command thousands of men and live in that sort of condition. One had to keep a wider perspective over a wider area, and naturally there became established this rather unfortunate split between the fighting men and I would say the 'thinking' men. It is difficult to say how it could be avoided. Certainly if didn't appear to the same extent in the Second World War but then we didn't have this perpetual living in mud and blood in front line trenches like we did in the First War.

I used to have a foot in both camps because, as I say, I had to live up in the front line trenches all night, and during the day on many occasions, and also I enjoyed the comfort of sleeping in a billet away from the immediate burst of shells, and one felt that there was this discrepancy in feeling and it just couldn't be helped owing to the nature of trench warfare on such a vast scale.

I can remember going up to a battalion in the front line in the Ypres salient when we were up there and it happened to be on the 5th Army front commanded by General Hubert Gough. The officers were living in the most ghastly mud and shell-holed area near Passchendaele and they used to say to me, 'Oh yes, we know all about it. We shall be ordered to advance again. General Gough will push his shooting stick into the lawn at the chateau at which he lives miles away and say, 'Yes, it is as hard as a bone this morning. Give the order to advance,' and that was the feeling in the front lines that higher command was out of touch sometimes.

On the other hand I think it was an exaggerated feeling. I don't blame Sir Douglas Haig in that way because I think he took a great deal of trouble to get as far forward as he could and ascertain what the conditions were and when trench warfare became still more a question of defence held in depth and he was commanding the whole of the British Expeditionary Force with over a million men under his command, he could not be expected to go and make himself acquainted with every sector of the front, but he did have a very good system of the divisional officers, majors and young lieutenant colonels who had been actually wounded in the front line and who he sent out as his liaison officers to tell him exactly what was going on in the front line.

I think before the opening of the Battle of the Somme, General Rawlinson, in command of the new 4th Army, which did most of the fighting in the Somme battle, was over-optimistic as to his chances of success. He thought that everything would go well. He thought that his artillery was going to cut all the German barbed wire and that his men only had to advance to capture two lines of trenches. As a matter of fact the wire was not cut. We lost 57,000 casualties on the first day of the battle and in very few places did we even get into the German line.

Charteris had a very wide range of duties which he collected under the title of Intelligence at GHQ. The principle one was dealing with the enemy order of battle on the whole of the Western Front. In that,

I had to keep in very close touch with the head of French Intelligence at their Headquarters. We used to telephone to each other every evening exchanging news about the capture of German prisoners or documents on the various sectors of the whole of the Western Front. And, from our own experience and from what I collected from the French, I used to produce for Charteris, who was my immediate boss, a map showing the order of battle as far as we knew of the German troops on the whole of the Western Front and the position of their headquarters whenever we could locate it and the position of their reserve formations in the rear.

Charteris gave me fairly free run over this and I was entirely responsible for it, and when he went sick for a month, went down with flu, and had to go to the South of France to recover, I had to go to Douglas Haig every morning at 10 o'clock and give him the intelligence picture in place of Charteris and I was then astounded at the completely false picture that Haig had in mind about the state of the German morale and economic resources.

When I told him that the Germans were still fighting strongly and that there was no real decline in their morale, he stopped me and said, 'But your Brigadier-General told me quite a different story about this,' and I had to say, 'Well, Sir, I have just got to give you the facts as I know them.' He thought that I was misleading him whereas he had been completely misled by Charteris. He thought that he had only got to break one hole in the barbed wire line and push the cavalry through.

I would present him with the map, which I had brought up to date showing exactly where the different German divisions were holding the opposite side of the line, and give him a statement of what troops were in reserve at any particular sector of the front, and give him a rough idea of what we could ascertain was the state of their morale, their equipment, from the prisoners that we captured at different points along the front, and telling him that there was a weak spot in one place or another where there were no German reserves behind.

One particular instance of that was Cambrai. Before the battle of Cambrai in November 1917, Charteris had consistently told his chief that there was no possibility of any German reinforcements behind the line and that there was a gap in their reserves behind

Cambrai and that no troops could be transferred from the Russian Front, which had then collapsed, for two months to come. Whereas in fact, a week before the Battle of Cambrai started, I had documentary evidence that three fresh German divisions had been transferred from the Russian Front and one of them was actually detraining at Cambrai. And I put these on the map and showed it to Charteris and Charteris said, 'Show me your evidence. I don't believe you. I believe this is a bluff on the part of the enemy and that they have given you wrong information, and I can't tell the Commander in Chief that there is anything in front of him.' Well that, of course, was the last straw as far as I was concerned and I went to Davidson, the Director of Military Operations, and said, 'I can't go on working with this fellow any longer and I want to go back to duties.' He said, 'Just stay where you are and let me know what the real facts are,' and within the next fortnight Charteris had gone.

Ten days later the Germans counter-attacked and captured 10,000 of our men – the result of the new divisions which had just arrived from Russia and which Douglas Haig was kept in ignorance of.

Of course it was never intimated to me that my opposition to Charteris had played a part in his removal but within two months I was moved up to number 2 to General McDonagh at the War Office in charge of the German Section of the Military Intelligence Branch.

Coming back to Douglas Haig, the very few occasions on which I had to go and report personally to him, I got very little verbal response from him. He was a man of few words and usually expressed his approval or otherwise by a series of grunts and his face was very impassive and it was difficult to say what impression anything one said had made on him. I got the impression that he thought that everything that Charteris told him was completely true and that he had no intention of accepting anything to the contrary. The Chief of Staff was a very nice fellow but a complete nonentity, and although he shared Douglas Haig's table in his mess I don't think Haig ever paid any attention to what was said to him by the Chief of Staff, and Haig himself, being a very capable staff officer, could draft all his operation reports and operation orders very capably without his assistance. Haig would listen to nobody but Charteris.

However in regard to an overall judgement of Haig in high command, I am of the opinion that the balance has to be in his favour. I have mentioned that he was badly advised and had completely wrong convictions about the use of cavalry and kept five cavalry divisions in France fully equipped and mounted –expensive and useless. As a Commander in Chief, I think Haig was a very fine and inspiring leader of men with all these drawbacks and the fact that he couldn't talk to the men like Sir John French could and seemed to the person who met him to be lacking in intelligence.

I feel very strongly that he had an enormous weight of responsibility on his shoulders. He was constantly been reminded by the Admiralty for instance, that he must at all costs capture the submarine bases at Zeebrugge and Ostend within a year or else. In fact he was told by Admiral Jellicoe that Britain would be completely starved out if the German submarine campaign was to continue. Admittedly from hindsight one knows that the destruction of the submarine bases at Ostend and Zeebrugge would have had very little effect because the only submarines that operated from them were in the North Sea, they weren't the submarines which were doing all the damage in the Battle of the Atlantic, and Jellicoe, of course, was wildly mistaken in telling Haig that the country would fall. But anyway Haig was given that from the horse's mouth and Haig believed it and he felt that it was his duty to carry on with the Ypres offensive in order to get those submarine bases.

He also knew, and with a certain amount of justification, (although the French didn't like to say it at the time) that owing to the mutinies which had taken place in the French army after their ridiculous offensive in April 1917, that the British must make every effort to divert the attention of the Germans from the French front by attacking even though he was bound to incur casualties by doing so.

I think that Haig was mistaken in continuing his Somme offensive after the failure of the tank attack in September 1916, and I think that he was also still more mistaken in continuing the Passchendaele attack after Gough's failure in September 1917. But, on the other hand, he was under these two very strong pressures during the Somme battle by the French failure and in the Passchendaele battle by this idea of capturing Ostend and Zeebrugge. I think he continued those unnecessarily far, but there again he was acting under the misleading influence of Charteris telling him all the time, 'We have only got to make one more effort and you will be able to go through.'

I think building up on this misleading guidance which he got from somebody whom he had the most complete confidence in, he felt certain that one more push would get him through and that he would finish the war in 1918 whereas people like Henry Wilson and even Foch thought the war could not be won before 1919.

For his choice of Charteris, Haig has to be seen as a very bad judge of character, just as Winston Churchill was a very bad judge of character and ability. I remember when I was reading through the whole of the Haig correspondence in the National Library of Scotland in Edinburgh, I found a letter from Lady Haig to him. I can't remember the date, but it said, 'I can't understand why you have chosen this stupid fellow Alan Fletcher as one of your ADCs,' and Haig replied, 'Well my dear, Alan Fletcher may be stupid but he suits me very well and I like to have him as my companion.' Well, he was that sort of fellow. He was only interested in a very small circle of acquaintances and with the rest of the world he appeared to be completely dumb.

Of course Lloyd George was more anxious than anybody else to get rid of Haig. He in fact sent Smuts to make a tour of all the Army Commanders in France and gave them the mission of finding somebody of better calibre than Haig to replace him. They came back and said that Haig was the best of the lot and Lloyd George had to accept that for the time being and I agree with that but I think Haig again demonstrated his being a bad judge of people in putting Gough in the wrong place commanding the 5th Army. I think that was a very grave mistake. He ought to have put Plumer in charge of the 3rd Ypres offensive. In fact he took away the Third Battle of Ypres out of Plumer's hands and put it into Gough's hands, which was a mistake and he had to try and correct that in the beginning of October by giving the major operation against Passchendaele over to Plumer when it was too late.

There were too many cavalrymen in top places. You see, Haig had a liking for cavalrymen and there he had Gough, and Allenby and they just weren't the people to be in high command because the cavalrymen on horseback were not the winning arm as they had been, perhaps, at Waterloo. However I must add that in the great crisis on the Western Front in March 1918, I was sent over from the War Office to France with the greatest haste to report on the response of GHQ to the dangerous situation and I found everyone very firm and confident that the attack could be halted. Haig was firmly convinced of this as was his excellent Chief of Staff then, Bertie Lawrence, who was calm and collected as was Edgar Cox who had replaced Charteris. I was very impressed.

Let us not forget too that August 8th was the turning point of the war, and Haig was its architect. The prelude to it, of course, was the counter-offensive in July down by Villers-Cotterets but the French armies were not in a really offensive fighting mood yet and it was only the British and of the British, principally the Canadians and Australians, who had the compelling impulse to go forward and attack at that time. And I think Rawlinson's attack on August 8 was the turning point and that Haig pressed the point and went on as far as he could after that. And Foch admitted that it was Haig's offensive in the North that had started the ball rolling for the final victory and Foch hadn't believed that it was possible to win the war in 1918, and Henry Wilson certainly wanted to wait till the spring of 1919 until the Americans were better trained.

But I think another winter of warfare in the trenches in the North would have absolutely finished the British army and I think that Haig's determination to carry on with his offensive in the North was the final drive which gave us victory, and it was only owing to his determination. I think men of lesser willpower like Henry Wilson would have dragged it out until 1919 and the Americans certainly would not have been in any more advanced stage then. They were dependent entirely on French artillery to help them on. They had no field guns of their own and they made a miserable show when they attacked in September, and I think Haig must be given credit for wielding the sledgehammer that really broke the German army.

5

BARON SHINWELL CH PC

Labour Relations

Over quite a short period of time I was able to meet and record three historically prominent figures on the Left, each with special claims to fame – Philip Noel Baker, with Friends Ambulance work in the war and then dedicated work towards the creation and development of an effective League of Nations; Lord Brockway, associated with the No Conscription Fellowship and all Pacifist causes and then post-war with a long lifetime of advocacy on numbers of great issues of the day as viewed from what he might have called a humanitarian perspective, most notably the abolition of the Death Penalty. The third 'catch' had been 'Manny' Shinwell. Though I had read two autobiographical works – *Conflict without Malice* and *I have lived through it all* when I met him in the House of Lords, I still felt a little uneasy. This was not least because I was coping, just as with Sir Oswald Mosley, with my own pre-judgements. In Shinwell's case this was in relation to how I perceived union disruption of the national war effort.

There is a second parallel, however unlikely, with Mosley. Charm, logic and conviction drew me into a feeling for a point of view which, hitherto, would have been too readily dismissed. My diary records of my meeting with Lord Shinwell that 'He was very, very good.' He was indeed!

Shinwell was born in London in 1884 to a Polish-Jewish family, his father, Samuel, being in the clothing industry and moving from Spitalfields to Glasgow not long after 'Manny's' arrival. Through upbringing and voracious reading the young Emanuel identified with socialism.

I was a member of the Independent Labour Party which I joined in 1903. I subsequently became a member of its administrative council and I was a member of that body for many years, intensely interested in its activities until it disaffiliated from the Labour Party. You have asked me about pacifism, and the Independent Labour Party was not essentially a pacifist organisation but it contained a considerable element of pacifist opinion. Keir Hardie himself was one of the founders and several others like Philip Snowden and Ramsey MacDonald, Bob Smiley, George Carson of Glasgow, Sean Maxwell, and a great many others were not extreme pacifists but they deplored armed conflict and protested against the possibility of wars among nations.

Before the First World War, to take an example, the Labour Party, and that included the Independent Labour Party, was associated with the international socialist movement. That movement held conferences in various parts of Europe. I have attended some of them myself as a member of the Independent Labour Party and a delegate from the Independent Labour Party and at those conferences they passed resolutions condemning hostilities among nations and in particular immediately before 1914 with the outbreak of war. In association with the Social Democratic Party of Germany and other social democratic parties in Europe, the movement passed resolutions even to the extent of declaring that in the event of war they would promote a general strike. In the event they did nothing of the sort. The German socialist movement, inevitably in the circumstances, supported the Kaiser, the German Emperor. There was no evidence of conscientious objection in Germany. There may have been incidents of a kind but it wasn't general in character.

Truthfully I was aware of the existence of people who advocated the cause of pacifism in Britain but read very little of their writings. I wasn't myself intensely interested in pacifism or resistance to war. I had other fish to fry. I was involved in disputes about wages. I was associated with the seamen and before then associated with the clothing trade and in fact in 1909, when Winston Churchill, President of the Board of Trade in the Liberal Government carried through Parliament, the Trade Boards Act, the purpose of which was to protect the interests of workers in the sweated trades so called –clothing, furniture, chain-making and the like – he accepted my nomination as the representative of the Scottish workers on that board. He probably didn't know anything about me. Otherwise he would have rejected my name and I was a member of that trade board for two years until I changed course completely and joined the seamen's movement arising out of the seamen's strike of 1911.

I was a delegate to the Glasgow Trades Council, the most influential trade union organisation in Scotland beyond any question. It was not only industrial in its outlook but political and after being a delegate I became vice chairman of it before the outbreak of war. Subsequently I became the President of the Council and held the post for several years until I went to Parliament. But to return to the ideological issues – the subject of policy – my thoughts about the world at large, about the future of our country, of whether we were likely to be involved in conflict with other countries and the like, the question of armaments or disarmament. I knew about the proposals for disarmament. Noel Baker was very young at that time and there were others. There was Lord Davies, associated with the movement. He was a Welshman, I think a newspaper proprietor, who expended considerable sums in the search for disarmament, and there were many others much more prominent than Noel Baker.

There was Norman Angel. There was Wilsford who became the editor of *The New Leader* which was the periodical associated with the Independent Labour Party and he wrote many books and was himself a pacifist in his views. I knew about that movement but when the war broke out I was associated with the seafarer's movement and the reason for that was, that when there was a strike in 1911 and Herbert Wilson the leader of the strike movement applied to the Glasgow Trades Council for assistance, two of us were sent down to assist the strikers. The colleague who was sent with me did very little but I was inclined that if I took on any task to put the whole of my heart and soul in it and so I spent some time with the men. Subsequently when the strike was won and I made my contribution to the victory in the Clyde, I became a branch secretary of the Seamen's Union.

Later we had difficulties over finance arising out of the peculiar financial operations of Herbert Wilson. He had many difficulties and we formed a breakaway union so called, the Scottish Sailors and Firemen Union. We then amalgamated with an organization which had been established in Southampton in opposition to Herbert Wilson, the British Seafarer's Union, and later we joined up with the Cooks and Stewards Union. We then became the Amalgamated Marine Worker's Union and I became the national organizer. So that is how I came into the seamen's movement. Of course, I had nothing to do with the sea but it was a venture which in the circumstances did me no good at all, because I eventually landed myself in prison arising out of the strike of 1918. The so-called 40 hours strike which was undertaken on behalf of the unemployed. The idea was to reduce the hours of labour and numbers of unemployed and I brought my men out on the Clyde despite opposition.

Returning to 1914, my inclination at the outbreak of war was to join up and I would have done so but for the request by the Ministry of Shipping, which had just been formed, and by the Admiralty, that I should render some assistance in their activities. So, as far as the Admiralty was concerned, the idea was to gather crews to man the auxiliary vessels. Numbers of liners were commandeered by the Government: they were transformed from passenger liners into auxiliary vessels, vessels of war. They were armed. They required very substantial crews particularly in the stokehold because they were not oil burning. It was difficult to get men to man them. They were not Navy men. Anybody at all who was available and could be got, I had to collect them and take them down to Southampton, in hundreds sometimes. Usually they were drunk all the way.

You ask me again about opposition to the war but I never was, as I have already said, intensely interested in pacifist views. It was never my line of country. I regarded the pursuit of socialism as being something that meant hard going all the time but it wasn't to be achieved simply by kid-glove methods. It was all very well to indulge in propaganda, to mouth very eloquent phrases, but it was another story to implement your promises and your aspirations.

I didn't believe, as some said, that the war was just a capitalist struggle, nor do I believe it today. Of course, all wars more or less have their economic implications. I recognise that but this was not just a capitalist struggle as it was suggested by many people on our side of the political fence but let us get down to brass tacks. What happened was that most of the prominent people in the Labour and Socialist movement were at loggerheads. To take an example, Ramsey MacDonald, who was one of the foremost leaders of the Independent Labour Party and who became one of the foremost leaders in the Labour movement, couldn't make up his mind which way to go. At first he was inclined to support the Liberal Government in its decision to engage in war. One must resist the enemy. It may be that if Ramsey MacDonald had been offered a post in the Government he might have continued along those lines but he wasn't offered a post and for many other reasons he decided to embark on a course which was described as peace by negotiation.

Now the strange thing, almost paradoxical, as I was not myself inclined to be pacifist, when Ramsey MacDonald initiated that campaign, peace by negotiation, I supported him. Not so much because of the idea, which I didn't think much of, but because of MacDonald himself. There was an occasion when he came up to Glasgow and we had a meeting in a hall called the Charing Cross Halls, when an attempt was made to break up the meeting, and I dealt very harshly with the leader of what was called the Scottish Patriotic Federation which had announced its intention to break up the meeting. They failed to break it up because I almost broke the jaw of the leader of that organization without MacDonald being aware of this: for which action I was summoned, went to court but the charge was dismissed by the Stipendiary Magistrate for the simple reason that he said: 'Here is a case of a man who alleges that the chairman of a meeting assaulted him. Although he admitted he went there for the purpose of breaking up the meeting and I dismiss the charge as grotesque and fantastic.'

So, this was the sort of life that I was leading but I supported MacDonald all the way through because I was very fond of him. I changed my mind later but I was then very fond of him. So, I didn't attach myself to the pacifist line. I knew about it. I knew about the very eminent people and very good people with genuine convictions and I recognised then as I have recognised ever since the genuine convictions these people hold and I don't quarrel with them about it. This is a free and democratic country. They are entitled to express their opinions and write about it and do as they please but don't ask me to accept it.

Now as for the Clyde, well, I was of course, involved to some extent in the Clyde workers' movement but not in a revolutionary fashion. I objected to many things that the Government was responsible for. I objected to the conditions under which the munition workers of the Clyde and the West of Scotland were operating under. There were many incidents that occurred of oppressive and retrogressive practices and in my view not at all associated with democratic ideas. I raised objection to them and spoke against them. So much so that the Sheriff on the Clyde who was responsible for dealing with exemptions against military service withdrew my exemption: an exemption that had been agreed because of my activities for the Ministry of Shipping and the Admiralty.

Well, you see, I was undertaking work as I have indicated for two government departments although I continued with my seafaring activities but then, as a result, the Sheriff withdrew my exemption and an extraordinary thing happened. George N Barnes, who was the member for the Gorbals Division (and I had assisted Barnes in 1906 when he had defeated Bonar Law, the Conservative future Prime Minister who had held the seat from 1900), recognized that there would be trouble on the Clyde if they persisted in withdrawing my exemption. He intervened. I didn't ask him to. I wouldn't dream of asking for an obligation of that kind but he recognized what had happened and he arranged to cover it up and so the Sheriff agreed not to interfere with my exemption on the understanding that I wouldn't make speeches about the war because I still went about talking about it and raised objections on all sorts of things.

It was usually about the conditions under which the conscripts were involved and the trouble with the landlords raising the rents and about profiteering and things of that sort. I said, 'Alright I agree,' but of course, I went on making the speeches and giving them an awful lot of trouble.

Then I didn't always agree with my colleagues of the Red Clyde.

I took my own line. Some things I agreed with. Other things I rejected at once: the revolutionary ideas. They started what was called the Socialist Labour Party, which was the forerunner of the Communist Party. I would have nothing to do with that. I believed in using Parliament and constitutional methods in order to achieve our objective and I would have nothing to do with their methods and I was regarded both by the Independent Labour Party then and by the pacifists and by the principal members of The Clyde Workers' Committee, as a loner you know. I was very independent and I have retained that almost the whole of my life. I do what I please. Not what other people ask me to do and of course, I dislike war intensely. I hate the idea of bloodshed: all that sort of thing. I would do everything possible to prevent it but I have got my own ideas about how to prevent it.

You have asked me to what extent in retrospect do I feel that the actions of the Red Clydesiders were specifically devoted towards the promised land of a socialist revolution by direct action, and to what extent was it merely taking advantage of the folly of the Government in handling badly a vital area of industrial effort?

The members of the Clyde Workers' Committee, members of the Socialist Labour Party, the revolutionaries, the militants, took their cue from what had happened in 1917 largely. Before then of course, there was the usual trouble in the munition factories. There was a committee, for example, with Davie Kirkwood one of the leaders. You had people like Tom Bell, Willie Paul and a number of others whose names for the moment I have forgotten. They were revolutionaries you know. They wanted revolution themselves without any clear-cut ideas of what the objective was. That was to begin with, but when 1917 occurred of course it boiled up largely because of what happened in Russia and not only for the Clyde, but don't forget that in 1917 there was a convention held in Leeds which was described as a convention of the Soldiers' and Workers' Council. I attended that. So did Ernie Bevin and a number of other people. I remember Ernie Bevin speaking there and so did I at that conference and we spoke in revolutionary terms but without having any clear concept at what we were driving at except that we were dissatisfied with what was happening during the war but largely because of profiteering.

All sorts of incidents had occurred between 1914 and 1918 in a sense, with nothing to do with war at all, just people grabbing and being greedy. Displaying all the vices of a capitalist system. This is what I objected to. My mind was always working on that social injustice. They only had to come to me with some case where somebody had been evicted from a house and I boiled. To take one or two examples. We had a rent strike. Now I need not have bothered because I was an official of my union and getting a reasonable wage and I could afford to pay my rent but I decided to join the rent strike. I was the last one out. Everybody else agreed to pay their rent eventually and I was left and was sued by the courts because I held to the principle you see.

Then there was this trouble: for some unaccountable reason the education authority, which had previously provided books free to schools, decided to charge for it. What do I do? I am President of the Glasgow Trades Council, or Vice President, I forget which I was at the time – I joined in. What happens? I don't send my children to school because of it and I am summoned again and have to pay my fine myself. Why do I do it? Simply because of this attachment anchoring myself to a principle. That is why I held on to the seamen's movement. I could have given it up at any moment. I could have gone into business with my father who was doing very well for the time, very well indeed, very prosperous. He would have been glad to have had me but I wouldn't have anything to do with it. This was my line of country. I didn't want to be a capitalist, a profiteer. I didn't want to wear a bowler hat and things of that sort. This was it, rough and ready. All this probably because of my lack of education; you see, I was never academic. I left school when I was twelve.

What education had I got? I had no instruction in composition or allocation or anything of that sort. I taught myself everything. Until the age of twenty I was lecturing to The Glasgow Philosophical Society. God knows what it was about but this sort of thing happened. So, of course, this was the time for rough and ready kind of business.

Now you have asked me about the meeting when Lloyd George came up to Glasgow. Well, that was a huge meeting. I think it was at St Andrew's Hall and I think if I am right that the chair was taken by David Kirkwood. He was either in the chair or certainly he spoke and he attacked Lloyd George but there is another example. David Kirkwood was in all appearances a revolutionary, a rebel, but he was nothing of the sort. He didn't have the slightest rudiments of socialist philosophy: nothing at all. He knew nothing about that. He just talked about rebelling against authority, against the King's men. This was the sort of thing but he was very effective and he told Lloyd George off and he said to Lloyd George, 'Look here. You treat us properly and you will get the munitions. If you don't treat us properly, you won't get them.' It was simply that, but he wasn't against the war: not at all. He wasn't against the war, and in so far as I can recollect some of our people were, like Jimmy Maxton and a number of others.

For example, as chairman of the Trades Council I took every meeting, apart from the Lloyd George one. When clients came up to address the workers up there I took the chair for them. I had to hold the meeting in control because they were very troublesome the workers of the time. This is what happened and you have a situation where there is an element of pacifism in the movement. You see, 'Down with the war.' You have got another element, which is patriotic, and they say we believe in our country and we don't like the other fellow and we have got to go on with this. We have got to see it through and at the same time we have got to see that the workers are decently treated. This is the sort of attitude; that kind of rule of thumb method. If I am asked the question was there any philosophy in it, any logic in it, I would answer there wasn't. You simply acted according to your sentiments.

I had a colleague, James MacKinley, one of the finest people I ever knew. He was associated with the Clerks Union but he was a colleague of mine. He came to work with me in my office in the seamen's movement. He was very useful. Taught me a great deal. He was called up. He was a conscientious objector. Now the first thing I had to do was to see that he was properly looked after. I did my best to prevent him being called-up but when he was called-up – he was unmarried but he had a mother who had to be looked after – and I saw that his mother was given so much per week while he was away. That sort of thing, and after the war he came back to the office but of course, naturally I was sympathetic to the conscientious objectors. Not because I agreed with them. How could I possibly agree with them because of my principles and my views? I didn't agree with them but because I hated the idea of a government or any authority oppressing people. A conscientious objector was a fellow fighting against authority and so I was with him.

In fact, when I went to jail in Edinburgh in 1919 arising out of the 40 hour strike, there was quite a number of conscientious objectors still there and I had to go and work with them in the coal hole. I remember them very well because they were the only people who got any food from outside. They used to give you a bit. Of course, I had no sympathy with the views of those people.

There are just two more things I would like to mention. First of all, there is the fact that I was an official of the Seamen's Union and we were losing men by the thousand. Every now and again I would get the information that one of our ships had gone: one of the Clyde liners or one of the Liverpool liners. My office was in Glasgow, right on the dock. We would get rumour, perhaps the whole of the ship had gone and according to our rules we had to pay benefit to the widows. The office would be crowded with people coming in. Lots of them of course, were people from different areas. Then of course I had to be notified by the Admiralty about the men who I had provided for these liners in hundreds. It was very difficult to get men to go into the stokehold and act as firemen and trimmers. I had to fight the Government to get decent wages. The basic wage of seamen at that time was four pounds ten shillings on deck a month and five pounds ten shillings in the stokehold. Well, I had to gather men. Dundee, Aberdeen, all round there, and I managed to get a trade agreement of seven pounds ten shillings a month. That was the wage. As for what happened, I would get notification that a ship had gone and of course, I had the lists of men provided for me. I had to look after them. Do all that sort of thing and I was very busy. The hardest work I ever had in my life and not very pleasant work. Now that was one aspect.

The other aspect was when I used to come up to London. Well, take an example. I would gather a hundred men and we decided to go by a certain train from Central Station to London and then change and get the train at Waterloo for Southampton. That was one of my jobs. Well, most of them would be boozed up before I got them on the train. We would have to give them advance money you see and I had to arrange that. Then we would get to London. Well, I would come back to London and stay for a day or two. Probably meeting some of the trade union people. I used to meet a lot of them at that time.

The Government had to get people who would tackle a job of this sort and I did it. Then as regards the Ministry of Shipping, later on in the war they were building standard ships. We were pleading for better accommodation, you see, instead of the ordinary fore-castle, and I had to go down to some of the ship-building yards and look at the ships as they were being built and see that they would get the right accommodation. In addition to that of course, I had to carry on my union activities and I was doing propaganda meetings all over the place which had got me into trouble with the Sheriff and at the same time, don't forget in 1916 I was nominated as the candidate for West Lothian for Parliament, and I was a member of the Glasgow Town Council at the time. Don't forget that I had that as well on my plate and Chairman of the Gas Distribution committee and Chairman of the Libraries committee. When I think of it, all these things, I begin to reflect on what I did at that time.

Then I had to go between Glasgow and Edinburgh, West Lothian stretching up from the Forth and I had to go there. I was selected in 1916 and from 1916 to 1918 when we had the election I was addressing meetings. I became very popular with the miners there and the agricultural workers and other people but it meant going back and forward there. You couldn't always get a train at the weekend. You would go on a Saturday, address a meeting on a Saturday night, there would probably be two on a Sunday and you had to stay on until Monday and stay with some miner in an awful hovel. Terrible sort of life it was: very embarrassing sometimes. This was the sort of thing I had to do and meantime I had my Town Council work as well and in 1918 we had a General Municipal election in Glasgow, just at the end of the war. I got the highest vote of any councillor in Glasgow. I was so popular at the time. I am saying that not because it bothers me now. It is no good to me now but I can think of it. I only had to get up and the meeting was called for me at a street corner down at Govan and the street would be packed.

We had trouble with the police for obstruction. They would come to me and say, 'You have got to stop this.' I said, 'It was not my fault. People come out.' Now I can talk of course, but in those days it flowed out like anything. Where did I get the damn thing from? It just came, that is all and I had debates on all sorts of things and I also used to go to The Secular Society and lecture. I lectured on the atheism of socialism. I lectured on the Jewish problem. I used to go occasionally and knock the stuffing out of some of the speakers on a Sunday morning. That sort of thing I did. One of these days I must write about some of these things.

6

AIR COMMODORE P J FULLARD
CBE DSO MC AND BAR AFC

Fighter Pilot

In July 1978 in Broadstairs, Kent, I met 'Peter' Fullard. I had worked with other fighter pilots who had achieved the recognized number of 'kills' – five to be considered an ace – but no one with a record approaching Fullard's. I remember being a little nervous because, from the first, the RFC was a technical service and specialist knowledge in this field was not a strength of mine. In fact we got on well. He was easy to interview. My respectful and warm memories of him are rekindled by both the transcript of the work we did together and my diary reference that he 'seemed embittered' by the non-award of a Victoria Cross, given the failure to take forward a recommendation for a Victoria Cross and the extent of his demonstrable achievement.

The recording includes reference to a cerious charge and a scandalous confession the nature of which make definitive research and conclusion elusive.

Fullard was born in Wimbledon in 1897, his father having been in the diplomatic service. His schooling was at King Edward VI in Norwich and he was there in 1914, returning in September after the summer holidays. He was intending to take up a career in Law and earned a place at Brasenose College, Oxford, but, on leaving school in July 1915, he applied to enlist in the Inns of Court Officers' Training Corps.

I was with them about ten or eleven months and was then commissioned into the Royal Irish Fusiliers Special Reserve

123

battalion. And, while I was waiting to take up my appointment, the Government agreed that people without air certificates, pilot licenses, could be taken into the Royal Flying Corps. I had always been keen on birds and flying ideas and had asked my mother to give me a hundred pounds to get a flying ticket at Brooklands or Hendon and she wouldn't. So as soon as the notice came upon the board that people without pilot's certificates would be accepted in the Royal Flying Corps, I rushed up to London at once and was accepted.

Training on the theoretical side began at Oxford. We had lecture halls all over the place and we were there about six weeks and then I went to Netheravon and learnt to fly on a Farman Longhorn and after two and a quarter hours I was passed on to Central Flying School at Upavon which was about four miles away and there I learnt to fly more modern machines such as the FE8, DH2, the Vickers Gun bus and various others which we borrowed from each other to fly and get experience. After a very short time, I think it would be in December 1916, I was made an instructor and although I was only eighteen I was given a flight in D squadron at Upavon which had the Henry Farman for initial training and I ran that for five or six months. Then I was posted to France.

From the pilots' pool there, I wanted to go to 41 Squadron where my previous squadron commander was now in command, a man called Lance Tilney. He had a squadron of FE8s (**a 'Pusher' plane with the propeller behind the engine**) and I was an FE8 expert but 'naturally' they sent me to a 'Tractor' squadron, (**propeller at the front**) Number 1 Squadron, a Nieuport squadron at Bailleul.

My CO was a Canadian, Major Dombasle, a very good man, a very kind man, and I can say advisedly that he was getting as good a pilot as there was. First, I had a total lack of fear; and then that I was such a good pilot I could get into positions which the German couldn't maintain and I would get so close to him that he was frightened. I was very conscious of what I could make the machine do.

However, I remember that on my first operation, I was part of a formation going over the lines, and I saw a squadron of Germans below, all different colours, and I was so keen on looking at them that I stalled and I spun right down almost to the top of them and afterwards my flight commander said, we thought you were a goner then. Anyhow, I pulled out and rejoined them.

It is hard to recollect on this precisely but I very soon became a leader of a pair and, in fourteen days of being in France, I was the senior pilot in my flight and I didn't get my flight because they thought I was too young or inexperienced. However, in a very short time I was promoted captain and I got a Military Cross in about five weeks. As far as I can remember I was due for leave in about four weeks after going to France. That is to say that all the people who were in France before me were either killed, wounded or had finished their time.

Perhaps I should explain the role our squadron, a scout squadron, had to play. Scout is really an inappropriate word because it wasn't a reconnaissance squadron. It was a fighter squadron whose two jobs were; first to escort bombers over the lines either to drop bombs or do photographic work, and second, to go out and attack the German reconnaissance machines which went up and down our lines through Messines, Roulers and Wervik.

At Bailleul we were just behind Ypres. We were the nearest aerodrome to the lines and we weren't quite in an apex but we were in a small rather flattened triangle and all the troops going up into the Ypres Salient went on the road past our aerodrome. We were just on the outskirts of Bailleul next to what had been an asylum and was now a casualty clearing station.

We would be called up just before dawn so we got the advantage of the sun. Yes, the prevailing wind was against us and we were always being drifted over the other side but we had the distant offensive patrol and the closer offensive patrol. One was actually on the lines so as more or less to protect our people and the other was as far as you could go, to Roulers with its railway junction, and beyond.

Our machines, the Nieuports, were the most manoeuvrable fighters of that period. It had a 110-horse power Gnome engine. It was immensely strong and could really be thrown about regardless. There was a theory put out by some journalistic people later that it was a very poorly stretched machine but I found it capable of withstanding the most enormous strains and dives and spins and rolls.

Its armament was one single Lewis gun fitted on the top plane on a quadrant and it was 15 degrees above the line of flight so that the bullets avoided the tip of the propeller. It was a cold machine. It was very thin, very thin plywood and canvas. The fuselage was more or less round and the seat was built into it. So that if anything dropped you couldn't get it. For instance I was once set on fire because a bullet came through and hit all my Verey lights, which I had in a row for signalling, and they all fell down into the false bottom and set me on fire, though I managed to get down. I would say that at that period, early 1917, apart from the SE5 which were only just coming onto the Western Front, the Nieuport was the most satisfactory machine there was and the proof of that was it went on right through the years and we weren't re-equipped until after I had left and the first SE5s came in January 1918.

I had about six months with Number 1 Squadron, until November 1917, and I had two leaves in that period and a spell in hospital with a burst blood vessel in the eyeball. Concerning the latter, I was at about 21,000 feet. It was as high as I could get in those days and I failed to get the German I was after who was a little bit higher and faster and I thought I would let myself spin down and see what happened. I put it into a spin. I came down about 9 or 10,000 feet and suddenly I went blind. A blood vessel had burst and, in sympathy, the other eye faded out and there was I at about 12,000 feet with no real sight, but there was a huge nursery just alongside the aerodrome at Bailleul and by watching for the sun flashing on that I was able to start the engine up again and cruise round until the pain eased and the sight began to clear.

Eventually I landed quite all right and my sight in one eye came back. I was immediately sent up to a big general hospital and there I was for about ten days and then I went on sick leave. I went home three times in those six months. So it really wasn't too bad. I did 250 hours flying and I got forty-eight Germans. Furthermore I never lost anybody who was flying with me in any formation, whether it was six, twelve or two. As to my own machines, I changed, as you can see from my logbook, two or three times because they were shot up but I was never shot down. Including the eye thing, I had to come down five times for one reason or another – through being on fire once, and through being shot through the engine another, a petrol failure another, but I came down twice just behind the lines. Once, upside down and once, in a shell hole, and I don't think I ruined machines except one or two of these occasions.

You have challenged me about the strain of such intensive combat, but no, I enjoyed it. I never felt worried. I thought there was always the chance of a stray bullet but it would be a stray bullet. It wouldn't be in hand-to-hand combat. My general tactics as a flight commander, were, when one met a formation, I used to get one Hun and make sure of it, and this would then shatter the formation. Then I would pull out and go above my flight and circle round like, they said, like an old hen and I confirm I never lost a member of my flight in the whole time because I was able in my position, and my presence if you like, to guard them and shoot, either effectively or warningly, against the Germans.

Now here I feel I have to say that during this six months or so I had a rotten squadron commander, a man called Barton Adams. He was an Australian and we didn't get on and then I had a very poor-minded brigade commander and when I was put up for the Victoria Cross, having got forty or forty-five enemy aircraft, he scrawled across the recommendation. I came back to the office and the recording officer, the same as the adjutant nowadays, he showed it to me. He had scrawled across it in crayon, 'Make him get some more.' I don't think that I really was fairly treated because after I got my DSO, I got eighteen more Huns and I was never rewarded for that and when you think that in that war and certainly in the second war people were getting smothered in decorations for fifteen and twenty.

I never claimed a Hun that wasn't confirmed either by the anti-aircraft fire or by other people or by a crash on the ground. I can say that without fear. Everybody except the commanding officer, every airman, every other pilot, was terribly proud of me and when I walked in the town of Bailleul I was saluted by all sorts of people who knew of me, or knew me, or knew my face. I was quite a striking young figure then, golden hair and boyish appearance and I became a little local legend in Bailleul.

The CO felt I did not treat him with sufficient respect and I didn't treat him with respect. Why should I? I mean he came along from some rather earthbound squadron. I never knew why he was given a squadron. They kept putting people in ahead of me. We had three senior flight commanders put in to take over from me as the senior flight commander and they all faded and all the time I kept coming through and popping up to the top again and yes, I was rather rude to that officer on one or two occasions, but still you must make allowances in a war.

You ask me if I were a difficult customer to work with and I accept I used to take advantage of being asked out. In those days you see, we had Amiens for example to have a night, I mean a dinner, out, and I think on one occasion I put some nude photographs up in the CO's room. Another time I answered him back about something but he was a very boorish man – an Australian – and he didn't fly. He wouldn't fly. Not that that mattered to me a damn. I mean he was supposed to be an administrator.

Oh yes and I was always consulted about things. About little ideas for pepping up the engines or something like that or when we got a new type of Nieuport because they had slight modifications which came along from time to time as they always do and I don't suppose this went down well either.

I must say something about the fitter and rigger looking after my machine. One was a very senior man from Devonport dockyard and the other a man called Copperstone who had been working with Martinsyde for years at Brooklands. The man from Devonport was a marvellous fitter and Copperstone was a very fine rigger. One had a great respect for them because they were keeping me in the air and they had a respect for me because I looked after their machine and brought it back most times.

To go back to Barton Adams, one of the reasons for his dislike of me was this: I had a great friend called Rooper. He was in the Yeomanry and was a rich man and he dressed very nicely. He had good breeches and he had suede calf-length boots and silk shirts and a gold identity disc before the days of wristwatches being so common, and altogether we were quite buddies and we were on an evening patrol and he got shot down or had engine failure. I was never able to confirm this and I saw him alight. Not land. He just sort of crash-landed and ran into a dugout our side of the lines in the Australian sector. The next morning his body was found and everything had been rifled from him. So I knew what had happened. It was in the Australian sector and so I took my flight up and I raked the Australian sector and killed a great many of them and I think it got back to Barton Adams. I said I had made a mistake, I am terribly sorry. I think that got back to him but these Australians had looted him. He was able to run. I saw Rooper. I mean when I came down in that district upside down into a shell hole before the people who came to me, these were gunners, English gunners, they took things from me and off the machine before they undid the safety belt and let me fall head first into water.

No my flight did not know they were strafing Australian trenches just that they were to follow me to attack a certain sector. You see part of our job was to go up in the evening and stunt over our trenches or the German trenches because they were quite close just to exhilarate the troops. You know, give them a feeling they were being looked after and therefore one knew pretty well where everybody was. We had the 16th and 36th Divisions up there. They were the Ulster Divisions and as I had been in the Irish Fusiliers we were quite matey. We had the nearest baths to the line. A friend of mine had put up in the Army Service Corps and he had built us a bathhouse, which was the one nearest the lines, and all sorts of people used to drop in and have a bath. We kept the water going all day and so we were, I should say without doubt, probably the best-known squadron in that area. We were astride the main road up to Ypres. Our quarters were on one side and all the huts and offices and the aerodrome and the hangars, which were only canvas erections leaning against the wall of the asylum, were on the other. A tiny little aerodrome, I shouldn't think it was more than 500 yards long if that and we always seemed to be taking off straight down a little slope and on the other side of the aerodrome was Number 1 Naval Squadron with tri-planes.

Perhaps I should say something now about squadron life. We had two messes. One was A and C Flights and the other was B Flight, which was the headquarters staff, which only consisted of the commanding officer and the recording officer. We didn't have an armament officer. I was in C flight. We were very respectable. I mean we probably went out and, for us, had a lot to drink but it wasn't serious drinking. We were all, well, about nineteen to twenty-two. We had very few middle-aged pilots because they had all gone, but there were some others a little older than us.

I can't remember high cockalorum or any such high jinks practised when we were at Bailleul. That came in after the war or much more when people were at home. Returning to the question of morale: I have seen people who never came over the line. They always had engine trouble or they went the wrong side of the cloud or something at the crucial time. Well, I got rid of one of them. We had two flight commanders and two sergeant pilots who couldn't take it any more. One of them said that the vibration hurt his arm because there was indeed a fair amount of vibration. You had to fly always with your hand on the throttle controls. You had a control and one was for petrol and one was for air and it did get vibrated sometimes if you weren't very careful because those rotaries, if they began to misfire through getting petrol or a plug malfunctioning, they got terribly vibratory as you can imagine. They didn't turn very fast. I suppose 1,200, 1,250 to 1,300 but if one cut out you got quite a nuisance and you couldn't really clear it because being a rotary the moisture, or whatever it was, was thrown outwards the whole time when the plug was in the cylinder head. I will say that we were fairly lucky. You see, in my flight, my people relied on me and relied on themselves and felt happier and we didn't have the failures in morale that existed elsewhere.

As for myself I just felt that I wanted to survive and my best way of doing it was to kill the other fellow. I think far too much has been made about 'knights of the air' and chivalry. I don't think it existed. You couldn't have operated like that. I can give you an example. I was on an early morning flight and I came across a two-seater and I got under his tail and shot him up properly and I thought oh well, he is alright (seen to). I will change my drum. I had to bring it down on a quadrant and while I was flying with my knees holding the joystick and fumbling because the air blast made it very difficult (there were ninety-seven rounds in a drum and we had double drums) the observer in the machine I thought I had dealt with conclusively came to life again and fairly shot me up properly. I had no qualms about going down again and shooting him to pieces. I mean I wasn't going to be insulted in that way, so to speak, being shot up. He was the one who shot my Verey lights down and, when I turned to look, he shot my goggles off and then another one went through here actually in my armpit. I got down and I shot him down and he was seen to fall in flames quite close to the lines. That is what I was saying about early morning because the sun was in the east and we came from the west and I could see him very well silhouetted while I was in the darkness more or less. Oh yes, I shot him down alright.

No, I never heard and I would never have dreamt of doing otherwise because you can always fake. I mean the old trick was to fall down, let the rear gun go in the air, and then the attacking man would think that is alright and pay no more attention as I did in fact but I don't think I saw the gun go up but I had seen my shots go in. My whole theory was to get so close that he couldn't dare turn. You see, I had a very small plane and those German two-seaters for instance were much bigger, probably almost twice the size.

As you got close to them I could see my shot holes moving up the fuselage and he would probably be so frightened at seeing these bullets and hearing it, because the noise of any gun, machine gun, firing at you, is terrific, in spite of your own engine noise and the rushing of the air, and I got most of my two-seaters that way. Getting in close. I mean I could see their faces and goggles and everything.

No I didn't carry a good luck token. I hadn't got any particular girlfriend. No, all I had was a little box made by my rigger with a spring-loaded lid in which I kept chocolate. That is about the only thing I kept up with. Oh I think I did once, oh yes, I met a girl who I think gave me a scarf. Her brother was in the other squadron on the other side of the aerodrome. But no, it was not a seriously kept charm.

In telling you that I was not affected by fear, that does not mean I was without apprehension in fact more than apprehensive about being taken prisoner and on the occasions when I did have to force-land either through enemy action or through engine failure, I made every effort to get back to our line even though it might mean landing in the trench area or in shell holes rather than take the easy way on a field for instance on the German side of the lines. I had an inherent and obstinate horror of being taken prisoner.

Returning to squadron life: we had a goat as a pet. That was all. We used to feed it on bread soaked in gin and watch it fall about but we hadn't any dogs and no parrots or anything else of that nature. We played football. We had a tennis court and we had a ping-pong table in one of the Nissen huts and we had a gramophone. We didn't have a photo-collage as some squadrons did. You know a screen with all sorts of pictures stuck on in various positions. I forget what squadron had that, 56 or 60 I think. Some very curious positions! No, we didn't have any pets except as I say this one goat and it was there when I arrived and it was there when I left. It was quite a happy old billy goat.

You were asking me about our knowledge then of some of the Germans who were having success against us, well at least I did wound Richthofen. He was wounded in the head and I had shot somebody. They didn't go down in flames or anything but I know that I hit them and two days later our RFC Commander in Chief, Trenchard, came up and congratulated me at the squadron on having wounded Richthofen. It wasn't a fight. He was simply going along. I don't know whether he was clearing a jam or whether he was looking for something else but he passed just above me fairly close and I let off a good burst at him and I knew I had hit him because I saw the shots going into the fuselage. I saw the bullet holes and although somebody else claimed it at another time I have got it in my logbook written at the time.

The German machines were all painted in distinctive colours. I knew where they all came from but I didn't know who was in each plane and I couldn't have cared less. We went for them hammer and tongs because we knew they were shooting down the artillery reconnaissance and photographic reconnaissance machines because they were very good pilots and very tough. They had a very good record but they didn't do very much against us after I arrived there and the funny thing is that although we got I think ninety-six or ninety-eight Germans when I was with the squadron, after I left I think that they got somewhere between six and twelve.

I think that reflects that I had instilled the squadron and trained the squadron how to fight. You see a lot of people were more interested in survival than anything else. People with families it is understandable. I was young. I hadn't got anything to lose except my life.

I trained them to stick together and follow me and when I drew out and went above them, they went on with their individual fighting. As far as general tactics were concerned, if you met say twelve or twenty-four of them, as you did sometimes, well then discretion is the better part of valour and it's no use just fighting and killing one and then being killed. That is not a fair do. You want to fight another day. I mean I didn't run away but you don't take on enormous odds just for the fun of it. You try to get a tactical advantage, the most obvious one is coming down in the sun, coming down from a height and being in a very close formation so that if you all start firing there is bound to be a bloody good cover of fire.

There are two interesting omissions in the interview given by Air Commodore Fullard, the first relates to the detail that his remarkable record to November 1917 was ended by a quite serious football injury sustained in squadron recreation. On recovery he was posted home as an examiner of pilots seeking a return to active service. The second is that while he was unwilling to accept that he personally suffered from the stress of weeks of sustained action in the air, a staff college auto-biographical essay he was required to write soon after the end of the war recorded a period immediately following the war of his being completely unable to concentrate, indeed being 'good for nothing at all'. Of course I do not know if there were to be a connection between this and any temporarily repressed strain in 1917.

7

HENRY MOORE OM CH FBA

Citizen soldier at Cambrai

When I went to see Henry Moore in May 1980 I was certainly conscious of the privilege I had been accorded and was excited by the opportunity, but, in retrospect, I think I should have been more conscious that in having for an hour and a half the undivided attention of arguably the most renowned sculptor in the world, I was interrupting his thinking or his actual work. What, creatively, may have been lost thereby I do wonder rather uncomfortably today?

Moore was warm, friendly, informal and altogether easy to interview. He shook my hand with a strength of grip which alerted me, in my own mischievous perception, to the power needed to create the holes in his monumental sculptures, such was the limitation of my vision of modern art. He did not move at all like an elderly man, his sense of humour seemed to me to be youthful and I relished his dismissive response to a question put to him about the likelihood of an artist being affronted by being surrounded by the destructive consequence of war. While I would hope not to be guilty of such intent, no words or concepts of the interlocutor were going to be put into the mouth of this man!

I remember beautiful things being in the room where the recording took place – framed drawings and paintings, shaped or natural stones in a dish. A particularly pleasant memory of this visit to Henry Moore's home near Much Hadham in Hertfordshire, was being shown round the large garden, an open air treasure house of some of his sculptural work.

I was born in 1898 in Castleford, Yorkshire, a little coal-mining town, not a village but nearly so and with an intensely industrial atmosphere. I mean within a mile or two of the centre of the town there were three or four coal mines, two chemical works, a glass works, potteries, in fact, there is a ware called Castleford ware that is famous like Leeds ware.

My father was for a period a coal miner. He was a very ambitious person and later he taught himself enough from books to pass his mining engineering and could have then qualified to be a manager or under-manager but still down the coalmines. However he had an accident to his eyes, which precluded his taking a position of responsibility.

I went to school at the elementary school in Castleford, Compass Street, first in the Infants' School. My father was ambitious for all of us. I was the seventh of a family of eight and my older three sisters and a brother had all qualified to be teachers before I was the age to go in for the local examination to go to the grammar school. In fact I failed the first try but my father then insisted that I make an excuse that I had failed because he was trying to make me take violin lessons which I intensely disliked. The noise I made was so awful for me that when I failed the first time at trying to get the county scholarship I said, 'Well, it's your fault, Dad, because you made me practise the five evenings in the week on the violin and I don't want that. I don't like it.' So he let me drop the violin lessons and I took the exam again and passed but another father might not have pushed his child but as he already had four out of the family become teachers by passing exams and qualifying and going to college, this is how he intended it surely for me and I did get to the grammar school but I knew at an early age that I wanted to be a sculptor.

Having heard a story of Michelangelo carving and so on – it's a long, long, story – this fired my ideas and my father at that time was taking fortnightly parts of a children's encyclopaedia which was coming out. Then eventually they were all bound into eight volumes but that took two years for him to do. Anyhow, it was just lucky that in one of them I found an article on Michelangelo and from then on I knew that I wanted to be a sculptor. My father wanted me to go through all the training that my elder sisters and brother had done and become a teacher but I knew I could wait. However, I did go to grammar school. I passed the Cambridge exam, which was the way to gain entry to University, but the war came in 1914 and in 1916, I was then just eighteen, and as for so many others, the war took over.

Oh it was exciting. I remember a Zeppelin coming over Castleford and causing great excitement late one night. We could see it. We were all out. I was about fifteen or sixteen. Now I had a teacher, a very good one, and a marvellous person really, and he was a conscientious objector, which was very brave. It took much more bravery to be a conscientious objector than just go with the crowd and join up. I admired him a great deal and he recognized that I could draw a little better than the average and he encouraged me and got me to design things for the school, the set-up of a new timetable, things like that and, oh well, teachers have been in my life a very important factor. He was one and also in the grammar school was the art mistress who was the daughter of a French mother and an English father and she had been to art school. She encouraged me a great deal. On Sunday afternoons I was asked to go up and have tea and was shown the studio or a colour magazine or whatever it was. On the whole teachers have been of tremendous importance to me.

By 1916, when I was seventeen, I was going on to be a teacher and I was a student teacher. A lot of the teachers had joined up and I was teaching in one of the elementary schools full-time. It should have only been part-time but the war circumstance determined otherwise. I remember the girls used to play me up like anything – it was a mixed school – because they would do all sorts of silly things and pretend to cry and, being a boy of seventeen, I couldn't keep order at all. However, I went back to the same school when I came out of the Army in 1919 when I was demobilized and, until I went to art school, I was teaching again in the same school and then it was easy. I mean I had already been a bayonet instructor and I had been in the Army. So, then I knew that you just pick out the one that looks like a bit of trouble and you make a fool of him or her and then they don't do it again. Yes, it's simple, but you have got to learn it.

Back to 1916, my father again thought all the time of his children and in my case he didn't want me to join, to be called up, when I was eighteen and a half. You weren't called up until you were eighteen and six months but when I was only eighteen and two or three months, he began to think and advised me that if I waited until I was called up I would be put into the local regiment, the King's Own Yorkshire Light Infantry, and I wouldn't have any experience with people different from Yorkshire people of the same kind and so on. He found out that there were regiments that one could join at eighteen and he gave me the names of three and sent me to London. The first time I ever went to London.

One of them was the Honourable Artillery Company, the other one was the Artists Rifles which he put on his list because I had told him that I wanted to be an artist anyhow, and he said, you will probably get experience there and the other one was the Civil Service Rifles. I went to the Honourable Artillery Company. They had a waiting list of over a year, which would mean that I would be called up before that time. I then went to the Artists Rifles. They had a waiting list, not quite as long as the Honourable Artillery Company, but it would still mean that I would be called up before they had a vacancy. However, the Civil Service Rifles, the 15th London Regiment, said there was no waiting list and so I joined up before I was eighteen and was called-up. That is why I got in the Army so early and was in France earlier than would otherwise have been the case. I was the youngest in the regiment.

In the trenches the older people gave me their rum rations just to see me drunk. You can imagine that to begin being the youngest I was given all the little jobs too that came along. For instance, the officer told me some time before the Battle of Cambrai, when we were in a quiet part of the line, that the battalion was going to be relieved and that I had to act as guide to the battalion coming in to relieve us. For some distance behind our position the communication ways were below ground for safety. Well I don't have a very good sense of direction so when he said, 'Moore, you go and meet them and bring them in. Will you remember the way?' I didn't tell him that I couldn't. I said, 'Can I start out now to find the way back because I might have got it wrong?' and I spent the whole morning finding the way back to the relief point that they would be coming to, chalking every corner with a little cross with my bayonet so that when I was coming back I could see the cross in the corner, otherwise I would be so ashamed if I couldn't find the way back and was leading the relief lot and taking them wrongly.

In November 1917 we were moved to Cambrai for the offensive there. You have asked me whether we did any preliminary training with tanks and the answer is no. I remember that the Colonel of the Regiment led us over the field with his baton and we did it just as though we had done it on Wimbledon Common where I had been trained and we advanced fifty yards, went to ground, flat down, and advanced another stage until we got to the spot required. Actually nothing happened much because the advance to Cambrai was over-done, took ground too far ahead and nothing much happened until we got to the part we were halted at. Then the next day a real German counter-attack began; first with a bombardment, which began I think in the night and the next morning it continued. The field we had reached was all grass completely. Within a day you didn't see a blade of grass with the shells that had fallen. They had begun to mix gas shells with high explosives. Although we had gas masks, we didn't know that the shell that dropped just behind us was a gas shell because of the noise of the other ones. Until you smelt it slightly and when you smelt something or saw the effects and could recognize that there was gas around, then you put your gas mask on but you didn't like the gas mask being on. It's uncomfortable. You didn't like it. So every now and then you would see whether it was clear by lifting your gas mask and sniffing a bit and if it was still there you would put it back on.

Well this bombardment of gas shells mixed with ordinary shells went on for three days. You didn't know it but a lot of us had been gassed. We were also being strafed by low-flying aircraft. I was a Lewis gunner, number one of a Lewis gun team. I asked the officer of our platoon if I could take the Lewis gun and try to fire at them. He said I could. 'If you go further away from us because we don't want them to pinpoint you near us. If you go a good 100 yards away so you can draw their fire, that's alright if you want to do it.' Well, I fired for I don't know how long but a long time. I didn't hit an aircraft. Even if the target is big its vulnerable parts are few and small and it flies past you at I don't know what miles an hour.

So, I fired for nearly a whole day as they came over. Nothing ever

Bellpool, a foreign–built (1904,) three-masted, square-rigged ship, docked in a British port. The sort of vessel in which Jimmy Hooper began his apprenticeship. [The National Maritime Museum]

Like Tom Easton working at a colliery near Ashington, these are Pit lads at Netherton, near Bedlington, Northumberland in 1908. [Beamish, The North of England Open Air Museum, NO30812]

Nellie Elson and her family attended a Chapel like this one – Huddlestone Street Mission in Sunderland, 1900. [Tyne & Wear Archives & Museums]

Regent's Street, London at the turn of the century as Howard Marten would have experienced it. (R. Wilkinson Archives)

J N Fletcher trained in Man-carrying Kites as in this photograph.
[Museum of Army Flying, Middle Wallop, Hampshire]

Margery Corbett Ashby (seated second right) campaigning for Women's Suffrage and photographed in New York in 1920.
[The Women's Library, London]

Restored Hebridean Blackhouse showing some of the features described by Donald Macdonald. [www.photoeverywhere.co.uk]

The sort of life which George Ives would have experienced in his first days in Manitoba, breaking the land which had never been touched by a plough. Probably from the Summer of 1903. [Photo courtesy of the Lloydminster Regional Archives/Barr Colony Heritage and Cultural Centre.]

George Ives tried his hand 'On the Trail'. A typical I M Barr Colonist Outfit along the Trail in 1903. Most didn't have the billowing white canvas top now associated with 'prairie schooners'. They were loaded high with 'stuff'. [Photo courtesy of the Lloydminster Regional Archives/Barr Colony Heritage and Cultural Centre.]

Victor Goddard became an airship pilot. Here a Non-Rigid Coastal-Type is being drawn with some difficulty from its hangar under stormy conditions. [Liddle Collection, (Goddard), Brotherton Library, University of Leeds]

Robin Money, on the 5th of May, 1915, in a communication trench near Houplines, Belgium. Engineers had installed the pump which Money is holding in an unsuccessful attempt at drainage.
[Liddle Collection, (Money), Brotherton Library, University of Leeds]

A letter written for Charles (Cecil) Hughes Hallett after the explosion and fire which injured the young midshipman. [Liddle Collection, (Hughes Hallett), Brotherton Library, University of Leeds]

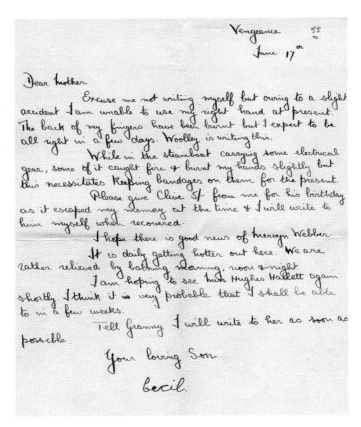

Vengeance

June 17th

Dear Mother

Excuse me not writing myself but owing to a slight accident I am unable to use my right hand at present. The back of my fingers have been burnt but I expect to be all right in a few days. Woolley is writing this.

While in the steamboat carrying some electrical gear, some of it caught fire & burnt my hands slightly but this necessitates keeping bandages on them for the present.

Please give Clive 5/- from me for his birthday as it escaped my memory at the time & I will write to him myself when recovered.

I hope there is good news of Mervyn Webber.

It is daily getting hotter out here. We are rather relieved by bathing morning, noon & night

I am hoping to see Hugh Hughes Hallett again shortly. I think it is very probable that I shall be able to in a few weeks.

Tell Granny I will write to her as soon as possible.

Your loving Son

Cecil.

Manny Shinwell (standing), with his Agent, J Salmon, and a Miner's Leader, campaigning at a 1918 General Election meeting. [The British Library of Political and Economic Science, London; Ref: Shinwell6/4]

The handsome, fighter pilot ace, Peter Fullard.
[Liddle Collection, (Fullard), Brotherton Library, University of Leeds]

James Marshall-Cornwall, as a Major General, c 1937.
[Middleton Family Archives]

Henry Moore in uniform, 1917.
[Reproduced by Permission of The Henry Moore Foundation; Ref: 00000009]

Elsie Knocker in Pervyse, 1915.
[Imperial War Museum; Neg No: Q105892]

Sub-Lieutenant Barnes Neville Wallis, RNVR, attached Royal Naval Air Service in 1915, aged 28.
[Mrs Mary Stopes-Roe (family papers)]

Henry Rich in the battledress uniform of the 120th Rajputana Rifles, Belgaum, India, 1914.
[Liddle Collection, (Rich), Brotherton Library, University of Leeds}

Henry Rich, serving with the Rajputana Rifles endured the tragic Siege of Kut leading to defeat and capture by the Turks. Here the Norfolk Regiment is in trenches during this long drawn-out engagement. [Liddle Collection, (WH Miles), Brotherton Library, University of Leeds]

James Grimshaw, VC, a Lancashire Fusilier at Gallipoli, wearing his new award.
[The Museum of the Lancashire Fusiliers, Bury]

Clare Vyner (centre), pre war.
[Liddle Collection, (Vyner), Brotherton Library, University of Leeds]

Gordon Jacob, 2nd
Lieutenant, The
Queen's Regiment.
[Mrs Margaret Jacob
Hyatt – family papers]

Gordon Jacob (with baton front row centre) and his PoW orchestra at Bad Colberg. [The
Liddle Collection (Jacob) Brotherton Library, University of Leeds]

Reginald Savory served with Sikhs, shown here in a Gallipoli trench. [The National Army Museum]

Always a hazard, as remembered by CG Phillips of the King's African Rifles, troops of this regiment making a river crossing in East Africa. [The National Army Museum]

Nurses and their ambulance off to the front. A Florence Farmborough photograph. It is likely that the nurse on the right is Florence. [Liddle Collection (Farmborough) Brotherton Library, University of Leeds]

H. M. Submarine B XI
Dardanelles.

Dec 21st 1914.

Dear Sam.

A line to thank you very much for your telegram of congratulations, it was very kind of you & came us a great surprise, also many thanks for your excellent scarf which has been most useful. The stunt was very ammusing & full of excitement. I hear I sent 100 Turks & many Germans to sleep. I am afraid it lies very lightly on my chest. I very nearly sank another steamer of sorts to day, the dirty dog just managed to escape me. Excuse short note but I have hundreds to write. Again very many thanks. Love to Buddie & John.

Yours always
Norman. D. Holbrook

'I hear I sent a hundred Turks and many Germans to sleep. I am afraid it lies very lightly on my chest.' A letter written by Norman Holbrook after the torpedoing of *Messudieh*. [Liddle Collection (Holbrook) Brotherton Library, University of Leeds]

Jack Smythe VC, photographed in 1920.
[The National Army Museum]

Victor Silvester in Italy. [Liddle Collection, (Silvester) Brotherton Library, University of Leeds]

Howard Marten, after the commutation of his death sentence and his acceptance of the Home Office Work Scheme, photographed in Dyce Quarry, near Aberdeen.
[Liddle Collection (Marten) Brotherton Library, University of Leeds]

Harold Macmillan,
Grenadier Guards.
[Grenadier Guards Museum]

A readily recognisable
image of Harold
Macmillan after his
interview by Peter
Liddle.
[Liddle Collection (Macmillan)
Brotherton Library, University
of Leeds]

happened because it was really very difficult. Anyhow, we went on for three days like this and then we were relieved. We had suffered a good many casualties. After having had a rest, we were told by an officer that those who had their voice affected in any way were to report sick to the casualty clearing area because we weren't going fully to the rear areas and I was one of those. My voice had all gone. It still is a little affected. We were marched actually back to a casualty clearing station, which of course, made the gassing a little bit worse because it was circulating. I mean if you have got gas in your system, to have exercise is the worst thing because it is spreading, you know, circulating.

Anyhow, it meant that when we got to the casualty clearing station we were sent back and I was marked for home, a Blighty case.

You have asked me whether, in your words, a 'sensitive young man who wanted to be an artist was not affronted by what he had seen on the Western Front, his whole artistic spirit rejecting what he had experienced?' In that sense I wasn't a sensitive young man. I meant to win a medal. It's a very different thing. I meant to do the best I could to win a medal. I wanted to come back as a medal winner, that is not I mean because one believed in the cause of England. I remember seeing my first dead body and it was a shock. I didn't know that the person was dead until I went up and shook him and he fell over. I was a boy of eighteen and I meant to win a medal. So it wasn't this kind of super sensitivity. This is what lots of the young people of that period felt. They weren't highly sensitive. I mean it was an adventure. I enjoyed it all. Perhaps I should add that I had not left the young artist behind me in England. Oh no, I didn't. I did drawings and so on in my spare time, especially when I got back to England as a convalescent, as a Blighty case, a stretcher case. After three or four weeks in hospital somewhere in Wales, I was allowed to get up and there I was drawing whenever I could. I mean people today don't understand what kind of response there was to that war, that First World War: the patriotism of everybody was unbelievable. I was very pleased when they said, 'Oh you are a Blighty case' but no, for me it was all a big adventure.

Well, what happened was, after being in hospital in Wales, we were sent back to the regiment as a convalescent and one morning we were all on parade and it was a physical training parade and the officer was looking on and he said, 'Moore, fall out,' and there were two of us and after this had happened he advised us that they were picking ten out of the regiment to go for instruction at Aldershot to become PT instructors. Physical training, and I went. There was a party of twenty of us in the class. I think only about ten passed. The course was intense and very tough and only about half of them qualified. Some got twisted ankles and so on because you were doing so much. They were testing you. They were only taking the real fit tough ones and I finished the course. Came back to the regiment and was very pleased. I was given a stripe, made a lance corporal, and the PT instructors in our regiment, and I think everywhere, we PTIs were specially treated because we were meant to sort of look especially smart and perky. You were allowed not to have puttees so you had a crease down your trousers. You had a white sweater instead of the ordinary khaki. So you were a bit out of the ordinary.

After a period I was chosen to have a special course in bayonet training and I became a specialist in bayonet instruction, which again was something that was a cut above the ordinary, just phys-ical jerks, because the bayonet instructors strutted around even more, but being young like that I certainly took to it. I mean a sculptor has to be a physical type. It's no good somebody wanting to be a sculptor and not being so. Michelangelo undoubtedly worked harder than any coal miners ever worked in England. I mean the carving and the hours that he would put in. I work much harder physically at my sculpture than ever my father worked. In fact, I remember my mother when she was getting on for eighty, coming down to me and my wife in Kent for a month in the summer and sitting out in the sun and watching me carve and she said, 'Henry, why on earth did you choose to do that? Your Dad had to work but why did you ever choose to?' She saw me physically working away and she thought that the one thing about education and going to grammar school and everything else, was to avoid physical labour but you can't. I mean if a person doesn't like physical exercise and doesn't like using his strength and fighting the stone and so on, it's no good him being a sculptor. It would be stupid.

Now as for bayonet instruction, in the main it's all a game when you are teaching and one rejoiced in the kind of physical display doing the thing that you set out to do and we had a course, a bayonet course, in which it was set up with sacks, which were meant to be bodies, which hung from a bar or in the trench. And this course was about 100 or 200 yards long and all the soldiers who were training had to do this course and I remember having to take a young second lieutenant who had just joined and was a very gentle type in that kind of way, not a pansy type, but I would have said a very sensitive sort. I remember taking him, this is a funny little story, and he wouldn't do anything properly at all really. I mean you had to pretend ferocity: it was like acting on the stage. You had to act as though you were a violent soldier and he couldn't do it. I took him over and said, 'Look, that's no good when you go there (France), you must jam the thing in and say "You bugger" or whatever. I mean you have got to swear.' So I said, 'Come on, we'll do it again.' I took him to the sack again and he jumped at it hard but I was following and when he got to the sack he said, 'Bother you, bother you.' I couldn't get him to say a swear word. I couldn't get him to do it.

I was not on this course until the end of the war. I was being sent along with a whole lot back to France and I was given leave and I went up to Yorkshire, to Castleford, and believe it or not, when I came back in the train to report at Wimbledon where the regiment was stationed, on the train I heard that the Armistice had been signed. And when I got to London that night all London was celebrating. I didn't get back to the regiment until the next day. I think it was the Cafe Royal that I went to. If not, it might have been a Lyons Corner House. People were dancing on the tables. All the girls were kissing the boys. It was tremendous especially for a soldier and I got back to the regiment the next morning and they still carried on and sent us out to France because I had been on leave to go to France and they couldn't change all the arrangements and so this contingent from the regiment that I had been chosen to go with, we still went back to France.

We went up to the front line and there we were, because although the Armistice had been signed nobody knew it was all absolutely over for sure. So we carried on just for a period and in any case they just couldn't simply disband the whole Army.

Fortunately being a student I was in the first batch of ten to be demobilized from my regiment and we had such a send-off from the rest of the regiment in France because we were the first batch to go. It was marvellous but being young and also being a student, because I was still a student teacher and my education had been interfered with or interrupted, it was especially marvellous. When I got back, this wonderful art teacher at the grammar school had found that there were new Army grants to help people in my position. I applied for one and I said to my father having then being away nearly two years, 'Dad, I don't care what you say about going to university, I am going to art school.'

I wasn't going to be thwarted in what I wanted to do and so in that sense the war had been a great help in my career and I wouldn't be without that experience. I wouldn't be without those two years or whatever it was. Of course, I wouldn't. I don't see how anybody can do without any of their experiences. Whatever experiences you have, they are part of your life and to imagine not having them, how can you? It isn't a period that I disliked. No, I enjoyed it enormously.

8

ELSIE KNOCKER MM
(The Baroness de T'Serclaes)

Front line nurse in Belgium, August 1914–1917

In August 1973, in Ashtead, Surrey, I met someone whose modern 'adaptability' (mending a leaking gas pipe with a condom I think can be called that) seemed to sit strangely with her readiness to communicate quite relaxedly with those who had passed on while under her care in 1914–5. My diary records that she was very much 'with it', and that is how I remember her, together with of course, as her Great War experience demonstrates, her independent spirit and courage.

This doughty lady was born in 1884. Her background pre-war was particularly sad; orphaned by the death of her well-to-do parents when she was but a small child, adopted, then, following a conventional middle-class girlhood, she commenced training for nursing but was led into an early marriage which proved disastrous. The marriage to a Mr Knocker ended in her suing for divorce on grounds of cruelty. As she said on interview, 'I was rather left high in the air with very little background and no foreground to stand on.'

I went through life just going to school and leading a normal, ordinary, girl's life until I was 21. I was a nurse in Sevenoaks Hospital where I met my first husband, Mr Knocker. It was not long before I had to leave him and went to live with my brother in Fordingbridge and from there I bought myself a motorbike and sidecar and I became very pleased with it and went in for all the motorbike trials.

I was living in Fordingbridge when war broke out and I thought I must go over and see what a war looks like, and offer my help in caring for our wounded troops. I went over by myself to France and found myself in the very heart of the conflict with all its terrors, troubles and terrible atrocities. Yes I know that sounds extraordinary but I had my motorbike and nobody troubled me or there were no restrictions or rules or regulations as long as you had a pair of capable hands and a good head on your shoulders and you knew what you were doing. They were only too glad to employ you. This was in August, right in the earliest days of the fighting.

I was literally told sort of 'first turning to the right and second to the left and you are in the war'. I found the war in Belgium and I found also that I could not turn back. Once I had got in the real war there was no turning back. Every pair of capable hands was needed for the terrible miseries that everyone was going through. I reached Ghent before it fell and helped in a hospital there.

In the next few days I should mention that on some mission out of Ghent I was misdirected and got amongst German cavalry. I had turned up the wrong road and came face to face with a whole regiment of cavalry and my heart beat very fast and I thought shall I turn and run or shall I go straight on? I was on foot at the time. I am very devoted to horses and I speak German quite fluently so I immediately made friends with the horses and then I made friends with the men and the men laughed at my amusing stories with horses and I waited until the commanding officer came along and he told me he would send me back to Ghent where I belonged and he gave me an ambulance and I drove that back to Ghent where I was to keep it until they turned up on Thursday morning which they did.

Yes, they turned up as they said on Thursday morning and I gave them the keys for the ambulance. Of course we were virtually out of Ghent at that time. We had to evacuate with our wounded but we left the German wounded in the hospital and I merely gave one of the Germans the keys to the ambulance which I had kept carefully and saw that nobody touched it.

The Germans were very strict on what they called military law and I promised them that I would keep the ambulance and I did against a lot of trouble, worry and bother but I did it. And they received their ambulance on the Thursday morning when they marched into Ghent but they were very hard and unfortunately a British nurse turned back in khaki uniform very bravely into Ghent after we had left. She went to look after a Lieutenant Field who was still in the hospital and unfortunately he could not be moved owing to his terrible wounds and the Germans came along and said, 'Who is this?' when they went round the wards. They said, 'He is a British officer and that is the nurse who is with him and they ordered that he should be turned out of the hospital. We have nothing to do with the British, he is not on our books,' and they turned him out with the nurse who had been brave enough to go back. Lieutenant Field died in lodgings. Somehow the nurse came back to join her unit, the First Aid Nursing Yeomanry, I think.

What I had experienced so far and, still more what I was to go through, in no way disturbed me and this was not simply because of my training as a nurse but because of my make-up. I am very sturdy. I came from a military family with generations of service. I suppose I have got the military structure in me that causes me not to be fearful of anything. I saw terrible things, too awful to speak about today. In particular what the Germans were capable of doing to civilians.

Never mind the propaganda now discredited. You can't forget a baby still crying and bayoneted up on a stable wall can you? I took it down still alive, and saw bayoneted women: dreadful and wicked.

Let me tell you about the work I became involved in. After the retreat from Ghent, I didn't like the fact that I was mainly working with civilians and I wanted to go up to the front line and I secured an interview with a Colonel Bridges, who was then head of The British Mission, and the French General, Foch. They both said it was quite impossible for me to go up to the front line. They wouldn't let me go and said that I would not be wanted but I was so distressed at seeing men coming down in the ambulances and they were put on the side of the street because there was nowhere for them to be housed anywhere. There was no hospital, no first aid station, nothing, and I said I want to stop them coming down from the trenches and that is where I will do my best work. General Foch did not wish me to go, Colonel Bridges did not wish me to go, nobody did, nobody gave me any help at all. So I thought, right, I will go on my own and I went on my own. Luckily I had my motorbike and was able to move about, and I went on my own up to the place where they said I might find accommodation which wasn't too destroyed or already being utilized and I went up to a place called Pervyse. There I settled in. The soldiers were so pleased to see somebody who had come to help them because they had no help at all. There were Belgian, French, Algerian soldiers, all kinds of nationalities and I didn't mind that as long as I could help and my one idea was to nurse them there in the trenches until such time that they could be moved down to a base hospital where they would receive proper attention and nursing of their wounds. This approach I proved to be correct because the famous Lord Dawson told me that that is essential because of the awful shock of being wounded.

I fed them by using the washing machines and cauldrons that they had in the funny old cottages there. Filling them with water and making a wonderful soup with the vegetables that were in plentiful supply round the houses and cutting off great chunks of horse flesh from the dead horses because it was all horse transport in those days and the horses had to die poor things because they were always in danger but we had plenty of meat from that and it made an excellent soup and I fed the men on that for perhaps as long as a week until I could get them back to a base hospital where they could receive first aid but that was exceedingly difficult.

There was absolutely no proper immediate first aid for those newly wounded. None whatsoever. Prince Alexander of Teck organized an old monastery, full of monks and took their lower rooms and in it he put an English nursing sister with a red cape. I don't know where she came from but she was a very astute and charming woman and she had this place absolutely filled with seriously wounded cases and anybody who could help, she was only too willing to employ and I took down by motor ambulance a load of wounded to her one day and I asked where I should put them. She replied that there is nowhere to put them. All you have got to do is to remove the dead from beside the living because we haven't even got the time to do that and you can have that spare space.

I had taken down four lying cases and two sitting and so I removed the dead beside the living and moved my cases in but it wasn't very sanitary. We had to put the dead bodies out into the courtyard where it was a very sad outlook and the smell was something frightful and so was the hospital. There was only this one sister and a few working wounded. Everyone else had left.

There seemed to be no organization in France or Belgium at the time. This Army sister couldn't even tell me where she had come from. She knew she had walked miles and miles and she was still in her white nurse's veil and white apron and dirty dress underneath. She said I don't know where I have come from except that we were turned out. So I walked and walked until I got here and somebody said there was an English lady trying to start up a dressing station in an old monastery so I came here and I was told that yes, there were some wounded here but she said, 'What chaos! What can one do with so many wounded and no one to help them? There aren't any doctors.' It was a hopeless state of affairs. That is why I stopped them coming down from the trenches to the base until there was room for them to come because what the ambulances were doing was bringing the wounded down and dumping them in the street side by side while they died or struggled for breath or to get a drop of water.

Now as regards the house I took over in Pervyse there weren't any stretcher-bearers bringing in wounded. There were just odd soldiers carrying them in or lifting them in and dumping them in the cellar. We had to go downstairs to the cellars of the houses. We couldn't put them upstairs because they would have been blown to pieces and so we put them downstairs in the cellars, on the floor, on anything we could find if we could find some odd blankets in a disused house. We would go and collect such useful things or anything we could find. The house or place I chose was empty; the village was too with regard to civilians.

If a man had just been brought in with a head wound I would put a light bandage round his head knowing that I couldn't do anything more but I would treat him for shock. Quiet, peace, very little food except a teaspoonful of nourishing stuff. All this came from my training at Queen Charlotte's, which was when Queen Charlotte's was in Marylebone Road, London. It was a sort of policy directive. They believed greatly in shock. It was to them like a golden goddess. We must treat patients for shock. Everything is shock. The human body can stand a great deal of battering but the heart can stand so little and that is what I was keen on. Never mind about their aches and pains and their cuts and bangs and no legs and so on. They can all be mended at a hospital at a later date provided you prevent gangrene from getting in but that you can prevent by disinfectant and we had this. We got it up from the military stores down in Dunkirk. It was all very primitive. I should think it was more primitive almost than the Crimea War up there.

Now this example of a wounded case I was telling you about, all we would do was treat him gently for shock by hot compresses, boiling water and seeing that he had teaspoonfuls of it. The hot compresses were put round his body. I didn't bother about his head very much. That was to do with the doctors later on. The wound was nothing to do with me. Kept him quiet and covered him over with rugs because we could get plenty of rugs because everybody had left their blankets behind in their houses and their cushions behind and there was plenty of straw. We could do a very good straw bed by two sheets and bales of straw between. Oh yes and it was not just soup, the Navy was very good at helping us with our hot chocolate.

I might keep wounded for probably two to three days because I would be going backwards and forwards all the time with a casualty that was alright for going back, and therefore down there they would have a spare bed ready, and they would tell me how many they could take at a place about fourteen miles from Pervyse. I would say have you any room sister for say four people if I bring them down right away and she would say yes. Of course we in Pervyse were virtually in the front line. There were trenches on either side of us. There were trenches all the way along. There was nobody in front of us except the Germans, but in the early days there were no trenches, there was no line and there was no organization. No anything and people came from everywhere. All I wanted was to save life and I knew I could only save it through my strength and belief in caring for shock.

Do you know we had a link to the Germans? Well, we had a black dog that used to jump over the trenches with a message to say we are coming over, or can we go over.

I think it was done through a prisoner of war who spoke German and I think he went halfway across no-man's-land and then came back again with somebody else and signalled to them that I wanted to come over and save life.

There was one particular occasion when I was in no-man's-land. This plane had come down and I wanted to rescue the pilot and I went out to rescue him and unfortunately he had left his plane and crawled in the bushes along the line. The man's name I was to learn was Campbell-Orde. I had to go of course. I couldn't go and pick him up by myself. We knew about where he was and I sent the two men who came over with me to find him and I went to see the commanding officer, which was my duty of course, to do. I reported to him what I wanted to do and he agreed that it should be done provided I didn't touch the plane. They are not my property, nothing to do with me at all. I don't want a logbook. I don't want anything, that is not my side. My side is purely Red Cross and I say quite frankly that is the reason why I was able to stay in the front line so long because I stuck to my word.

It may seem extraordinary but on one occasion when we wanted to go forward to collect wounded, the Germans sent a message over to say that they could not agree to not hitting us if we came on the front line in khaki uniform, which we had, and a khaki helmet. They can't tell in bad weather if we were women or men. If these two ladies will guarantee that they will only wear their veils, which will flap about in the wind, we shall never fire on them and they never did.

You can imagine that with bad weather and the churning up of the ground with shelling, mud became a great problem. Once a man had got into it, it sucked you in and it was nothing else but to dig with our hands until we got him out. If you got two or three men to help it wasn't difficult to get him out. Our horse fell off the duck-board once and got in the mud. That was much more difficult believe me. I had to get off and get the saddle underneath him but still everything seemed easy when you had to do it out there because you had to do it. It wasn't a case of shall I or I don't think I can. It was a case that you had to.

Then the shelling: it got so dangerous where we were we couldn't stay there – it was absolutely impossible. We were shelled night and day. We should have certainly been killed ourselves. Well, they said there is a little house further down. It is in the village, it isn't right in the front line: it is about 200 yards' walk. I said that doesn't matter as long as we can keep the wounded safe that is the great thing. So we went down there and that is how we got that, and the men sort of turned it out and cleaned it up. A Colonel Padgett of The British Red Cross Society decided we had to have protection for the entrance to our cellar and he went to Harrods to arrange for an armoured door to be made and sent out. It is still in existence, preserved in The Imperial War Museum.

The wounded men were awfully courageous. They used to always say, 'Don't worry sister,' and I am sure that the desperately wounded always had 'somebody' with them and they always saw beautiful things in the sky. They saw faces, they shook hands with people and they were all people willing to help them 'over'. I have seen a man on the table, brought in, cursing blue murder. I have never heard such swear words, terrible words, everything you could think of. All of a sudden when he was put on the funny little table that we had, he stopped and he said, 'I am sorry mate, I didn't mean all that, I am sorry. Yes, I will come quietly now, yes I will.' You see they always had somebody with them.

You might like to hear of one man, clearly well educated, who came into the cellar with a wounded hand. I dressed it and he wanted to return immediately to his post. I pulled him back from the door just as an enormous explosion went off very near. I said something like, 'Oh my goodness that was close,' and he replied in a totally different uncultured way, 'You shouldn't have done that, Sister, that was for me.' Yes and I said, 'Well it would have been bad luck if I hadn't brought you in.' 'No, you see I am over the other side.' I said, 'It is alright, you will be alright in a minute. Come in and have a cup of tea.' Of course, I was looking for shock not thinking of anything else. I was much too young to think about the spirit world in those days. He wouldn't sit down and he stood there absolutely to attention. I asked him if there were anything he wanted. 'No thank you, I see I am over the other side.' That is what he kept saying and I said, 'Oh well that is alright, you will be alright when you get to hospital.' He said, 'I shan't go there.' Well, I told him the ambulance would be here in a minute and then suddenly he asked for paper and pencil and wrote this extraordinary letter to the men. I must find a copy of it. It simply stated that he was no longer with us, he was over the other side and everything was wonderful and beautiful within and he asked his fellow comrades to take courage and believe that there was nothing in death and it was merely a walk over to the other side and that the soul which is the mainstay of your body is never injured. That is God's work and that no one can ever touch that one particle which is your soul.

He said my soul has gone and I am merely human flesh and then I said well luckily they have stopped firing now. Would you like to go and he said yes. So I opened the door and he just dropped dead on the spot where the shell had dropped. He just crumpled up. He was dead.

I remember another man who had come in and wanted a dressing done and I did it and then he said that he wanted to write a prayer. 'Have you a paper and pencil?' I said yes, I have and I gave him mine and he wrote down this wonderful prayer. 'Oh God, my most merciful Father who created all things in heaven and on earth.' I know it because I say it every night and every morning, but my son Kenneth who was killed in the Second World War, has to be standing by me as I say it.

One man lay in no-man's-land frightfully badly injured, and he said to me, 'Oh what a lovely red cross in the sky. Can you see it, Sister?' To avoid confusion or disappointment I said I could. 'Yes isn't it lovely,' I told him as I held his hand. He said, 'It is coming towards us now and it is getting much brighter and nearer.' He clasped my hand and said thank you and then he died.

One thing I remember which may be of interest is that a Colonel Maitland of the RFC came up to see me and he said, 'Look you can do us such a lot of good if you will let us put up a field telephone here and use it to let you know immediately we have a boy leaving to go over German lines and you would keep a check on him all the time he is over German lines and on the way back and let us know of his progress using the telephone?' I said I would willingly do that. So I did it for several cases and I saw boys come back happily enough.

With a Lieutenant Busby however, he came back quite happily and was quite alright, came down quite low and waved to me but unfortunately somebody shot and killed him. I saw him in the cockpit. He was such a nice boy, Lieutenant Busby, and then another time I saw this boy right up miles up just over our lines and I watched him, the machine caught fire and I watched him come down. Of course, he came down like a log. It was about 2,000 to 3,000 feet into the Flanders mud. So I reported him as killed in action. Lord Dawson then came up and said you can't put him down as killed in action, you have got to put him down as missing. I said, 'Look Bertrand you can't do that. The mother can't sit at home expecting her son to be missing when he has jumped 2,000 feet into that mud: he's dead.' His reply was to the effect that we have got to put him as missing if you can't find the body. If you can find the body then we will do as you say. 'Very well, then I will find the body. There is no question about it.'

So, with German permission, I took our own men and Germans with our dog in hand. I said we have got to find this body, no matter what happens and we found it after a long search. Mind you the body was a good fortnight old by that time, after we got all these orders through. We found it and dug it up and brought it back to the dugout. You know, there wasn't a single man who would go near that body. I was the only one. I had to take my tunic off, my shirt off, I was just up to there in body lice. He was covered in them and there was nothing really but skin and bone except in his inside pocket there was his wallet and inside was a picture of a very well known actress in those days, I can't remember who it was, wishing him all good luck and a letter from his mother and a few coppers and his identity card. Of course, I said not to touch him, leave him as he is, put a sheet under the stretcher so that all these lice can fall on the sheet and we can burn that and I said I am getting Lord Dawson up to see for himself. So Lord Dawson came up and he was turned nearly sick and he said, 'My God what a sight!' and I told him, 'Yes, but we get these every day, you only see one in a year. There are his papers,' and of course, his mother was then told he was dead. Thank God, she was saved years and years of waiting for him and he was such a charming boy. Such a shame but I did a horrible necessary job there.

Yes I did have another woman helping me, Mhairi Chisholm. I never looked upon her as anything but a stooge to me, a cleaner up, and she was quite a good driver of an ambulance and she was a good motorcyclist but she didn't know anything about wounds or anything like that. I think she was quite keen on the photographs we took. Yes, we worked together for three years until I was gassed in 1917. We were just friendly and she did all the donkeywork, the scrubbing of the floor or anything like that.

You ask about the relationship between us, well, it was just the friendliness of an older woman with a great deal of knowledge in her head, to a girl who knew nothing, training her, and telling her what to do and where to go. We didn't have rows: I couldn't be bothered. There was far too much work to do to be bothered with a row.

In fact, as the reader will suspect or may know, there was more to Elsie Knocker's difficulties with her colleague than is directly related here. Miss Chisholm had actually been invited to accompany Mrs Knocker to the Continent in August 1914. I did explore the dismissiveness with which she spoke of Miss Chisholm and certain charges were made. Subsequently I recorded Miss Chisholm too and further pursued the matter. It is my belief that nothing constructive emerges from developing this sub-theme here, but both recordings, unedited, can be studied in The Liddle Collection.

You have asked me whether we had doctors able to assist us in the cellar, and we did, Belgian doctors, but they were not always available and on occasion yes I had to undertake essential surgical procedures as for example the amputation of a completely destroyed foot. I was wounded myself by a shell fragments in my legs and later on I was gassed too.

In response to your question about recognition of my work, I was awarded the Military Medal in the field. That was for the rescue of Campbell-Orde. The medal was presented by Prince Alexander of Teck. He wanted me to go home to England and be given it at Buckingham Palace but I wouldn't go. I said, 'I can't leave work now. We are right in the middle of the (**1917**) offensive.' He gave it to me with a slap on the bottom. He was Queen Mary's brother and a great friend of mine. He was sweet.

On invitation by someone in the RAF in 1918, I joined The

Women's Auxiliary Air Force to drive ambulances. I went to Hampton Court Palace and lived in the stables there with all the WAAF, and they were the girls that did the driving of the big ambulances.

They took them to London one night and put them all round Piccadilly and we had calls at 9 o'clock at night that all our drivers had absconded leaving all the cars in the West End because they objected to not being able to put them under cover because it was a very cold winter and they had to crank them up. There were no electric starts in those days or anything like that. We all had to crank our own engines up and it was very hard. I was the commanding officer of the station at Hampton Court. I had got this position as squadron officer because of my work in Belgium. I was well known and they wanted a capable woman who was able to command and look after girls and who could drive an ambulance and so on and so they appointed me.

It was when I was at Hampton Court that I learned that my former comrade at Pervyse, now also in the WAAF, was causing trouble again and I went to report the matter to the WAAF Commandant I went up to say that she was behaving very badly and I had the authority of the commanding officer to come up and see her and see what we could do because it was demoralizing the whole station. She looked up when I had finished. I was much younger then. She said, 'You have got a pair of very beautiful eyes. There is a mirror over there, go and look at them in the mirror.' I went over and looked. 'What you want is to keep them shut. There is the door.' I thought to myself, 'My God is that what goes on?' So I got a drafting from there.

In 1916, Elsie married an aristocratic Belgian pilot and became the Baroness de T'Serclaes. That this marriage was not a success is the explanation for the absence of reference to it in the interview.

9

SIR BARNES WALLIS CBE FRS RDI FRAeS

Rigid Airship Designer

Of course the anticipation of meeting and working with Barnes Wallis in March 1976 was something to savour. My diary has the reference that might be expected: 'A very good day. A technical rather than a personal/social tape. He is working on a revolutionary aeroplane design and my visit could well be imagined as an interruption, as angle-poise drawing instruments had to be swung away to let me into his study for us to work together.' Then there is a reference to a light-hearted interchange I had totally forgotten. He must have asked from where I had travelled, my response of 'Sunderland' eliciting: 'Where is that?' 'He laughed when I affected shock and dismay that a man of his record did not know where Sunderland was.' He seemed to me a gentle, quiet, pleasant man with a nice sense of humour as well as with an undiminished passion for innovative engineering.

I was born at Ripley in Derbyshire where my father was a doctor and the date of my birth was September 26 1887. I went to school at Christ's Hospital when the school was in Newgate Street, London. I suppose it was as a senior schoolboy that I began what I would call a 'drift' towards engineering and innovative design rather than my moving along some defined plan to such an end. I went as an 'improver' apprentice to the Thames Shipbuilding and Engineering Company of Deptford because my father's practice was at New Cross, which is the Deptford area.

My work here was on sorts of 'bits and pieces'. The first I can remember is working on a 6-cylinder steam engine for a high-speed launch but one only worked on a very small part under a fully-fledged fitter. This was shop-floor experience, but then I moved down to John Samuel White's who were builders of destroyer craft doing about 40 knots and there I acted as a general fitter and worked in the engine-rooms on trials. After about a year of doing that they moved me up into the drawing-office because one got to be known as having some general mathematical education from attending night classes which were held by one of the senior draughtsmen of the firm.

I worked there with a man called Pratt with whom I had formed a considerable friendship because we were both physical exercise enthusiasts. Pratt had been trained at Vickers, Barrow-in-Furness, and had been there at the time that Vickers built the original Mayfly rigid airship. She broke her back after being increased in length because she was too heavy to fly altogether. Pratt came down to join Samuel White's having shipyard experience and there we formed this friendship and when the Zeppelin menace became so great that the British government decided that they also must have rigid airships, they nominated Pratt as head of the new department in Vickers, the airship department. That would be in 1912.

Pratt spent a month or two visiting Germany and the Zeppelin works and when Vickers got an order to produce another rigid airship, the first man he took on his staff was myself, with the position of assistant chief of the airship department in Vickers and then I moved to London and worked with Pratt in two rather secret offices in the old Victoria Street, now of course pulled down. Pratt and I produced the design drawings for the first successful rigid airship, the R9. You will understand that these curious gaps in the numbering was not due to any attempt to build rigid airships in between but the government simply gave consecutive numbers to any airships whether they were little non rigid 'blimps' used for scouting at sea or whether they were rigid, and the number which came after number 1 happened to be number 9. So, our first ship was number 9.

This was a comparatively small ship, only some 550 feet long – something of that sort – and we found that the executive at Barrow-in-Furness, which was Vickers' principal shipbuilding yard, resented very much the design drawings being made in London under the authority of the London office and some difficulties arose in the manufacture. So, our London office was split up. I was sent to Barrow to smooth the way there and interpret any ambiguities in the design and became head of the airship department of Vickers, Barrow-in-Furness. We built our first ship of the Zeppelin type of rigid airship which had been continuously developed since the beginning of the war and flew her from a shed built for her on one of the islands The British government decided that we must enter into the manufacture of rigid airships because they were so useful as long-range naval scouts capable of remaining at sea with the fleet for some considerable time and therefore the Barrow design office became of major importance and we started the design of long-range airships covering very much the same ground as the Germans and learning quite a considerable amount about how to set about the job from what we could find out about their ships.

A great deal of information was supplied to us by the French government because before the war a German Zeppelin had made a forced landing due to running out of fuel somewhere in France and while they entertained the Germans to a lavish luncheon party, swarms of technologists crawled all over the German ship taking particulars of the construction which the French subsequently handed on to us.

The story of Count Zeppelin is of course well known of how he expended the whole of his private fortune in developing the rigid airship, a process which went on slowly until, his funds being exhausted, the German people were taken by a wave of enthusiasm for the work that Zeppelin himself was no longer able to carry on and produced with publicly subscribed funds a very advanced type of airship which really marks the time when Britain seriously came into the rigid airship world. The type we produced for use towards the end of the war was the rigid type based on the German designs.

Perhaps I should have made clear that in fact when war broke out I dashed out of our drawing office in London to the nearest recruiting centre and enlisted in the ranks in The Royal Naval Air Service where my experience with airships gained me ready entry. After a few months the government learned of my defection and I was yanked out and sent back to work with Vickers on a further rigid airship programme.

If you ask me what are the things which I remember best today about those war years, it has to be taking up seriously the design of a high-performance rigid airship and we gradually gathered a staff of suitably trained engineers in London and commenced with the detailed design of the first rigid airship to be flown successfully in this country. That is the R9. I would need to check on this but I think the first flight was December 13 1916. If you judge, as you say, that it looks beautiful, it is certainly nothing to what we produced afterwards.

It is tempting to share with the reader the continuation of these memories into the inter-war years concerning airship, aeroplane and later still special purpose bomb design, but that lies outside the remit of this volume. However I cannot resist recording the answer given to a question on the achievement in his life of which he was most proud. The reply: 'My marriage.'

10

MAJOR-GENERAL HENRY H RICH CB

Indian Army, Mesopotamia, and Turkish POW

In June 1973 when I went to stay at Gosfield Hall in Halstead, Essex, as the guest of General Rich, I knew from correspondence that we shared a consuming interest in the war but he had a particular justification for his commitment to the Mesopotamian Campaign and its conduct, 1914–16.

By origin to secure Britain's oil supplies from the Persian Gulf, a divided authority in its direction, questionable competence in its commanders in the field, disastrous in its outcome, Rich had experienced the campaign as a junior Indian Army regimental officer from beginning to end, the end being the privations of a three month siege followed by two and a half years of Turkish captivity.

With regard to his memory, his erudition in the area of our mutual interest and his undiminished passion for all matters related to the Mesopotamian campaign, General Rich was perhaps the most exceptional man I met in my researches. I got the clear impression that he was a man who set exacting standards in the study of a subject he himself pursued with rigour.

Rich made his own assessment of command in the field in what was arguably Britain's most humiliating defeat of the war, the fall of Kut after siege in April 1916. It may not rank with the significance of the fall of Singapore in February 1942 but it has resonances with the US/British invasion and occupation of Iraq, modern Mesopotamia.

Presented here is the record the General made of his soldiering and captivity but the five cassettes from which this is drawn have much more to offer the student of the campaign.

I was born in Mauritius in March 1891. My father was a gunner officer. I went to a dame school in Cheltenham and then to Bradfield Junior School for a year or two finishing up at Aldenham in Hertfordshire.

As far as I can remember back I was always intended to be a soldier and quite literally I just kept that as my objective and anything I didn't want to do because I thought it wasn't of any use in my career, I just didn't do and I got away with it.

So from school I went straight to the Royal Military College at Sandhurst. I would have been rising nineteen. The term I was there was unique in that there were more vacancies than there were candidates so we had no Army entrance exam at all. As long as you passed the medical test you were admitted. The first three months were concerned with drill and of course the academic side, dealt with by officers from the Army. We had a major in command and four captain instructors. When the drill was over its place was taken by riding. I had never ridden a horse before but I had had the sense to talk to someone and he said, 'Well you say that and you will get right down to the bottom of the class!' which was where I wanted to be, where all the old docile horses were.

Of course Sandhurst included cavalry and infantry officers. We did a lot of practical work, digging trenches and doing military sketching and that sort of thing but we had, as far as my recollection goes, no field days as such. We shot a course there, just rifle.

It was still the days of influence. If you wanted to get into the Guards Regiment, you had to have a certain amount of influence as well as money and that was the case too for all the better-known line regiments. As far as The Indian Army was concerned, which was the only way I could soldier because my father couldn't give me an allowance, you had to pass out in the first twenty-five. The passing-out examination involved everything you had done, that is the drill exam, the riding exam and the exams in the military subjects and military law. I passed out fifteenth.

Now the procedure for the Indian Army was that you had to do a year with a British battalion in India and at the end of that time you were given your choice of an Indian regiment but again unless you had influence or someone who would ask for you, you didn't get it. I served with the 2nd Battalion The Royal Welsh Fusiliers.

edge of our camp and tried to keep warm. I had heard that paper kept you warm so I took all the maps out of the handbook on Mesopotamia and put them over me but they were quite useless and I did what everyone else did, lay down for about ten minutes and then walked about for an hour to get warm again and then laid down. When the news that the Turks had evacuated Basra was received, the general sent up a sloop and the Norfolk Regiment in a river steamer to control the looting.

The Turks had blocked this channel but the Navy had little difficulty in finding its way round and it only required a couple of shells from the sloop and the landing of the first battalion to stop all the looting. Our battalion was left behind to cover the disembarkation of artillery horses. At that time I was the quartermaster of the battalion and responsible for seeing to things like rations and baggage and everything like that. One night we had rather a shock. During darkness there was a crash and a number of heavy bodies rushed through our camp (we had our tents ashore by then) knocking down most of the tents but doing no damage to anyone. In the morning we found that our artillery horses had stampeded so the gunners spent the next couple of days rounding them up.

Our next orders were to go to Basra by river steamer and we had our first experience of a means of travel that we were to get to know very well later on. The river steamers were shallow draft and could get practically up to the bank of the river anywhere but the only means of getting from the steamer to the shore was a couple of planks. When we got to Basra we were billeted near and in the Turkish government offices. Our job was to collect all the arms and ammunition we could, round up bad characters and on general guard duties.

This was still in November 1914. Suddenly we realized that something was on because one of our battalions moved off. Two days afterwards we got orders to embark that evening to go upstream. I spent the time loading the steamers and we embarked at dusk. In the morning we were anchored off the junction of the Tigris and Euphrates. The two sloops and a number of smaller vessels had been armed with 3-pounders and they were all collected in the river. It was only then that we found out what had happened. Two battalions, from different brigades, had been sent up in the hope that they would be able to cross the river. They had started off from their camp, pushed the Turks out of an advanced position but when they got to the riverbank there was no means of crossing the river and on that the rest of the brigade was ordered up.

Directly we landed we were given a sector of the camp to defend and we had hardly started to do any digging when the Turks made a feeble attack, which was easily driven off by our outpost. Next day we started off to collect for the battle and I can remember sitting there feeling very blue about the gills, waiting for orders when the commanding office of the Norfolks turned round to me and said, 'They talk about mice in their stomach, I have got rats in mine,' and I felt much better after that.

When we got the orders, the commanding officer told me to come along in the rear. All the 'followers', transport etc were there and finding what I could, I followed along behind everybody encouraging and if necessary kicking reluctant reservists to go into battle. I was assisted in this by the very lowest caste in the Indian Army, the sweepers. My head sweeper who I had known quite well, used his brush to great effect.

On the way up I saw in front of me what looked like a medieval castle, ramparts and all sorts of things like that and it was really my first experience of a mirage. What I was actually looking at was the reed and mud huts of an Arab village where the Turks had their front line and by the time I got to it the Turks had disappeared and the troops were down on the riverbank shooting it out with the Turks across the river at about 300 yards. I strolled down to the riverbank to see what was going on. It wasn't very much and at nightfall we were withdrawn to the village, which was only a mile from the bank leaving outposts on the banks.

The next day we were sent down to the river again to engage the Turks while another force went up and managed to cross the river well north of the Turkish position and the result of that was that the Turkish commander there surrendered. We had our first British officer casualty in that battle which is always a bit shattering because if it is a friend of course, it is a bit upsetting. When the Turkish commander gave up the town, the troops entered it. We were left behind just to clear up the battlefield and in a very short time we went across at the junction of the Tigris and Euphrates. It was during this battle that we had a spot of bother with our stretcher-bearers who mostly were Christian bandsmen. They had dumped the wounded in the open and fled for cover themselves and so the adjutant, decided that we ought to do something about it. He didn't want a court martial or anything as rigorous as that because it would have meant losing the stretcher-bearers. So he decided the best thing was to give them an old West African punishment of six lashes.

So he took me as support, the Sikh major, his own assistant adjutant and a very tough gym instructor and a guard of Sikh boys and we took these bandsmen out of sight and sound of the camp and we gave them six apiece. It was very effective. The wounded were well looked after in later battles and one of the men we had beaten actually got a commendation for bravery.

As soon as the battalion had dug its defences round the camp, we pitched our tents and started to dig down about a foot inside each tent. The Norfolk soldiers laughed at us but we continued. That night the camp was heavily sniped and we felt quite snug being that foot underground that we were. The next morning it was our turn to laugh while the British soldiers hastily dug their tents down that foot which gives you confidence. One night there was a panic in the camp. There was a certain amount of shooting. We didn't know what had happened. It was far too dark, but in the morning we discovered that some Marsh Arabs had attempted to steal into the camp and one of them had been killed in our lines. It was the first time I had ever seen one of this type of Arab – very powerful, very squat. They led primitive lives just in the marshes on the sand hills, which were only just above the water level.

After a short time the rest of the brigade returned to Basra leaving us in a smaller camp, which we christened Fort Snipe. The object of the camp, apart from being an outpost, was to give protection to the sloop, which anchored off our camp with the task of taking on the Turkish gunboat if it ever appeared. We got on very well with the Navy. We visited their wardroom and they came across to our mess. In addition, every day one of the armoured tugs used to go about five miles upstream to watch for floating mines which the Turks were reputed to possess. We were encouraged to go up with the naval officer in charge to keep him company and it really was quite a hilarious occasion. When we got to our anchorage about two or three miles upstream we anchored and a camel was seen in the distance. The commander ordered the gunner to shoot at it. The first shot fell about halfway. His next order was to cock it up a bit which was duly done and that again was nowhere near the camel. The final order was 'all hands to the stern' which we did and that just gave sufficient elevation anyhow to frighten the camel.

In our camp we felt very secure. The floods were starting, there were no Turks nearer than forty miles and it was just impossible for us to be surprised. Our only trouble was from Arab snipers. We would see a light coming down the river. It would stop somewhere upstream of us on the riverbank. The light would disappear and a few minutes later a dozen or more shots would be fired at the camp. Whoever he was he never hit anything and after he had fired his ration of shots you would see the light appear again as he walked down to the riverbank and disappeared upstream. We tried at times to encourage him because we knew he was doing no harm and we hoped that he was getting some ammunition or pay from the Turks. Another recreation there was to go out shooting. The marshes all round the camp had a certain amount of duck and snipe and a few wild pig. Those of us who had sporting guns would go out with an escort of soldiers armed with rifles, always with an eye cocked on the horizon, and as we got further from the camp we would see figures collecting and shortly afterwards there would be a boom in the distance and a bullet would hit the water some hundred yards away and we knew it was the Arabs after their sport. So that was the signal to turn for home.

The floods were now beginning to get quite serious and we had already erected a very thick bank around the camp to keep the water out but it was a losing battle. Some time while we were in Fort Snipe that would be between January and the middle of March, the Viceroy of India came out to visit us. Strangely he was the only member of the Indian government or the Army Headquarters in India who came out to see what was happening in Basra. When the floods became so bad we had to retire to a little bit of higher ground where we had already erected a smaller fort, which we called Fort Snippet.

In the middle of March we were recalled to join the brigade in

Basra. At that time there were signs of the Turkish army coming down to attack Basra where one brigade of the division was already entrenched. My battalion was sent out to reinforce. It was a journey of twelve miles, six of them across flooded water well above the knees. It was an extremely tiring march. When we arrived in the entrenched camp at Shaiba we were given a detached post, which we proceeded to fortify and prepare against the Turkish attack. Shaiba was a nasty place altogether. It was beginning to get hot. We had dust storms which would sometimes last the whole day. The water was brackish. We had great difficulty in getting the animals to drink it at all but necessity eventually forced them to. Our only excitement was the cavalry brigade would go out periodically to reconnoitre where the Turks were building up their troops some six or seven miles away and half a battalion of infantry would be sent out to see them home.

On April 11 we had news that the Turks would attack the next day. We were ordered to pull down our tents and be ready for dawn. Just before dawn there were two shots fired and in an instant the whole of the horizon in a semicircle was covered with the flashes of the Turkish rifle. They didn't do much damage. They put in one heavy attack which was easily held off. They attacked in open order. Their fighting tactics and lines were not very much different from ours. They were obviously much tougher than the troops we had met before and much better disciplined and although they couldn't get any further they didn't attempt to withdraw. During the night they made another attack. They got as far as our wire, about twenty yards from our trenches, but they couldn't get any further.

I should add that during the day we could see on each flank of the Turkish attacks, standing well out of range, masses of Arabs and on our flank we saw for a few seconds a cavalry charge by one of our cavalry regiments against a detachment of Arabs who of course, didn't stop. The Arabs could have made victory certain for the Turks but they always hung about to see which side was going to win. If they got at all menacing a couple of shells usually sent them back.

We took no part in our counter-attack the next day but we did pick up about twenty or thirty Turks who had had enough and came in to surrender. It was only then that we knew what we were up against. It was the Turkish Military Fire Brigade and quite different from anything we had met before that. After the Turks had been cleared from around the camp they withdrew and on 14 April General Mellis took the force to find out where the Turks were.

As soon as he had located where they were, our brigade, the 18th, was sent to march round behind the other brigade and take up position on the right flank. I don't know what happened there because I was sent off to be galloper to General Mellis and as a subaltern I saw the conduct of a battle from the commander's point of view. I was always within earshot of General Mellis' headquarters.

I was sent off with messages all over the battlefield, sometimes to my own brigade. All the troops managed to advance towards the Turks a certain distance but they were on a grassy slope going right down onto the Turkish position with not a spot of cover anywhere. A cavalry brigade was on the right flank, quite the worst place they should have been. The Indian cavalry brigade at that time was not composed of the best cavalry regiments, which were in France, and it was very badly commanded and General Mellis had not the slightest confidence in them at all. And I remember being sent off on one occasion with a written message from the staff for the brigade staff and just as I was going off the General turned to me and said, 'And give this personal message to the cavalry brigade commander, for God's sake do something.'

I found my way eventually to the cavalry brigade headquarters and found that they had knocked off for lunch. There was the general and the staff sitting against the limbers of the guns (the gunners being the only people taking any part in the battle in the cavalry brigade) having their lunch baskets in front of them. I handed over the message to the staff and I got on my horse and turned its head towards force headquarters and said to the commander, 'And General Mellis sent you a personal message; for God's sake do something.' I then spurred my horse and disappeared. When I got back to force headquarters I found a very anxious lot of officers. The advance had been held up indefinitely. There were hordes of Arabs on the right flank and the left flank taking no part but we knew that if we were defeated we hadn't a hope.

General Mellis ordered the guns, which were two Field Artillery regiments, to move further forward, which they did. He sent out messages to the two brigades that they could put in every man they had into the firing line and at the same time he ordered the 48th pioneers from the fort to come up and take up position halfway out to see us back if necessary. At the same time he ordered all the transport carts out from Shaiba to bring in the wounded. Well, the tension at force headquarters was really terrible because nobody knew, I think even Mellis himself didn't know he was going to win the battle, and then suddenly one staff officer picked up his field glasses and looked at the Turks and said, 'There is movement.' In a flash everybody had field glasses, including me, on the Turkish position and there we could see one or two men getting up and retiring, and a gasp of relief went up from the staff. The Turks were going and shortly after that our forward troops saw what was happening and practically the whole line went after them.

I can't say they dashed after them because it had been a terrifically hot day. Water bottles were empty and the troops were done in but they did fix bayonets and the officers drew their swords even, however the Turks had gone before they got into the trenches. Pursuit was impossible because the cavalry brigade had also been out in the sun all day but it turned out to be completely unnecessary because the hordes of Arabs then turned on the Turks and did far more damage than ever we could have done. I must have been sent off somewhere to do something because when I got back to headquarters it wasn't there. In fact there was nobody I could see at all, so I started to go back because I knew where the camp was and on the way I found strange mule leaders leading mules about and I directed them back on to the camp and incidentally got a drink of the best water I have ever tasted from one of them. And then in the dark I found my way back to my own camp where I learnt that we had three officers killed and a tremendous number of soldiers as well.

General Mellis I remember from this day as a man without fear. He had got a VC for some very heroic exploit. He was anxious of course but he was very much of the school, 'There is the enemy, go and hit him,' sort of general but he was always there when there was any trouble.

The Turks had been so badly mauled by the Arabs they didn't stop until they got to Nasiriyeh which was fifty or sixty miles away and they were in no condition to take us on again in an attack. After the battle, the main forces were recalled to Basra leaving us not at Shaiba because the place was so horrible that we were moved to a small village a couple of miles away which actually had a little greenery. It was the only greenery and wells that I saw in Mesopotamia. It was a very pleasant little spot and we stayed there while resting for a month or two.

Somewhere at the end of June or the beginning of July, the battalion was recalled to Basra to join the brigade again. The hot weather was then in full force and wherever you were the heat was really appalling. We were about a month in Basra and the brigade got orders to join General Gorringe's division, which was attempting to capture Nasiriyeh on the Euphrates. As quarter-master I spent a whole day in the sun loading at Basra. When we arrived at Qurna we had to transfer into shallow vessels as the water in the Hanna Lake was getting very low. Again another terrific day in the sun and when we got across that lake which we did with difficulty we found that we had to cross a bank in the river Tigris.

The ships couldn't do it on their own power and men had to be landed with ropes on both sides of the bank to pull the ship over the small embankment. That was done successfully and we arrived where General Gorringe's force was encamped. After disembarkation the bulk of the brigade was put on the left bank of the river and we, the 120th, were attached to General Mellis's brigade on the other bank. As I was unloading the ship to get our stores ashore, I suddenly realised that the world was going black in front of me. I told a very surprised Sikh boy to pour buckets of the Euphrates over me, which he did and I recovered to a certain extent.

The next day I realized that I was very sick indeed and I had to go to the commanding officer and say, 'I am very sorry, sir, I don't think I am able to march.' He said, 'You are still quartermaster, you better stay in the ship,' which I did. I knew very little about the battle and in fact the next day I was sent down to the base with dysentery. I first of all arrived at Qurna hospital where I spent a couple of days in the heat of somewhere around 120 and finally got down to the base hospital in Basra. There were no amenities, no nurses. We were looked after by orderlies of British regiments or by the Indian Hospital Corps bearers. When I had recovered from that I was sent on board an ocean-going ship in the river to have ten days' convalescence. That was the only time in Mesopotamia that I had a decent bath and good food. At the end of ten days I was sent up river again and I joined my battalion at Amara just before the advance on Kut was ordered.

In the battle, which we call Es Sinn, some other people call it Kut, our brigade was the holding force on the riverbank while the rest of the force went wide round the Turkish left flank. My job as quartermaster was simply that I was responsible for seeing that the troops got their food and water up. As far as our brigade was concerned there was little fighting but the moment the Turks evacuated their position from the threat of the rest of the force, we were ordered into river steamers in pursuit. The Tigris was so low at that period of the year that our ships kept on getting themselves stuck on the sandbanks in the river and we spent a whole day on the sandbank outside Kut and then managed to get free but by that time the Turks had got well away and when we had steamed about eighty miles above Kut, General Townshend ordered the brigade to disembark on the left bank at a place called Aziziyeh. We were there by ourselves for a fortnight or so and then the rest of the division with Townshend himself came and joined us. The weather was now beginning to get a bit cooler. We were pretty well done in. Very few officers had any leave at all in the period. The men had had none.

We had had a year in quite unpleasant conditions. Food not always full rations and we had been through very bad hot weather. So this period in Aziziyeh, as far as the troops who had recently joined the force were concerned, was very necessary for them to build up their health again and we were also made up to strength, both British and Indian from home and India. The British troops, who were mostly territorials who came out from home found conditions extremely trying. At one time the Turks came and occupied a position about six miles from the camp and Townshend took

171

the opportunity of having a practice attack. We all went out with the hope of catching the Turks but they disappeared before we arrived. It was during our stay in Aziziyeh that one morning we heard the general alarm blown. We immediately all rushed to our positions in the trench camp and waited for the attack. Townshend who had built himself a very fine observation tower, climbed up it and nothing happened. Eventually the brigade was sent out. What Townshend had thought had been an attack from mounted enemy turned out to be a flock of sheep. That was the effect of the mirage, even as late as October.

Orders were eventually given to move forward. We advanced some twenty miles to a village near which we knew the Turks had taken up a defensive position. One night the bulk of the force made a night march away from the river towards the Turkish position with orders for an attack to take place on the Turkish position the next morning. The night march was a complete success. We all got to our different rendezvous in time, for some of us anyhow, to have a short sleep. In the morning there was a thick river mist and we suddenly heard a jingle bit and a Turkish cavalry patrol rode right into the midst of us but unfortunately although they were fired on they got away. So the Turks were warned that this attack was coming in on their right flank. When the mist cleared, we had our only glimpse of the arch of Ctesiphon and a small village. Of the Turkish position we could see nothing. That is in front of where I was. We were ordered to advance, the battalion being in support that day. Two battalions were in forward and two were in support, of which one was ours.

I was sent by the commanding officer to hang about brigade headquarters in case there were any messages for us, which I duly delivered, and the attack went in. You could see nothing, you could hear a lot of firing, you could see a lot of shells bursting but I saw absolutely nothing of the attack at all. When we had gone a certain distance we were held up and half a company of ours was sent off to protect some cavalry guns, which were on our right, because there were hordes of mounted Arabs in the distance. We stayed put more or less till nightfall unable to advance and at dusk we received orders to concentrate on a bit of the Turkish position, which Townshend called 'VP'. I was left behind by the commanding officer to pick up and direct any of our men or other men that I saw on VP. On these occasions one always feels you are the only man on the battlefield left but there were plenty left. I directed a lot of men back and I couldn't see any more and it was now pitch dark so I made my way to VP, or the direction of where I thought it was, picking up on the way an emergency ration which was an absolute blessing because we had had no food since the night before.

When I arrived in VP there was utmost confusion. Nobody quite knew where anybody was. Men were wandering about in twos and threes asking where their battalion was and we didn't know and we didn't sort ourselves out till the next morning. We then collected what was left of the battalion. The whole force there received very heavy casualties and almost ceased to exist as a fighting force. Having got the battalion collected, we remained in VP till the late afternoon when we were ordered to concentrate on a feature which Townshend called 'high wall'. It was a wall of sorts about eight or ten feet high. On our way down we and the Norfolks were ordered into the trenches as the Turks were making a counter-attack on the troops left in VP. They pressed their attack home with considerable vigour, not on us but just on our right, but during the attack a Turkish infantry battalion marched across our front in a column of four. Well, we practically obliterated them with small arms. There weren't any left when they came out.

After having spent the night in those trenches, the next day we were ordered again to get to VP where the remnants of the division were collecting. We arrived there during late afternoon, hungry and thirsty. We were settling down for a night when out of the blue came our mess sergeant with some food. We asked him how he had got it up here. He said, 'I put it on an ammunition limber and it is the General's dinner.' So we were one of the few lucky people to have any food that night. Next day we were ordered to withdraw.

The whole force was ordered to withdraw on Aziziyeh: we stopped on the way after a fairly short march. Our morale was good. The whole withdrawal was quite orderly and we arrived at a village where there was an advanced depot and so we then got our first real rations for four days. We continued our retirement towards Kut and came upon a place by the Tigris where our river steamers, *Comet* and *Firefly*, were anchored.

During the night there was a sound of wheels and we could see the campfires of the Turks all round us and there I, like many others of the force, decided that this is where we finish. When daylight came in front of was an astounding sight. The whole of the Turkish force was in camp about 2,000 yards away from us and of course it was a gunner's dream. Every gun opened at practically point blank range. The Turks mingled about that camp all over the place. Townshend made a feint attack with the infantry in their direction while he got away all the transport that was left and the field ambulances. When they got well away, we were then ordered to withdraw and I found myself with perhaps thirty men of my regiment and our major. We were followed up by the Turks and we shot it out occasionally at about a couple of hundred yards until the Turks, who were just as tired as we were, gave up the struggle and then I just went on with my small party of men through the night and I came across where the troops had halted. So I told my fellows to lie down and I went off to try and find battalion headquarters, which I eventually found, and was told by the commanding officer to just bring that detachment in when we moved on again. I better add that I was adjutant at this stage, no longer quartermaster.

Then the march started again, we went all through that day and into the next night. By then we were perhaps ten miles from Kut, and I gradually moved back in the direction of Kut. I didn't meet many stragglers. I met a lot of Gurkha troops who were obviously done in. They had done an extra march to us. We offered to help them or carry their rifles or anything like that but the little men would have none of it, they just stolidly went on. We picked up quite a number of exhausted men. I always had someone on my horse and was usually carrying a couple of rifles and we got into the outskirts of Kut some time in the evening where the garrison there had arranged for food. We had done about fifty miles in thirty-six hours. It wasn't till the next day that I managed to find out where the battalion was and then it had gone over the river to this small village on the right bank, which was called Woolpress, to turn the Arabs out of there. I came back that evening and I rejoined the battalion on the next day. We spent the whole siege in this spot.

The man who was commanding our regiment at that moment, Captain Miskin, turned every Arab out. We didn't have any nonsense about it. Every Arab had to leave the village, which they did. We couldn't have existed with them because it was very small. I think the area was probably 600 yards by 300 yards.

The Turks gradually worked up to surround the village. In our sector on the riverbank – we were the northern sector – the Turkish trenches at the nearest point were about a hundred yards away and it then went off at an angle until opposite the other brigade they were quite a distance away. We then spent our time digging in, putting in barbed wire and the Turks occasionally sniped us and we sniped back at them and eventually we settled down to that line. Christmas Day or just about that time, the Turks made a determined attack on our sector of the village but we managed to hold them off and that was the last time the Turks did anything determined against our village, but they built up their trench system.

Communication from the town was by one of these armoured tugs and, of course, signal communication. As for the siege, we had our moments because the sappers and miners produced some homemade mortars out of the Gnome engine cylinders of two broken down aeroplanes and they sent one across to us. It was just this cylinder stuck on a wooden board, a hole punched in it in which you put a little bag of powder and a little bit of slow fuse. You then had a bomb, which was made of jam tins on a wooden base with another little bit of short fuse. You aimed the thing at the Turkish trenches, you lit the first fuse at the top and you rushed round the nearest traverse and waited for what happened. It was great fun firing it. Sometimes it didn't go off at all, sometimes it just dropped into no-man's-land, and once it sailed right over and went into the Turkish trenches and exploded.

We were to come under aerial attack but not until the siege had been on for two months or so. German planes started to come over, perhaps three. The first time they came, they bombed a lot of troops at the rear of our village but after that they directed all their attacks on Kut itself.

I remember clearly the main infantry attack we faced. It was during the night and I was sleeping and the Sikh major came up to me and said, 'Listen'. So I listened and suddenly realized there was no noise going on at all. We had got accustomed to noise and we thought something must be up. So immediately we got everybody out into the trenches just before the Turkish attack started and it didn't get very far. Some Turks got on to our wire but not very many. We suffered few casualties as we were in trenches. They were in the open!

Concerning food; at the beginning we had more than our allotted ration because apparently Townshend had decided that the troops wanted building up, so for roughly the month of December we had a ration and a quarter. Related to this is a funny story. When we got over to our bank of the river there was in the village two or three mounds of barley waiting to be shipped. We reported it at once to headquarters over the river and nothing was done about it until halfway through the siege. By that time the top four inches of every mound had sprouted and when they eventually took it over to Kut, which was well in the halfway stage, we were accused of eating something like 300 tons of barley, which was about a ton a man!

From the beginning of January rations were systematically reduced until the last fortnight of the siege we were receiving four ounces of bread and ten ounces of horse but on our side of the river we were slightly better off than the other side because there is no doubt that although they didn't take a ton a piece, our men of both regiments had a good deal of that barley. We had a very wise mess secretary and we had a few mess stores and he wouldn't let us eat more than one tin of anything a day. It had to be divided between us so that we were that much better off but we were pretty hungry at the end even then.

There were two scales of rations for mixed Indian and British troops. The British troops had their scale, which is food suitable for them, and the Indians had their scale of food, which is suitable to them. The main items of the British troops' food is bread, meat, vegetables, jam, small portions of butter, bacon, tea. The Indian troops had the Indian flour, lentils, they didn't have our butter, they had the Indian equivalent, and they had a sweet material which was made of sugarcane, and they had a modicum of chillis and things like that. They did have meat but their meat was always goat to comply with both the Hindus and Muslims and the scale of it was not so big as that of the British troops because the Indians are not great meat-eaters.

As the scales reduced they were reduced in proportion and Indian troops at the end had four ounces of their flour and ten ounces of meat but as it was horse they wouldn't eat it and not till the very last in spite of having permission from their religious leaders in India to eat it, a lot of them wouldn't. Some of them did but by the time they started to eat it, it was too late and I think you can say that the Indian troops in the end were not quite as fit as the British troops but no one was fit, nothing like.

Morale on our bank was quite good throughout. We had in my own regiment one deserter only. A Muslim went over to the Turks who were always trying to get them over. Everybody opened fire on him irrespective of whether he was a Muslim or a Hindu as he tried to get across.

As for our eventual surrender; as I saw it at the end of April, we knew a couple of days before that we were going to have to surrender. We had guessed it from about the middle of April when the relief force's attacks on the left bank of the river at Hanna were held up. We were told to destroy everything except a hundred rifles, which we did, and most of our ammunition was just thrown into the Tigris. On the morning of April 29 1916 when the white flag went up, we went and sat on the riverbank and just waited.

We were lucky. We were taken over by a well-disciplined Turkish battalion and we had none of the troubles on our bank they had with looting and beating-up of people on the other. A Turkish major who could speak a little French, came up to us. We opened our last tin of biscuits, gave him some and he produced coffee and we just sat about until the afternoon when a Turkish ship came across to take us up to the camp at the mouth of the river.

My feeling at the end of the siege was one of relief. I suppose one had been living on nerves. A second reaction was we will get out of this enclosed space and that is all I can remember about my feelings. We went up in this steamer to the camp where the rest of the division had been collected. We had no tents. We were all terribly hungry. The Turks produced their troops' rations – practically impossible to eat. It was a hard biscuit thing, about six inches in diameter, about two inches thick. Some people tried to bite it but you couldn't. The only way I managed to do it was to get a couple of stones and beat it up in small pieces, soak it in water and eat it as porridge. We spent a day or two there and it was arranged that as the Turks couldn't feed us, a ship would come up from the British lines with sufficient food on it for the force.

The British sent a ship up with the object of producing rations because the Turks said they couldn't feed us, and also to take back as many wounded and sick as the Turks would allow to go back. In this cargo of food was our Christmas order, which had been sent to Bombay – every luxury you could think of, far too much for the five of us who were left, all of whom had some sort of tummy trouble. We ate what we could and anyone who wanted it could come and have the rest.

The officers were divided into two parties to be taken by river steamer up to Baghdad. I was in the second party. The men, after we were separated from them, we didn't see again. It is now well known that they had a desperately grim march into captivity. When my party of junior officers in the main got to Baghdad we were paraded through the main streets to the cavalry barracks. As a young man I felt no shame or anything like that at all. All I was interested in was here was the city of the Arabian Nights. The barracks were reasonably clean. We were given our first pay, which for a subaltern was three gold sovereigns and four pounds in paper money, and that was supposed to last us until we got the next lot. Under the Geneva Convention a capturing force has to pay the officers and treat them as they do their own forces and that seven pounds a month was the pay of a Turkish lieutenant.

From Baghdad we went on to Samarrah, about eighty miles by train. After Samarrah we had to walk, first of all to Mosul and then to the next railhead, which was about 200 miles beyond Mosul. For our transport we were allotted one donkey between two officers and an orderly. We had Indian orderlies then, they were taken away later.

I had not really recovered but I managed to march most of the way, sitting on the donkey occasionally. When we got to Mosul, we were put in foul Turkish barracks but we were allowed out into the town to feed ourselves as best we could: a nominal escort but more or less free. There was a good Greek restaurant and I just ate everything I fancied, milk puddings, meat cooked in grease and at the end of three days I was completely over my tummy troubles. When we did the next trek of 200 miles to the next railhead I walked the whole way becoming fitter and fitter as we went. It was a pretty unpleasant trek but it was beginning to get cooler because we were going north all the time.

From that railhead we went by train to Aleppo where we spent a couple of days shut up in the barracks and we weren't allowed out for food until the next day but there were a lot of little boys outside the barracks who would sell us bread, so we didn't starve. From here we went by train through the plain of Tarsus to the next gap in the railway, which was over mountains. When we got to the railhead we were allotted quite a number of carts to go in, but we preferred to walk and got our way.

On this journey in stages I came across my only personal sight of the murdered Armenians in some ditches at the top of a mountain. There were hundreds of bodies.

Nobody had thought of escaping at this stage and I don't think anyone was in a fit state to do it. After we had crossed the Tarsus mountains we did a long railway trip because the railway was then continuous to Constantinople. Our railhead was Ankara where we spent a couple of days and then we had the most pleasant march of the whole trip, about 200 miles over very pleasant hilly country to a town called Kastamuni which was my first prison camp. The party I was in was billeted in houses from which the Armenians had just been turned out. They were furnished for us very reasonably by a contractor who also fed us at a cost. We had a tremendous number of arguments about food and eventually decided that we would do what we could to feed ourselves and we got rid of the contractor and bought the odd bits of furniture he had given us.

Our freedom varied: to begin with none at all, we were just allowed to walk up and down the hundred yards of street our houses covered. At that time most people were content to lie on their beds and take a thorough rest. As we began to get fitter we agitated and were eventually allowed to take walks under escort and play whatever games we could in a certain field nearby. We were guarded by Turkish reservists whom we brought to heel in about four days. They were delightful old men, honest, friendly and would do messages for you into the town and buy food. There was a guardroom somewhere in the street and there was usually a sentry or possibly two, one at each end, but as far as anyone wanted to walk out was concerned, it was easy but there was no object at that time in going out. There were a hundred and twenty of us, mainly junior officers, one or two colonels and we had a certain number of British batmen we were allowed to bring with us, it was about one between every two officers.

For recreation all sorts of activities were organized by individuals. One house, not ours, had a good orchestra. We had a tailor, boot mending which I did, and we had somebody who did inlay work from toothbrushes. A lot of people did nothing at all. A lot of bridge was played. I played whatever games there were and later on I was allowed to go and buy leather in the town for shoemaking.

Concerning escape from Kastamuni; four officers escaped. I knew they were going because I could write a little Turkish and I made out a pass for them. It wasn't absolutely accurate but it got them on alright. They walked out quite comfortably one night. They went towards the Black Sea but they were recaptured. They were then attacked by tribesmen who released three of them, the fourth didn't get away, and those three got right away to the Black Sea, over the Black Sea just before the Russian Revolution and got back home.

As a result of the escape, we had a certain amount of trouble and were moved to a barracks at a place halfway between Kastamuni and Ankara. We spent an unpleasant winter there and during that time, the early part of it, the Turks offered us parole for anyone who would promise not to escape. They would be taken to a wonderful camp where they would have absolute luxury. Before this had happened we had a great deal of trouble with the commanding officer of our camp who wanted us to give our parole to him that we wouldn't escape. Some did, some didn't. There were a few die-hards against giving parole and the colonel said he was going to report them to the Turks. It was impossible escaping in the winter anyhow but when a second lot of so-called troublemakers declared that they too were ready to be reported, the result was the Turks offered official parole. That of course, took time.

From January to March the temperature never went above zero and conditions were bad. We had no money. The Turks couldn't give us any because it was impossible to get anything through but we got our interpreter to get in touch with the Greek merchant I had bought my leather from and we asked him if he could help us. His answer was to send £300 asking for a cheque. He eventually sent us something like two thousand Turkish pounds. It really was astounding. Any Armenian or Greek, if you would get him alone, would cash you a cheque on the current rate of exchange. In addition, I was doing the purchasing in the local town for one of our messes and I dealt with a Turkish butcher. I would tell him I had no money, we want half a cow and two sheep and he said that is perfectly alright because I know when you get some money you will pay me. When we got some money we paid him and that was the state of almost any camp in Turkey. At the end of the war I met in Constantinople that Greek merchant I mentioned. He had the sense to buy up all the English cheques that he could find in Turkey and he had something like £8,000 all of which was borrowed. Without him I think many would have perished in that cold winter.

Turning to our escape; numbers of us were determined to escape. The barracks were built with two walls with a large gap between them. We dug and got right down through one of the inner walls into the floor below the Turkish guardroom and were starting to dig down again, to go under the outer wall, when we were moved to another camp. Here we were told in no uncertain terms by our fellow officers that they didn't approve of anybody escaping. Those of us who were determined to escape before were still more determined to do so then, and we gradually built up enough food. We were organized by an escape party leader. We were in three different houses and it had to be organized so that in a certain period in one night we all broke out.

We got out without the slightest difficulty. I climbed out into the garden on a rope ladder with my escape mate. We had to pass a Turkish sentry and then found ourselves in the open but to our horror in the morning when it got light, we discovered that we were in a place which was only about four miles from the camp and there wasn't a shade of cover at all. However we managed to lie up in a small place in the hills without being seen and then after that we were aiming to go east to join up with Dunsteforce, the British independent operation in the Caspian region. We didn't know much about it but we thought they would be there and we went east and we were out altogether for about eight days before we walked into a village in the middle of the night and were picked up.

We tried our bluff of being German officers but unfortunately we met a Turk who knew what Germans were like and we were dragged back but we were shown no brutality at all. Our particular guard was a renegade Armenian which was about as low as you could get but we watched him jolly carefully and if he had shown any signs of trying to shoot us or anything else, there was always one of us walking within easy reach of him. He would have been the one who would have been shot. We had one or two unpleasant experiences. He insisted on leg-ironing us together at night which was a bit inconvenient but we had no hostility from the Turkish villages we went through at all. In fact, one woman came up and talked to us and said her son was a prisoner in British hands and was being well looked after. On our way, we found the country-side terrified. There were brigands around and we ran into a gang of brigands but we couldn't talk to them. They could only talk Russian and so that opportunity went. When we tried by signs to explain what we wanted all they said was you go back to Kastamuni and get as much money as you can to take you away. We got back to Kastamuni to find that, except for the party of eight who got clean away, everyone else was taken back.

Those of us who had been naughty were now taken to the Officers' Prison in Constantinople. Here I developed Spanish flu and was taken to a Turkish hospital and while I was there the rest of the party were taken off to a place in the middle of Turkey. By the time I got back out of hospital the war with Turkey was virtually over. You could read the Turkish newspapers that we relied on. They were turning round from pro-German to neutral to pro-ally. Just before the Armistice I was sent off to another camp and I had a very pleasant Turkish officer escorting me and when we got across the Sea of Marmora to a railhead and a gun went off he said, 'The Armistice,' but it wasn't. I then landed up in another camp and after a couple of days the commandant came up to us and said, 'You are free,' and that was all he said or did.

We then went to the stationmaster, who was a Greek, and said we want trains to Smyrna, which was duly arranged and the newly freed officers went off to Smyrna. A major, myself and a doctor remained behind because we knew that there were other troops who hadn't come through and we wanted to see as many people through as we could. We did all that and then finally ourselves took the train down to Smyrna.

When in due course we met some of our men who had had an infinitely worse time than us, they were very pleased to see us and we were terribly pleased to see them. There was no resentment among the men at their worse treatment and that was the end of it. I think they knew just as well as anybody else that the first thing an enemy does when he captures people is to separate the officers from the men. After all, a gang of officers and men together can do quite a lot because they have got the initiative there, and if you get a gang of men together you may get one or two who are capable of doing it but that is all.

Was I in any way changed by my experiences during these years? The only way I think I had changed was that before 1916 I was a very light-hearted soldier and in captivity I think I decided that I better take my profession a bit more seriously and I did what I could. I managed to get out from England some of the older military history books and that was the start really of my career as a serious soldier.

11

LIEUTENANT-COMMANDER
C G VYNER RN

Jutland

I have numbers of reasons clearly to remember Commander Vyner but first among them has to be his phone call out of the blue with its succinct message: 'If you want my Jutland diary and memories you must come up to Ullapool in the next fortnight as I am clearing up and moving abroad.' It was April 1981 and I was to be married later that month.

After a week filled with wedding activity and two days travelling to North-West Scotland, Louise and I had the pleasure of meeting and staying with Clare Vyner in his beautiful remote sea-viewing home. He was eighty-seven and was looked after by two nice New Zealand girls whose accomplishments, I remember, did not include cookery. My diary records the Commander as 'remarkable' and I remember him as just that. The quiet way he spoke of his experience at Jutland was somehow the more effective in conveying the high drama faced by officers and ratings of the destroyer HMS *Acasta*.

I was born in London in 1894. My father started in the Army having been the second son of the then Lord Northampton and as was the wont you either went into the Army or the Navy or the Church and he went into the Army. He started in the Grenadiers and later transferred to the 10th Hussars and saw service in Egypt, service which included the Battle of Omdurman, and then on to India. When my father died, my grandfather invited me to take the name of Vyner in order to continue that name. He only had two daughters and it was obviously going to disappear from the family. My elder brother couldn't be invited to do so as at that time he was in some way heir to the future Marquis of Northampton.

After prep school I was examined at the medical school on the Thames Embankment where everybody always went in those days to do their examinations for entrance into the Navy. I think I got through by the skin of my teeth and I went with seventy other boys to Osborne, the junior establishment of The Royal Naval College the following January of 1907. I absolutely had no influence on any of this whatsoever. I was always given boats at Christmas and for a birthday present and so forth and it was always understood that my elder brother would go into the Army. Both of which happened. He served with the Scots Greys and I was in the Navy. It was as simple as that.

Generally speaking I really enjoyed Osborne. It was extremely tough. You got up in the morning and went straight into a cold plunge. Everything was done with a gong. There was a gong to say your prayers, a gong to get into the plunge, a gong to get dressed, and a gong to get out of the place.

You always went to Osborne a day early on your first term and then the whole college arrived the next day and it was the custom – there was a very large hall there called Nelson – and it was the custom for the first term to be up against the wall in Nelson and then the other boys when they returned, who were not very much senior to yourself, to come and quiz you about your life and your home and your pets and this and that. The older ones didn't bother because they were too high and mighty by then and they weren't interested in you.

There was the most stringent discipline all the way through and if you did get into trouble it was always very serious trouble and if you were beaten, which you were if you did anything rather out of the way, it was a most painful experience as your term would be drawn up for the process and you were lain over a gymnasium horse to receive your beating and the doctor would be present and the whole thing really was extremely high powered. I remember the captain at Osborne, later to become Admiral Sinclair, had his son there with me and he was always in trouble. He was very unlucky. The thing was that he was dealt with just as strictly. The fact of his father I think made it worse for him; he couldn't be seen in anyway to be let off or anything. He had to get the full treatment.

The Duke of Windsor was a term below me but due to my getting pneumonia at Dartmouth I joined his term for one term in my fourth year as a cadet at Dartmouth. But he did not come to sea with us in the *Cornwall*. He went to Oxford. I knew him but I didn't have much to do with him. Prince Albert, the future King George VI, was only there for one term with me. He was first term when I was sixth term and I am sure he was liked much more than the Duke of Windsor as a cadet, but of course the Duke of Windsor was always difficult. I don't think he was very clever, in fact he couldn't have been for he was below me the only term I was with him.

At Osborne, I have to say, everything was done there, to get you going and liking the Navy. Your first term you went to sea for a week in a cruiser. You went to sea for a day in a destroyer. During my time there I was taken over to see the launch of the first dreadnought, a tremendous occasion.

At Dartmouth, the senior establishment, you did your engineering training and the place was much more like a public school beyond the fact that you wore a uniform all the time and so forth. And it was a rather depressing place I found. The very fact of the railway opposite having come to an end because it couldn't go into the sea obviously and one rather used to see the train leaving for London out of the window and rather wishing one was in it at times.

No, I never really cared for it awfully. One certainly had a full life, wonderful gymnasium, swimming baths, I suppose everything a boy could want but I found it depressing. Cultural activity was non-existent anything. The whole object was to make you a naval officer and nothing else and nobody was interested remotely, and I doubt very much whether any of them were capable, of that sort of interest. I don't suppose for one moment that the instructors and people were particularly chosen for any real reason of that description, that would be just one of so many, you know. The officers were chosen with care undoubtedly because it was their job, so as to speak, to bring you along, and you had a term officer, and the commander again was the right sort of person. When I was there, the college commander at Dartmouth was later to become an admiral and he was a splendid sort of county chap. He belonged to Devonshire and hunted and all that sort of thing but I don't think he was particularly interested in anything academic or cultural.

One little incident you might like to know about in these years at college took place at a hotel in Paris to which my mother had taken me. Also staying there was a party of Japanese. It was a Japanese Naval deputation seeking to place orders for armaments from France, Britain and perhaps elsewhere. They had made their headquarters at this hotel to do their work in Paris and of course the fact that I was wearing a naval uniform intrigued them enormously and so much so that they invited the management of the hotel to introduce us to one another. Having done so they invited us to take coffee with them in their apartments because they had a whole suite of rooms at their disposal and we really made quite friends with them so far as one could in such a short time. And one evening the admiral who sat and talked with me – he spoke very good English – said that he had been responsible for appointing Admiral Yamoto to command the Japanese fleet which sank the Russian fleet when they came from Europe to Vladivostok, or hoping to get to Vladivostok which they never did, at the Battle of Tsushima. Before we parted company he produced for me a very beautiful series of etchings of the battle and explained to me what the various ships were and so forth all of which was of great interest and I held them for many years. Unfortunately they got burnt when my house burned down in Yorkshire.

As a result of pneumonia I went down from Grenville Term to the Exmouth Term. The Exmouth went to sea three months later in the cruiser, *Cornwall.* The cruise lasted six months. When we were returning from Newfoundland to Halifax, Nova Scotia, we got a message that the *Novaya Bay* had gone ashore somewhere south of Halifax and that we were to go and see what we could do to give assistance, which we proceeded to do. But when we reached the vicinity of the *Novaya Bay* the fog was so thick you literally couldn't see fifty yards and although we were proceeding very slowly we hit a rock and that was it. It ripped the bottom out of the ship and the next scene was rather like the *Wreck of the Birkenhead* because all the cadets were considered to be an extremely valuable cargo, being no fewer than seventy future officers and in case the ship sank we were all lined up on the quarterdeck, with a view to being rescued I presume. Well actually, we sat there for quite a long time and we obviously weren't going to sink so we resumed our normal life.

After service in a cruiser I was appointed to the battlecruiser, HMS *Indomitable*, and then to the new battleship, HMS *New Zealand*, in January 1913. She was destined for a cruise to New Zealand to show the people what they had invested in. It was of sufficient importance as a cruise that King George V came down to Portsmouth to see us off. We went to Ascension Island, St Helena, South Africa, Australia and then Wellington, New Zealand. We were welcomed by Lord Liverpool, who was the Governor-General, and during the next three months we toured every possible place we could get into. We always kept a check of our visitors coming on board and when we had completed the tour we had over a million visitors and the population at that time was about 900,000, which was quite interesting.

From my own point of view I was quite delighted to meet an old crofter from my father's home in the Isle of Mull who had emigrated there some years previously and who was determined to meet me when he saw my name in the paper. He came on board bearing a huge stag's head as a present, stuffed of course, and this now hangs in my old home on the Island of Mull. In addition to that we had another very old gentleman came on board and said that he would like to give himself up as he had deserted from some ship about thirty or forty years previously so that was quite a big joke.

Politically a more significant cruise was the one in July 1914. We went as a squadron of course, battlecruiser squadron, with Admiral Beatty in command, flying his flag in HMS *Lion*. We anchored in Kronstadt. From there we visited St Petersberg and were entertained by Sir George Buchanan, the British Ambassador. *Lion* and *New Zealand*, moored side by side, put on a special ball. We, that is *New Zealand*, were the supper room and *Lion* was the ballroom, and Sir George Buchanan and his family as well as the Russian Royal family were there.

The following day we left and it has always impressed me since that the Admiral was told he was not to take his heavy ships at high speed in close proximity to the Tsar's yacht as it might cause a dangerous rolling on her part. But when you think that she must have been at least 4,000 tons, as big as the modern *Britannia*, probably bigger, it really shows the degree of inefficiency on the part of the Russian sailors if that were really the case. Another thing I remember is that there were no incinerators in ships before then and the sailors were terribly profligate with food leftovers and whole loaves of bread would be thrown overboard after a meal which would float away astern. And when you think of the size of the fleet which went North after the Royal Review at Spithead, you can imagine what a quantity of stuff there must have been thrown overboard. Well, the Commander-in Chief's destroyer, *Oak*, was coming up astern to join the fleet and her commanding officer commented on it to the Commander-in Chief that it really was an impossible situation, and he immediately gave orders that every ship was to have incinerators and that nothing was to be thrown overboard.

We were in action less than a month after the outbreak of war at the Battle of Heligoland Bight. I was at that time an acting sub-lieutenant and my battle-station was in the aft turret with Lieutenant Battenberg (the future Lord Louis Mountbatten) who was in charge of the turret. One of the things that I noticed, or we all noticed really, was that nobody really quite knew what would happen in battle and in point of fact you could see absolutely nothing and we had to put our heads up above the turret (twin 12-inch guns) and direct the turret by word of mouth in order to get any kind of target at all. And immediately after the action we organized open sights, open V-sights, to be put on top of the turret which one of the engineer officers did on his own because we were just sort of friendly, and in any future action they were there in order to get you onto the enemy target because of the fog and the cordite smoke. By the time Jutland came along of course all the big ships had got director firing.

In December 1914 I left my battleship for service in a destroyer, HMS *Acasta*, in the 4th Destroyer Flotilla: a big change for me. As it happened I was quickly informed that it was a change! Coming from a fairly efficient ship like the *New Zealand*, I was really very struck with the way everybody dealt with everything separately in a destroyer. I mean each gun was entirely on its own and so far apart that you couldn't tell what the others were doing and there was no means of telling anyway. I did suggest to my captain that I thought it would be a very good thing if all the guns fired at the same target more or less together so one could see where the shells went but the reply to that was, 'Keep your big ship stuff to yourself. We don't want that here,' and that was very interesting.

Before Jutland there were no brushes with the enemy for us but there were plenty of alarms because weather conditions were always so bad in the North Sea that people were always getting into trouble. And if you got into trouble it could be pretty serious trouble, like when the *Opal* coming in off patrol in a snowstorm hit the entrance to Scapa Flow and there was to be only one survivor. In bad weather there were no lights anywhere. You had absolutely no help of any kind, no radar of course, no nothing, just yourself finding your way home.

I think in many small ships, and certainly in ours, morale was good. We were very cheerful. Of course you always lay in pairs when you were in harbour, I mean *Shark* and ourselves were always next door neighbours. And the flotillas were divided into divisions of four boats, and subdivisions of two boats, and that's the way they moored. And occasionally one would give electric light to both ships because you were supposed to economize always and sometimes of course you didn't have any at all, you just had candles and things, but generally I think everyone was very happy, much more so probably than the big ships who got more and more frustrated.

Quite frankly, as for warning about Jutland, I would say we had absolutely none. I think everybody was of the opinion that things would develop and you could do very little about it and I think that was really as far as it went.

I would say myself that you would approach the enemy simply and solely as an anti-submarine guard on the big ships you were with. From then onwards I would think in all probability you would be guided by the senior commander of the group of destroyers that were together at the time. There they probably would take to spoiling action, in other words, had they seen a German flotilla starting to attack, they would immediately have gone out to oppose it and break it up. Certainly in the event that is rather what happened in our case when we arrived at Jutland.

We certainly had an idea of what was to come when we left Scapa. We ourselves, a division of four destroyers, left with HMS *Invincible* under Admiral Hood and his squadron, which were of course battle-cruisers, and they were destined to join Beatty and their battle-cruisers who were already at sea. The Grand Fleet came to sea afterwards, well more or less the same time, but they were astern of us as we left Scapa Flow and the approaches. I don't know what happened in the way of signalling between the various ships. We ourselves simply continued on our way, screening the three battle-cruisers and then we sighted a great deal of smoke and so forth in the distance and we realized that things were about to happen so we went to action stations.

I was on the bridge with the captain and my particular job was to fight the foremost 4-inch gun and do anything else the captain wanted me to do. The first lieutenant, who was the second in command, he was always on the after-gun so he would be as far away from the captain as possible, in case one end of the ship blew up I imagine, and the other didn't so there was somebody who survived and that was the arrangement in every destroyer I know about.

Almost immediately, it happened fairly quickly at least, the *Invincible* instructed *Shark*, who was our commanding officer of our four boats, to act independently and he immediately launched himself at the enemy and the enemy appeared to be almost innumerable to my eyes. I wouldn't like to say how many ships one could count at any given moment, but a great many. In fact I think it was the German first scouting group and all their destroyers, probably some light cruisers and also the German High Seas Fleet coming up astern, and in a very short time we had a hole in our fo'c's'le which you could easily drive a motor car through. We ourselves of course were steaming more or less directly at the enemy; they on the other hand were crossing, as you might say, from south to north as they were still proceeding in a northerly direction, not having yet discovered that the Grand Fleet was not very far away.

The shelling was extremely intense but the chief trouble was, from my point of view as I was solely at this particular time busy trying to hit them with my 4-inch gun, was the number of shells dropping in the sea short of us was so many that you could see nothing much of what happened to your own shell. And that is why originally, months before, when we had done practice, I said I thought all three guns should fire together. It was certainly most apparent when one got into action of this sort that one little gun became really a peashooter firing at the enemy and perfectly useless, and that was extremely depressing. In fact my own recollections were that at no time was one particularly frightened in any way, one merely got frustrated. It wasn't as if one was particular brave or anything of that sort, it was just the way things happened. You wanted to be winning the battle and you really couldn't see you were doing much about it.

Things then proceeded to happen to us fairly rapidly as we suddenly realized that *Shark*, our senior officer's ship, was in very serious trouble, not very far away. So we went to her and when we got there we saw that the ship was in a complete shambles, and really was totally destroyed as you might say. We went round her to see if we could take her in tow or anything, but of course we weren't ready to take her in tow – we had nothing to do it with – and the captain, Loftus Jones, who was in command of the *Shark*, told us to clear out, which we proceeded to do. But before we had got very far, we received two shells in our engine-room which more or less finished us, although we went on a little way. We couldn't get into the engine because of the steam and eventually the ship petered out from lack of steam, and that in a way was the end of the battle as far as we were concerned as a fighting unit.

We lay stopped as the entire Grand Fleet passed us firing over our heads at the enemy beyond. And just a little bit I rather missed out – one little bit – is that just before we eventually drew to a close, in the proceedings, the German first scouting group came out of the fog really not very far away from us. I think we thought at the time four or five thousand yards and that allowed us time and opportunity you might say to fire our torpedoes at them and the gunner, the torpedo gunner, claimed that we did get a hit but whether that was ever allowed or not, I wouldn't know.

Whereas *Shark* had much worse damage to her top hamper (superstructure and deck) you might say, sort of funnels and guns and so forth, apart from the shell through our funnel we were entirely hit in the hull. All the shells that landed on us, which weren't very many, were all on the hull. *Shark* was totally wrecked by gunfire and of course the volume of fire directed at both of us really was such that if you were stopped you obviously had no future of any kind.

And we were stopped, but by the time we were stopped, of course, the Grand Fleet had appeared out of the haze on the other side. We were between the Grand Fleet and The High Seas Fleet. I remember that the explosion of the shells on piercing our hull had had the effect of opening the now jagged plates outward and we had great difficulty placing a collision mat over such a hole. The number of casualties in point of fact was surprisingly small for the amount of damage done to the ship. I think we had eight killed altogether including the engineer officer who was killed in the engine room when the shell hit the engine room.

All the ships around us for their own reasons left us and carried on with their battle and when darkness came we were alone. There was a ship on fire about a thousand yards away, a German light cruiser I think, and my captain suggested that I go across to it in the whaler and see what was happening to it. So we duly got our pistols and so forth and climbed into the whaler and set off. After a few strokes in the whaler, the German ship blew up, so then we had to go back to *Acasta* without having discovered anything, but it was a German cruiser. During the night our wireless was still operating and our leading signalman, the only one we had because the other one had been killed, was able to read signals all night, including one from the Commander-in-Chief in the *Iron Duke* to another destroyer to steam north and endeavour to locate *Acasta* and take her in tow. And when daylight dawned, lo and behold, there was a destroyer coming towards us and did precisely that and we were slowly towed home to Aberdeen. Anyhow we managed to limp home and we were put alongside a jetty and it turned out we were nearly sunk and then the Admiralty decided that she should be broken up and that was that for *Acasta* but she doesn't go down as a loss in the battle.

My next ship, immediately after the battle, was to be HMS *Nizam*, which was building on the Clyde. She was being finished off as you might say. She was a destroyer like *Acasta*. I remember that later on she was fitted with a winch for a kite balloon and on one occasion the fleet went to make a sort of intrusion into German waters you might say, towards Heligoland, and we were ordered to put our kite balloon up. But it got stuck and the poor fellow (the observer in the basket) was flying at 4,000 feet with a rising wind and a rising sea and the winch completely stuck. And we, of course, down below rather laughed about it at this stage thinking of him up there. Well in the end we had to turn round and heave with the wind and try and take some of the weight off the balloon, force the winch, and by fitting on another wire we were eventually able to clear the winch and get the poor chap down. He was really rather flattered at all the endeavour because he knew what was happening because he could see out of the balloon with his glasses. He could see us working on the winch down below.

The only other incident to which I should make reference was when through the illness of my captain I was in command of our destroyer on a North Sea sweep in the summer of 1917 and so thick a fog came down that I couldn't see the buoy we released astern to avoid collision. We completely lost contact with the fleet but managed to make safe passage home.

12

LIEUTENANT-COLONEL
JAMES E GRIMSHAW VC

Lancashire Fusilier at Gallipoli Landings

It should not be surprising that someone engaged in the same work for many years reflects on his earliest efforts with the conclusion that he could have done better. As I look today at my questioning of Colonel Grimshaw, I wince uncomfortably at my lack of knowledge of the Regular Army pre-war and at my putting forward questions which allowed for single sentence response. However, rescue was at hand in the form of the Colonel himself. My diary for the day in February 1970 captures something of the occasion at St Margaret's, Twickenham. 'He is the sole survivor of the W beach six Lancashire Fusiliers VCs on 25.4.15. I explained why I had come to see him as clearly he gave no time to journalists etc. Soon he and his wife warmed and he said quite frankly he had enjoyed it. 2.30 to 7 pm! I enjoyed it too.' I only wish I had recorded what is still a vivid memory, that Mrs Grimshaw, showing me to the door, said she felt she knew her husband far better as a result of being present at the interview.

James Grimshaw was born in Wigan in 1893. He was to be one of twelve children. With that number of mouths to feed in his working-class family, the Army offered a way forward. He joined in 1912 and was with his regiment, the 1st Battalion the Lancashire Fusiliers, in India the following year.

Well, from first arrival in India, when you disembarked from the troopship, I don't think one will ever forget that smell. Peculiar, nice, I really liked it. Exciting, something of the atmosphere of the East.

I also remember the religious ceremonies. I have seen plenty of those but I saw quite a lot in Karachi of the Parsees and the burial of their dead. They don't in fact bury their dead. They take them to big towers, which they call Towers of Silence, and the bodies are put at the top of this tower, and the flesh is eaten from them by the vultures, and then the bones drop down to the bottom. It is a rather morbid subject really but that is their practice.

I was in Karachi when the war broke out. There had been rumours that it would be against the Russians. We really didn't know anything at all about Germany and I didn't know anything myself regarding the political state of affairs in England. I don't think any of us knew but we left India under convoy and in due course found ourselves in England at Nuneaton in Warwickshire and after a couple of months we were overseas bound again from Avonmouth. We didn't know where we were going but it proved to be Alexandria.

The First Battalion the Lancashire Fusiliers was in the Regular Army, British 29th Division, and had been chosen with a recently formed British division, and with Australians, New Zealanders and French troops, to land at different beaches on the Gallipoli Peninsula, neutralizing Turkish opposition in the forts guarding the entrance to the Dardanelles and thus enabling an allied squadron of warships to get through the Dardanelles into the Sea of Marmora and thus appear off Constantinople ready to bombard unless the Turks threw off their alliance with Germany.

In Alexandria we spent some time in camp reorganizng ourselves and the Commander in Chief, General Hamilton, walked down the line and inspected us. He was a slim man. Typical type of general fellow with moustache and I remember one little thing about him. A man stood a few ranks away from myself and he pointed at the man's breast. 'That medal there you are wearing, you are too old for this war aren't you nearly?' He said, 'No, Sir, how do you know that, Sir?' 'Well, it's the medal for The Boxer Rising in China in 1900,' was the General's response. In fact we did have Boer War soldiers in our ranks.

Well when we left Alexandria for Mudros harbour, preparatory to the landings, the harbour was thrilling; absolutely full with ships of all kinds and nations and one thing that was outstanding there was the Russian ship. It had five funnels and actually I saw it a few times afterwards in different parts. It was soon christened the packet of Woodbines.

On the island we practised disembarking from ship's boats and coming down from the gangways on warships and even rope ladders down the side of the ship. It is not a nice feeling climbing down a ship on a rope ladder unless you are a good climber when you are fully equipped with extra weight and so on. Later on it was approximately seventy pounds with our equipment and extra ammunition, 150 rounds of ammunition in their pouches, and so on that we carried.

I should have told you that my regimental number was 2609, that I was a corporal in C Company of my battalion, which was in the 86th Infantry Brigade of the 29th Division and we were taken to make our landing from the cruiser, HMS *Euryalis*. We sailed on the night of the twenty-fourth April, stopped for a while outside the island of Tenedos, I believe, and I could faintly see the Gallipoli Peninsula.

It was just after dawn that we were to land. It wasn't a rough sea. We were crowded into ship's boats, the boats roped in a string of four or five for towing ashore by a little steam-powered Pinnace or whatever it's called by the Navy. Of course I cannot be sure but there may have been fifty or more in our boat with its two or three sailors. After a certain time the tows were cast off and the sailors rowed us in. The Navy was shelling the Turkish positions and we had been issued then with plugs to plug into our ears to try and deaden the sound of the bombardment.

Well in my own boat the sailors who were rowing us ashore were killed as they were rowing. The enemy fire burst all at once. It was organized fire, practically all machine gun and rifle, and a certain amount of shrapnel. The sea was all spurting up as we were moving in, but the men were so packed in the boats that you couldn't tell that men had been hit but people to the right or left of me in the boat were killed or wounded. I was sitting on the left hand side going in to the shore. Men hit, just slumped forward, they didn't fall overboard. I should think twenty must have been killed or wounded.

When we jumped overboard there was about three and a half feet or four feet of water. The barbed wire stretched right from the edge of the cliffs right across the beach to the water and our bombardment had done little to destroy it. The wire was thickest near the bottom of the cliff and as to its height I would say from a tripwire to waist height.

I simply don't know how long it took us to get to the bottom of the cliff. It was our baptism of fire and we were so busy with one thing and another really you couldn't gauge the time. There was a little mound above the shoreline about forty yards in length and I managed to get a little bit of cover there. Later I found out that it really was a miracle if you were not to have been hit. My cap badge was shattered. My water bottle was riddled, the pack on my back, the same thing, and so on. I am making comparisons with other people.

We had been told beforehand that our objective was a hill, Achi Baba, which dominated our end of the Peninsula. Nothing could move on the Peninsula without it being seen from Achi Baba and that was the objective we were told.

Now amidst all the confusion on the beach and the sense that it was every man for himself, my company commander stood out, his demeanour controlling us. The trouble there was that we didn't know whether people were dead or wounded or not and the thing that was needed was to try and control the whole show. We couldn't do anything about the wounded at all. We had to leave everything. If we had have known who was wounded we couldn't stop. You had to get on with what you were doing. One thing paramount was the effect of water and sand on your rifle mechanism and the only way to deal with this was to try and urinate on the rifle bolt.

There were few clear targets to fire on, only stray ones, snipers only. So by the time we got to the top of the cliff, I don't know how long it took for that, just the remnants of the defenders were left behind and the Turks had retired to a couple of hundred yards behind the top of the cliff. When today you see the relatively low height of the cliffs you need to bear in mind the April 1915 circumstance and clambering up it, weighed down by rifle and equipment making the climb seem like Everest.

From the top of the cliffs we could see Turks. They wore a sort of balaclava helmet and a grey uniform and we saw them in the act of trying to retire to prepare trenches a few hundred yards in from the cliff. We rushed those trenches and cleared the people out. I didn't actually use my bayonet: I just pressed the trigger. You are carrying your rifle either at the trail or held in front of you so it is ready for immediate use, firing from the hip or anywhere. It all depended on where the object is.

This was part of our training. You don't lie down to take position like we do on a firing range. You just fire and that is that. We took their first line of trenches and we advanced about a couple of hundred yards further. We then got more or less sorted out and a few reinforcements linked up to us.

A few days later, on April twenty-eighth we made an attack on the village of Krithia, which stood between us and Achi Baba. We got into the outskirts but that was all: we got orders to retire. I know there has been criticism of poor liaison between the commander in chief and his senior officers at the landings and later on, but I attribute that to hindsight and to the fact that a lot of the trained staff officers were actually killed at the landing.

By the way, although we suffered heavy casualties in an attack on June the fourth, we made a big attack on the twenty-eighth which was successful when we advanced about 1,000 yards on the right of Krithia. And that was the time when we went over the top fighting that day, biscuit tins had been cut up in triangular shape and fastened on our backs so that the reflection of the sun could be an indication to our artillery and the ships at sea to give us covering fire. It wasn't, as has been written, bayonets flashing in the sun. It was the biscuit tins which had been cut up and put on our backs. After this the division took up commemoratively the triangle of blue cloth as our divisional sign.

I think with regard to being in battle action or in the time awaiting it, one gets used to it and more or less becomes a fatalist. I would like to put it that way and you have no feeling in the matter at all once you get over the top. It is the hanging on before the actual assault takes place, that is the worst time and some people do a bit of thinking. Personally I always had my own faith, and that was between myself and my maker. That is all I can say and yes it was a help to me. This and being a fatalist – what has to be, will be, kind of thing: a soldier's Christianity.

As for the Victoria Cross, well I heard about three weeks after the landing that something was up but I didn't know what recognition there was to be. I was told by my Company Sergeant Major Jackson, 'You have been up to something haven't you?' or words to that effect but he wouldn't tell me any more. I didn't hear any more until November of the same year that I had been awarded the Distinguished Conduct Medal. I didn't hear for eighteen months after that that it was anything different. My wife was the first one to know. I was on leave, out playing football, when a reporter came to the door of the house with the news that I had been awarded the Victoria Cross. Well naturally as a regular and trained soldier, identified with my regiment and with my country, I had always taken a pride in my reading and history, and I had read a bit of military history and naturally it was a confirmation of everything really when something like this happens. It isn't the sort of thing one can plan for or arrange. It just happens and there you are.

The Regimental History makes it very clear that it was the sheer courage and determination of a few men to cut the wire under intense fire and so assault the cliffs successfully which merited the award and, unusually, it was to be on selection by their comrades that a number of awards was made. Corporal Grimshaw was one of those men so recommended.

13

Dr GORDON JACOB CBE D.Mus FRCM

Western Front and German POW

It is possible that one of the reasons Gordon Jacob, the distinguished composer, has left a particularly pleasant general impression in my mind is that neither in his home in Saffron Walden nor by his conversation did he make the slightest endeavour to hide things which were psychologically important to him. I remember being warmed by his pride in his successful mastery of wind instruments despite some physical disability in a lip. Proof to him of this successful struggle lay in his becoming a Royal Academy of Music Examiner in this class of instrument. Second, he clearly had an obsession with pigs. Everywhere I looked, even to cabinets on stair landings, there were glass pigs, china pigs, clay pigs and I dare say plastic pigs though I didn't see any of the latter. It gave me some delight to put Dr Jacob in touch with a veteran I knew who had a similar obsession but with cats. I was told they were to keep up an agreeable correspondence.

The interview took place in February 1977 and I believe it justifies my diary judgement: 'Very good tape.'

I was born in 1895 in a London suburb, Upper Norwood, and I was the youngest of ten children. Seven brothers and three sisters we were and my father was in the Indian Civil Service and he died at the immature age of forty-eight and left this large family, but the India Office treated my mother with generosity and we all had pensions up to the age of twenty-one and that took care of things, so we were looked after well originally. I went to Dulwich College which was only a mile or so away from us at Upper Norwood but as for any development of my interest in music there, of course in

201

those days music wasn't looked upon as a possible source of liveli-hood and my mother was very much against my taking it up professionally and she had advisors among the people we knew, mostly retired officers from India and that sort of thing. She'd spent a lot of her time in India you see and they said, 'Oh no, music's no good, you can't let him do that.' But I did have piano lessons from the organist of our church, and other people, and also later at Dulwich itself, and I played the percussion in the orchestra and that sort of thing to try and get a knowledge of the orchestra, which I always was immensely interested in. In fact I have written one or two books about orchestration, which has been rather a speciality of mine. But anyway, to go back to the home, some of my brothers and sisters were keen on music and two of my brothers were rather more than that. They both tried their hand at composition and in two very different ways: one in the very conventional Victorian way, the other in a more avant-garde type for that time in the '20s and '30s.

I always wanted music to be my life but I didn't see how it could be because my family were so much against it and they planned I should become for some unknown reason an analytical chemist. Well I was some good at science at school and chemistry was my strongest subject, but of course the war broke out when I was nine-teen and I was just leaving school that very summer in July 1914 and went straight into the Army.

I can certainly tell you why and it was because of the immense war enthusiasm. I, and my friends at school who were the right age, we all wanted to be in it before it was over. We thought, 'Oh dear, it will be over very soon,' and we thought, we have the spirit and have the experience (**School Cadet Corps**) to fight for our country and we were very patriotic. I enlisted in August 1914 about three weeks after the war had started. I was away on holiday when it actually broke out and when I came back I enlisted at once. I was told that educated men were required in the Royal Artillery but I found that they were real rough, tough, East End types and they used to burgle houses in Folkestone and that sort of thing. I came across the sort of people I didn't know existed, and I remember talking to an Army chaplain down in Folkestone and he asked me what I was doing before the war, and I told him I was at school and

I joined the army straight from school and he said, 'Oh you're taking your degree in the University of Life.' That was very good I think.

I used to write very amusing letters home, which made my family rock with laughter. I looked on the funny side of the thing but I learned that these men were rather admirable in some ways and many of them in every way. I mean quite a lot of them were honest and serious-minded chaps and they didn't resent me coming from a different background and in any case I never advertised it.

However, Gordon Jacob was not to remain in the Artillery because 'strings were pulled' as he wrote to me, and his application for a transfer to the University and Public Schools Brigade was accepted. He joined this officer 'preparation' unit at Epsom Barracks.

This was a tremendous relief after the rough conditions in the RFA and I really enjoyed my time at Epsom and the people I was billeted on were very nice and kind, and I had a billet with one of my own school friends who was in the same battalion, so that was rather nice. Then we moved to wooden huts, a camp in Woodcote Park, Epsom, and things became rather more 'military': official and military as it were.

After more training at Clipstone and Tidworth, we, that is in our new designation as the 18th Battalion the Royal Fusiliers, went to France on the fourteenth of November 1915. I always remember that date and I was in the front line a week later.

Gordon Jacob has written in an unpublished manuscript about his experience in 'holding the line' but did not speak of it on interview.

Well all the time really up to the attack in which I was taken prisoner I didn't take part in any offensive action, but during this period of holding the line, as it was called, I spent some time in an officer cadet battalion at New College, Oxford, and got my commission. It was about this time, September 1916, that I learned of the death of my brother on the Somme at Flers. I would like to speak of him soon.

On being gazetted at the end of September 1916 I was ordered to report to the Queen's Royal West Surrey Regiment at Sittingborne in Kent and I remember feeling that we newly commissioned officers, though in many cases we had been in France, were considered as rather 'amatuer upstarts'. In due course I was to join the regiment's 1st Battalion on the Somme where in very muddy trenches they were, with the offensive over, sticking out the winter.

My first action, and the one in which I was to be captured, was on April 23rd 1917 in the Arras offensive, but you have asked me whether whatever creative spirit was within me were not revolted by all the destruction I had seen already, even before it could really be said that I had been in action. I was not so distressed about myself in that way but I was distressed at the tremendous waste of talent in general and how the best young men seemed to be the ones who were killed. This is not something which I only thought later because I remember how very upset I was about my brother being killed, and he was a such a talented chap too. He was a scholar at St John's, Cambridge, and he was a brilliant young man. He was only twenty-three when he was killed and he would have done something I think in a literary way probably, and that loss seemed to me to be quite appalling and still does, but I didn't worry about myself very much because I was completely an amateur you see. I didn't know that I had as much talent if you like as I found I had afterwards so I didn't take myself too seriously in that way. After all I was only twenty or so.

Now where I did feel pressure, as I am sure all the young officers did, was that whatever happened they mustn't show any signs of fear or anxiety however frightened they really were and I was very frightened. I wasn't a brave man, I never had to do anything extra-ordinary or anything like that but I think I've always had a rather pronounced sense of humour and that helped a lot in keeping one's spirit up and of course in our little company mess in the line we were all very friendly, and it was a very good atmosphere altogether.

In my mind I can see the circumstances in which I was captured very clearly. We'd been in action since dawn. We'd crept up to within a few hundred yards of the German line during the night and we were told we mustn't make a sound. The men were very good, they didn't make a sound and we just lay down and waited for the barrage to start and it started just at daybreak. Immediately the barrage started we got up and it was a creeping barrage and we advanced under cover of the barrage through the German wire, some of which had been destroyed enough for us to get through, and the Germans had to keep their heads down because of the terrific barrage. It seemed like all hell let loose and then we got to their front line, which was very lightly held, and we occupied that and it gave us some shelter, but I never got any further than that and the Germans kept throwing hand grenades and if anyone showed a square inch of themselves, they got a bullet. The whole thing was rather confused and I didn't even know some of the men I found myself with. I mean we didn't keep together in a platoon or anything after a few hours, just carried on with anyone who was there.

There was a small party of us, of about a dozen I should think, and we were in this very shallow trench, in fact I've got the sort of feeling we were almost out in the open. And we had a bag of bombs, Mills bombs, and we handed it rapidly from one end of our little line to the other until there were no bombs left and we had no ammunition of any other kind. And I was the only officer in the group and I said, 'Well there's no point in us waiting to be killed we'd better give ourselves up,' so I got hold of an old canvas bag which had held ammunition and I put it on the end of the rifle I had, the end of the bayonet as a flag of truce, and the Germans were standing ready to throw bombs straight at us. They had those stick bombs and we should have just been wiped out so I didn't see the point of that, we just gave ourselves up.

I thought they might kill us because that was what we'd been told, but later I could see that that was to prevent us giving ourselves up. In fact they treated us quite well. The front line Germans were quite good. I mean we were all rather sort of miserable together in the front line, friends and foes, and we had sympathy for each other. We knew how awful war is and they treated us much better than the Germans behind the lines who hadn't seen action at all. So all they were interested in was whether we had got any English cigarettes and various things like that. Of course they took all our equipment away and our weapons and things naturally; and they tried to get hold of some people's wrist watches and things like that but on the whole they treated us reasonably well.

We were taken along tunnels wonderfully constructed, with great caverns of billeting space and beds with wire mattresses and we marched, after being in action for all that time, from dawn until about 1 or 2 o'clock in the afternoon. We were interviewed by an officer for a short while and then we were taken back to the rear and marched, or walked anyway, miles. We were so tired we went to sleep as we walked and we were taken back to some village where there were some empty houses and we were put into them: there was no furniture and nothing on the floor. We just lay down on the floor and went to sleep, and then the next day we were taken to a railway station and put on a train. And I remember we had to change at some large station, I think it was at Frankfurt, and went into another train, and were taken to Karlsruhe which was the sort of distributing centre for prisoners, so they didn't waste much time taking us to a camp.

From Karlsruhe we were taken to Strohen in North Germany, a sort of 'blasted heath' actually. And later we were moved to Bad Kolberg, a much more comfortable place, with hard tennis courts and other amenities. There were three pianos in the camp, one of which I managed to get put into my room, which I shared with about six other prisoners and really life was very much more comfortable in there than it was at Strohen. There were a great many escape attempts from Strohen, some of which were successful by means of tunnels or by means of just going and cutting the wire and taking a risk of getting through.

I was a new prisoner when we were there and the only people who could contemplate escaping were people who'd been prisoners for a long time and had collected some material somehow; German money, compasses, maps, enough food for a week's trek. The only people who were actually punished after escape attempts were the people who had attempted to escape, not the rest of us. I cannot remember which camp I was in when I was present on that well-known occasion of a commandant who could speak a little American/English lecturing us at the roll-call following an escape saying that we might think he knew nothing about the activities we were getting up to but in fact he knew 'damn all'. I think his name was Niemeyer.

I had in fact had the short-lived satisfaction of successfully hiding a map myself in the peak of my cap. It was only a spoof map. They had some civilian detectives in to search the camp because there'd been so many escapes and attempts, so I got hold of a piece of paper and I drew a rough sketch of the camp, and then I did a little map of surrounding imaginary countryside and a little sort of signpost saying 'to England' or something on it, you see. And I put it in the lining of my cap and these German detectives looked in all the most unlikely places they could whereas on the table under some cigarettes in a box were some maps. They never touched that, but they got hold of my cap and they took this out and as a matter of fact they saw that I'd only done it for fun so they said, 'Take all your clothes off.' So I had to take all my clothes off and be properly searched. I took my clothes off and was completely naked and did a sort of war dance in front of them and they were highly amused at this, so it wasn't a serious escapade even their rather limited sense of fun was tickled. That was at Strohen I remember now.

Bad Kolberg was such a long way from any frontier it would have been impossible to escape. As a matter of fact there were one or two attempts. I saw two chaps go straight up to the wire, cut a hole in it and go and they ran for their lives but the Germans got them, they shot at them but they didn't hit them, but they recaptured them. Then there were two other men who had made twelve attempts at escape I think and on the thirteenth they were taken and shot from Bad Kolberg. One was in my regiment and I had to help to be a pallbearer at his funeral. Whether they were shot in being captured I really don't know but we thought that they had been shot after they were captured which of course is against the laws of war. But I think that was only because we wanted to think the worst of the Germans probably, because there was no proof of that, but the rumour went round the camp that they had been shot and the Germans I think got to hear this and they gave them a really slap-up military funeral and fired shots over the grave and everything.

On the subject of music at this camp: I had the idea of forming an orchestra. You see, musical people sort of gravitate towards each other and I used to play trios with a man who played the clarinet and another man who played the cello and they attracted other people and I heard people practising instruments from time to time in the camp and I got to know them. We were able to buy instruments through the canteen at enormous cost and I think my first violin had his instrument sent from home via the American Red Cross before America came into the war. I am almost certain he had his own fiddle and I'm not sure that another man didn't but we bought a cello I know. At least one cello, and I gave a benefit concert so the clarinet could buy a clarinet in A because he only had one in B Flat and we managed to buy him one in A, which he never used because he liked his old one which was all tied up with string.

You may be wondering how we had money. We were able to cash cheques on the American Express Company in Holland and after America came in we were able to cash cheques through Holland and they eventually got to our Bank, Cox's Bank in London. But they cashed cheques for us whenever we wanted to and gave us *Lagergeld*, prison camp money for them which was no use outside the camp, you see. We charged, I don't know, 5 marks for a seat or something and we probably had somebody at the door collecting the money.

I don't know who'd been in the camp before, but it was really a spa, and our concerts and theatre performances were given in the spa itself, which was quite a posh sort of place, and we built a stage, quite a good stage, and there was a piano there. There were two pianos in that hall, and then I managed to get the third piano put into my room because I was the sort of official musician at the camp. And then nobody minded me having it, and there was the piano ready, and we were able to buy the instruments and music stands and anything we wanted through the canteen. They got the instruments from some large town. The canteen belonged to a civilian firm in some town. I could get anything we wanted. I got manuscript music paper there and anything except food, no food.

I think in my case the provision of music for the prisoners was pretty selfish. I'd always had this passion for music. I'd got this little orchestra together. I didn't have one at all in civilian life, but I used to do what music I could and play piano duets with another chap who was quite good at the piano, and things like that. Well anyway I had this overwhelming desire to write music, which I did. I wrote some in the camp and I arranged it for the instruments we had, and also arranged other music for them and really I got wrapped up in that. I never even thought about trying to escape or anything. Music was the thing I'd always wanted to do, and here was an opportunity of doing it in spite of the straightened circumstances of the prison camp. And that sometimes I'd work twelve hours a day writing out parts for the orchestra, and arranging music and writing my own music, all that sort of thing. And I really managed to lay the foundations of a technique in that way, because we had to play all sorts of different types of music, and I think that's always good for students, not only to concentrate on one type of music, but to have experience of even the lighter types as well, because they all have something to contribute to the general training of a musician.

I got to learn the actual technique of composition and scoring for instruments, about the technique of strings and woodwind. I already knew the brass technique because the brother who was killed played the trumpet – he was very good – so I was conversant with that; but apart from that and the piano, I didn't play anything. I'd never played a stringed instrument, but I was able to learn a lot about writing for these things, and what was easy for them to play, and all that sort of thing.

From the serious to the light-hearted, I should mention that in the ranks at the canteen in Tidworth I played the long-suffering piano for soldier sing-songs by the way, a whole row of pint pots put there for the pianist – me! I couldn't get through them all and everyone spilt beer in the piano and that sort of thing. I remember taking the works out on a hot day and standing the action of the piano in the sun to dry the beer out. Those memories are marvellous – and then men would want to sing their favourite sentimental songs: things like *Don't go down the mine, Daddy* and all that, *My fiddle is my sweetheart*, that sort of thing. They'd come up to me and in a rather tipsy way, 'You know how it goes, mate, don't you, der-di-der-di-der-di-der.' I would say, 'That's alright,' and then I'd vamp away, you see, and they were quite happy.

I played percussion in the theatre at Tidworth once, and I was rather pleased about that because they paid me about ten bob a week for doing it in the evenings, and that was tremendous when I was only getting seven shillings a week.

You ask whether the experience of captivity found any expression in the music I wrote as a prisoner. Well, yes it did, and actually at the time it did, because I wrote a rather ambitious piano sonata when I was in the camp and I headed it with that rather sententious verse about 'Out of the dark that covers me, thank whatever God sent thee for my own unconquerable soul' and I put that at the head of this piano sonata: a thing I wouldn't dream of doing now. But that showed that I was feeling that, and I also wrote an orchestral work not for my orchestra, but for a full orchestra, an overture which I called *The Song of an Exile* I think, and I introduced into it one or two old English folk songs.

I might even have it somewhere, I'm not sure. I've got a lot of old music and old attempts at music, which I wrote before the war when I was at school and that sort of thing and it's an awful hotchpotch of styles of course. I went to one my piano teachers, he was the organist of our church and he was a composer – liked music himself – and I used to take him my efforts and play them to him. And he'd sit beside me and he'd say, 'Bach, Beethoven, Debussy, Elgar,' as these composers were suggested to him by my music you see, and where it had all come from.

The German officers came to our concerts, and I remember playing the Chopin *Funeral March* at the funeral of those chaps who were shot by the Germans. I played the Chopin *Funeral March*, and when one of the German officers, a middle-aged man, came round, they always came round to see that we were all in our rooms you see, no one missing at night, and he said, 'Herr Lieutenant Jacob, you are a great artist, *sehr grosse* artist,' which I thought was rather good coming from a German because they usually said, at that time, that England was the land without music, and he evidently was sufficiently musical to listen. They thought that I played very well, and, of course, he knew all about the orchestra and he always used to come to our concerts.

As for getting music from home, I knew I shouldn't get much sympathy from home about anything to do with music really. They didn't actually discourage me from doing it, but my mother used to tell my teachers not to be too encouraging, because she didn't want me to get the idea that I'd be a professional musician. But through this same canteen I mentioned I was able to buy scores, miniature scores. I got some of the huge works of Richard Strauss, and studied them, written for colossal orchestras and all that, and I collected quite a little library of scores out there. I've still got a few with the censor stamp on them.

Of course I got no opportunity to play music outside the camp. We didn't have parole. We didn't go anywhere outside, though at Coburg we did. The reason why we didn't at Bad Kolberg was that they demanded on our little passports that we had if we were on parole, a photograph, and we said we wouldn't do that, because that was an insult, and if they gave you parole that's enough, no one breaks his parole. But they didn't trust us, so the senior British officer had us all together and he said, 'I'm going to refuse to do this. You can do what you like about it, but I'm going to refuse to have my photograph on my parole card,' and we all agreed with him so we didn't get out. But at Coburg I went to a village church once or twice, only once or twice, because we had services in the camp. We had an occasional service in the camp. We had a man there who was organist of a church in Birmingham I think, a man called Tucker. He got together a male voice choir in the camp, and he gave concerts with that and also they sang at services, which we conducted for ourselves. Occasionally an English chaplain would come because some English chaplains who were taken prisoner were very good at getting to other POW camps. By the laws of war they were at liberty to be returned if they were taken prisoner, but some chose to stay and minister to our men in their camps. They would make a sort of round of the camps and occasionally one of them would be with us.

In my experience, as prisoners of war, we were fairly treated. Of course we hated the Germans and wanted to think the worst of them, and there were a lot of petty, rather spiteful regulations, which we resented. There was never any brutality at all as far as I know, and nothing really very bad. They behaved well I should say on the whole. One or two of the non-commissioned officers were rather unpleasant in their manner, but that's as far as they went. The officers, the old type of German Prussian officer, we had one of them at Coburg, he was brutal to his own men, but he wasn't to us. I mean he'd go up and slap men in the face on parade. He did resent us laughing at the Germans and I don't blame him for that. But we used to laugh at him and we used to laugh at the interpreter because he wasn't very good at English really, and he got fed up with this and he got the guards with their rifles, and he said, 'Now you've got to parade for so long every hour. The bugle will go and you'll turn out and parade every hour, and these men will stand in front of you and behind you with loaded rifles, and if there's a shadow of a smile on anyone's face they have orders to shoot,' so we didn't smile then. But the funny part was that if these chaps in front had shot it would have gone through us and hit their men, men who were aiming at our backs. No one had thought of that.

Of course some people took very badly to the constraints of life as a prisoner. I was almost sorry for the men who had no real interest. There were plenty who did handicrafts. There was one or two who drew very well and painted, and there were others who were studying for degrees and working hard, but I should say the majority were the other type and they deteriorated physically. I remember one man of very good family. I won't tell you his name because they're quite a well-known family, but he was a chap of only about twenty-three and he looked at least fifty, and he was going bald and I think he actually died in captivity. He drank: we could get German wine at the canteen if we paid for it. He was drunk most of the time, as many of them were, and they played cards for high stakes. One man, I think, was quite sorry when the Armistice came because he was owed about £1200 or something.

There was a certain amount of quarrelling but I don't think I came across any serious issues of that nature. There were one or two who weren't very nice to me actually, and, of course, they hated music. They hated the feeling that anyone could do some-thing that they couldn't do I think, and they used to make sarcastic remarks about it and that sort of thing. I didn't mind, but apart from that I don't think there was much jealousy or ill feeling anywhere. I think there was a little homosexuality. There were one or two rather good looking young chaps who made up as girls when we had our plays, and they looked marvellous, just like girls, and I think some of the men would be keen on them. I remember catching one of them in a room one day in what might be called compromising circumstances, but I don't think there was much of that sort of thing.

The reader will not be surprised to learn that Gordon Jacob's 'musical opportunity' in captivity set him inexorably upon the career he had believed out of reach.

14

LIEUTENANT-GENERAL SIR REGINALD SAVORY KCIE CB DSO MC

Indian Army at Gallipoli

Before I went to record General Savory in April 1972 at Seale near Farnham in Surrey, I had seen him and heard him speak on a number of occasions. It is difficult to imagine a man with a more soldierly bearing, nor one who so exuded presence, an aura of command. He had too, a deep, resonating, voice. For all those manifestations of power however, he was easy and helpful to work with.

He was born in London in 1894, his father a manufacturing chemist. He went to Uppingham School but in his own words was a 'bit of a rebel' and did not distinguish himself. He was sent to a 'cramming' establishment in Germany to improve his academic progress. He was impressed by the 'supreme confidence' he saw all around him and by glimpses of a 'magnificent Army'. Savory regarded the eighteen months he had in Germany at this English-staffed crammer preparing him for Sandhurst as the 'best education I ever had'. He had not just learned the language quite well but had come to realize that 'there were other people in the world, outside the British who had ideas of their own'. He used to ride, shoot, and visit the homes of officers in the locally-based cavalry regiment, and had made lasting friendships. Savory was keen to emphasize the impact of the propaganda of two world wars in giving British society a distorted image of the German. His friends were 'military to the backbone but so was I'.

I thought the Royal Military College, Sandhurst, was tremendous. I was very impressed by my training there and very happy. Military thinking was led from there, but when I got out to India at the end of January 1914 I was horrified to find how far practice was behind precept. That is always the case isn't it wherever you go, military life or civil life or anything else? In fact soon after joining my Indian regiment we were inspected by the local brigadier and to my amazement we were all dressed up in full dress and we had an order stating that we were being charged by cavalry from the right whereupon we formed square and adopted sort of Waterloo tactics, which was rather off-putting when you consider the war was quite obviously on its way then.

When the war broke out I was in a hill station in the Himalayas in India serving with the First Battalion of the Duke of Wellington's Regiment. There was no wireless in those days and no Reuters direct. Any news we got we had to get from headquarters, so to speak, and every day in that obviously critical period we used to send an officer riding ten miles or so in to headquarters at Murree and he used to come back with various reports. Until one day one of our captains, by name Horsford, came back to the mess, took off his belt, flung down his cap and said, 'It's no good sir,' talking to the commanding officer. 'It's no good sir, there's not going to be any war. Paris is placarded with notices saying order de-mobilization.' Well, it was quite clear to us that Horsford had got hold of the wrong end of the stick. So we sent in another officer who came riding back and saying to the commanding officer, 'It's alright sir, it's alright sir, Horsford was wrong, the placards didn't say order demobilization but *ordre de mobilization*.' I think that's a rather good little story don't you?

Well now the moment the war broke out I was transferred from the British Army to the Indian Army, to the 14th Sikhs. In February 1915 I went off to Suez with my regiment and arrived just in time for the tailend of the Turkish attack on the canal. Real action awaited us on the Gallipoli Peninsula. The initial landings had not been as successful as had been hoped. We went ashore at Cape Helles at 'V' Beach beside the SS *River Clyde* early in May.

Of course we could both see the evidence and hear accounts bearing out the fact that war was a pretty stern and tough business but we were very proud of ourselves. We were all regular troops, we were four long-service battalions in the Indian Brigade. I think we kept up our morale pretty well. It was rather a good thing that our men you see, being Gurkhas and Sikhs, couldn't understand what the British soldier was saying, so their complete non-comprehension of what the British soldier was saying about war being so bloody and everything else passed them by completely.

The Turkish sniper was magnificent. He put the fear of God into all of us. They were wonderfully brave men. They would sit up in trees and somehow even behind our lines, you know, and shoot away. We used to shoot them down from their trees. We never took any prisoners in the early days, feelings were running pretty high. I can recollect the taking and shooting of a whole batch of Turkish prisoners but I would rather not talk about that.

You know what it is in war. You potter around, you do patrols now and again, you come back and have some supper or some breakfast and you go out on patrol again, you lose the odd man here or there, you might get hit yourself. And so it goes on day after day. Then one day you're told to go in for the big thing: so it happened with us. Our first successful show was a little thing called Gurkha Bluff, and the Gurkhas went round the Turkish right flank and got in behind them. And we followed them up, which was good. It was at the end of May. This attack, to my mind, set an example which might have been copied for the whole of the rest of the campaign but just wasn't. Well, then you see things were obviously boiling up for a big assault and we had our orders for this for the fourth of June astride of Gully Ravine.

I was still a second lieutenant. My company, of which I was second-in-command, was on the right of the gully, in the first line. We had to lead the way. Well, one watched one's watch ticking away there. You did what you could to get the men in the right place and instructed and one was too busy to be very afraid I think. What did shake us a little bit was when one of our shells fell in our own trench and it buried the company commander and me and I remember my ears buzzing. Eventually we were dug out. We were still intact. I lost my watch but I managed to borrow a watch from the nearest signaller. And then we watched the time. Zero hour: blew the whistle and over the top we went. Awful feeling. It's rather like a sort of magnified feeling you get just before you start off for the hundred yards, butterflies in your stomach. And when you got over the top I'd never known anything like the roar of fire that came at us, just a roar.

Well, I was young and fit and I had all the bravery of the novice. It's always the novice who is the brave chap. And I ran ahead of my men. I had a rifle with a bayonet and I suddenly found myself standing on the edge of a Turkish trench with a Turkish soldier down below looking at me rather surprised. So I bayoneted him, I stuck my bayonet into him poor devil. I got him through the shoulder and I skewered him to the back of the trench, I can watch that chap's face today. I don't know what happened after that. I got my bayonet out and I popped into the trench and I went along and met someone, and the next thing I remember was lying on my back on the Turkish parapet with some Turks using my body as an aiming rest and firing at the rest of my chaps coming up; not very pleasant. I suppose I had fainted. And then I came to, on and off. Then the fire stopped and I looked around and got up.

And then I had a look around and I saw my little bugler, whom I had with me as a runner, rather a young chap who was such a good looking young Sikh, and they'd got him and they'd mutilated him in the most foul way. The Mohammedan doesn't like the Sikh, you know, like me and like the devil. They'd got hold of his John Thomas and pulled it out and tried to cut it off with a blunt blade: a horrible sight. Anyhow I got up and there was nothing for me to do with no men. They'd all gone. So I trotted back to the trench we'd left. I was bleeding a bit in the head and I was lifted up. An old Sikh came out from the trench and picked me up. One of our regimental wrestlers, a grand fellow with a red beard, he looked like a Greek wrestler. And he took me down to the doctor and they patched me up and I went down to the field ambulance and they put me to bed there. I was very shaken. It was a bloody experience. And when I was better they talked about sending me off the Peninsula and I wouldn't go and I came back, joined my regiment and found there seemed to be very few of us left. I don't know what our casualties were, but something pretty heavy.

What do you see when you're in your first battle? Nothing very much, dust, smoke, your men spread out like that. You can't control them, you couldn't see them, you couldn't shout, nobody can hear: extraordinary business, appallingly bad tactics. So all I could do was go and fight my own private battle. There's no leadership, you're living just with the men. It wasn't much fun, it shook me. But then you see I came back and I found myself with the commanding officer and he said to me, 'Savory, it's an ill wind that blows nobody any good, I'm going to make you adjutant.' Well, I think I must have been near twenty-one, tremendous to be made adjutant at that age. And that kind of thing, you know, improved one's morale and one had responsibilities to fulfil and things to do.

For example, I had the battalion's war diary to see to. I wrote it up about once a fortnight when I remembered it and then very cursorily. I don't think an awful lot comes out of war diaries, you know. That may not be the case for brigades and divisions but in a battalion the real descriptive value is from diaries and letters and all that kind of thing. The war diary is irrelevant. The regimental soldier, he doesn't bother about paper and writing and bumph and all that kind of thing. Our war diaries were very, very cursory things. Probably just nothing except 'two men killed and thirteen men wounded today' or something like that.

On twenty-eighth of June we were back again in action and we did quite a good advance up to a place called Fusilier Bluff and then the Turks counter-attacked us. I think they counter-attacked us for about four solid days, I'd never known such fighting. We slaughtered those Turks, I'd never known anything like it. I took a rifle myself. They came on and on. Bombardment, attack: bombardment, attack. There was no room for both us and the 6th Gurkhas in our trench, they came and stood on the trench behind us and fired over our heads. I don't think a single Turk reached our trenches. I should think there must have been two or three thousand of them piled up about fifty yards away. I'd never known such slaughter.

At the end of that the Indian Brigade had suffered severe losses too, so much so that we all had to be amalgamated. My regiment was amalgamated with a Gurkha Regiment and the other two Gurkha Regiments were amalgamated and we went off to the island of Imbros for rest and recovery and then we got ready for the August show.

Savory's unit was to be involved not at Cape Helles but at what had become known as 'Anzac', further up the Peninsula where the

Australians and New Zealanders had made their landing, on very different terrain from Helles, trying to take a series of steep ridges above their beach, but had similarly been stalled. Further up the Peninsula still, a new landing was to take place at Suvla Bay while at Anzac a diversionary attack on the right was designed to draw attention away from a plan on the left to make three separate assaults at night on the heights which commanded the Dardanelles as well as the allied beach-head.

The Suvla show was frittered away by sheer gutless performance, there was no leadership. I'm talking now, of course, after the facts, but we broke out from Anzac and things didn't go quite as fast as we had hoped, they never do at night, things are awfully slower. And we got round behind the Turks and then we got rather bogged down because our guide, an awfully brave New Zealander called Overton, took a short cut, which was fatal, and he lost his way. And we instead of carrying along the path we knew we had to go, wandered round the countryside. The Turks were on the run. We captured a German Army officer in his pyjamas. We captured some Turkish guns and we were well on the road to the north and then we went wandering around, you see, we'd lost our way. When daylight came, the Turks recovered, had a look at the situation, got up the hills and they saw us all down below in the valley, which was easy meat as far as they were concerned.

So, that night advance which might have settled the whole thing didn't go off very well. Then we had some more attacks to do and the Australians on our left were not very good, they came running back and left us open and we came back. And then we, the Indian Brigade, were then switched off to the top of Anzac, the Sari Bair Ridge, with the Sixth Gurkhas in advance and my regiment just behind in reserve. My God that was heavy fighting. We didn't have to do much, but the British troops did. They got to the top of the ridge after the Gurkhas had been shelled off.

Anyhow one of my recollections is the Turks counter-attacked and these troops came running down the valley, sheer panic. I'd never seen anything like it. Panic is a terrible thing. That was the end of Gallipoli. It was the 8th or 9th of August.

We had got onto the lower slopes of Sari Bair and were looking out over Suvla Bay. What were they doing there? No move, nothing. The whole plan was beautifully organized, but there was no general or brigadier there to say, 'Is anybody on that hill?' The answer would come back, 'I don't know, sir.' Well, in the last war somebody would have been told to bloody well go and find out. If those chaps at Suvla had been ordered forward immediately after their landing instead of their footling about to find water, the battle was won.

In general on the Peninsula, food wasn't bad. Mails were remarkably regular when you consider the conditions. Sanitation, that was a problem, what sanitation can you really do when you've got thousands and thousands of men in a few square, in a square mile or two. The flies, of course, were simply too ghastly for anything. And the corpses, the stink was terrible. I think one of the greatest shocks of my life was going out before the serious fighting had started and wandering around no-man's-land and seeing my first corpse, real corpse, blown up and black and on the point of bursting, you know, and flies wandering in and out of the chap's nose and mouth. It was a ghastly, ghastly sight. But then you see you can't do much for the sanitation under those conditions. You can dig latrines and so on but you can't dig latrines all round the corpses can you? I think one of the nastiest sights I ever saw was vultures appearing in no-man's-land. It wasn't very pleasant to feel one's going to be picked to death by a vulture.

Soon after this big show I went away sick. I had a very bad go of dysentery and I was away in Egypt, sick, thoroughly enjoying myself incidentally. I was away six weeks or so and I came back just in time to take part in the evacuation. I remember the simply magnificent, detailed, plans the careful carrying out of which enabled us to get away from Anzac without loss. It was one of the most highly planned and efficient things that I've ever known all my life.

Well now I go from the sublime to the ridiculous. We organized a very good system with Fortnum and Mason's for our mess supplies and they used to send us out a regular fortnightly hamper, you know, whisky and all that kind of thing which was dumped on our regimental dump on the beach at Anzac. And before the evacuation, a lot of Australians were wandering around, and thought it would be a good thing to salvage things rather than their getting into the hands of the Turks. And so we sent some men down to guard our dump against the real enemy, I say jokingly, the Australians, and when we got on board the boat, every single bottle was in the great-coat pockets of one of the officers or one of the men of my company. When I stepped on board the lighter a Sikh handed over my bottle to me so we got all our whisky away.

But the things that interested me so much were enormous dumps of ammunition on the quay. They were hollow. The outer boxes were all like that. Inside the ammunition dump, all the boxes had been taken away and evacuated. The field ambulances were kept there right until the very end and they were left behind and the flag still flying, the Red Cross. Men had been kept until the very end still walking backwards and forwards from tent to tent pretending there were sick there and the whole place was absolutely empty. The guns were withdrawn until there was only one gun per battery left and they fired off four rounds a time hoping to deceive the Turks. We had rifles stuck up on the front line and a man walking up and down firing them off one after the other to make the Turks think we were still there. It was so very well organized. And when we walked out of our trenches on to the beach to get eventually on to our boats we found ourselves walking into a long queue with a gap left for us. And we worked out at night that you've got to get the head of your regiment into the tail of the gap in front and that your tail must just about fit in the head of the regiment coming along behind in the dark, and if you can achieve that you've done pretty good staff work. And so far as I know nobody was left behind at all. There was a small gang of sort of final ditchers left behind but they all got away: perfectly amazing.

Following the Gallipoli Campaign, Savory was to see Great War service in Egypt, Persia, and Mesopotamia before post-war involvement with the British Military Mission in Siberia. Though materially advancing the cause of the White Russian opponents of the Bolshevik Revolution to success proved beyond the endeavour of the British Mission, Savory himself was to facilitate the escape from Vladivostok of Marie Zorabov, who became his wife and whom I also recorded on the occasion of my visit to Seale.

15

MAJOR-GENERAL C G PHILLIPS
CB DSO and Bar MC

King's African Rifles in East Africa

I had recorded other veterans of the East African Campaign when I met General Phillips in July 1980 so I think my vision of the gruelling endurance test of war in this theatre, which was indeed the case, was not unduly coloured with the contrasting, popular image of hide and seek played with an adventurous, chivalrous, imaginative, and usually more successful foe. There was, for me, great interest in learning about the qualities displayed by East African native troops and the challenge of leading them in relatively small detachments in semi-independent operations over such varying terrain. From General Philips I felt I was brought nearer to what pre-occupied a commander at his level in the field.

General Phillips lived in Nairobi but the interview took place in Chidham, near Chichester, West Sussex, at the home of his sister.

I was born in 1889 at Chatham Barracks, my father being a captain in the Royal Engineers. I went to a prep school at Upshot in Surrey and then to Repton in Derbyshire. From Repton I went to the Royal Military College, Sandhurst. My father had been killed serving in Somaliland in 1902 but I was quite sure I wanted to maintain our family Army Service tradition.

I was commissioned in 1909 and appointed to the Second Battalion the West Yorkshire Regiment, at that time in Aldershot, but we moved to Colchester in 1910 and then in January 1912 to Malta. Now Malta proved to some of us a pretty boring station. We didn't get on with our commanding officer and three or four of the officers of our regiment applied for colonial service, to go to join the King's African Rifles. Because there were few vacancies, to advance my case for East Africa, I said my father had been killed serving in Somaliland and that certainly seemed to help. Permission for my secondment was given, I went on leave from Malta and was shipped out to East Africa – I was now a lieutenant attached for a limited period to The King's African Rifles – and I reached Nairobi in October 1912.

The regiment I was joining, the 1st King's African Rifles, consisted of one battalion. Four of its companies were in East Africa and four were in Nyasaland, much further afield. I was posted to B Company in East Africa. Now to get there I was sent down to Mombasa and was told to take up to the company six months' stores. Well, I had no money to start with. However, I ordered what I thought was 6 months' stores and I was to go up to a place which was about 400 miles away up country, and I had to get on a boat, and when the water failed us and there wasn't enough water, I then had to walk up. Well, I walked up with a convoy of porters. We arrived at our destination and there I stayed and fought against the Somalis. We had several small engagements with them. We were there until 1914 when my time was up with the King's African Rifles.

One funny thing I remember from this time was learning from the Italians in their part of Somaliland that they had picked up a British Government wire (we had no such facility in our part) that His Majesty's Government wanted no fighting at all involving British troops in the area. In fact three or four such engagements were then in full swing! The Somalis used to attack our camps at night. We always formed squares. They fired on us, we responded and then attempted to chase them but they always ran faster than us. What we were trying to do was to quieten the country and try to stop more and more people crossing its borders but we had no power of stopping them. We went up to the Abyssinian border and at the point where we were we had a hell of a lot of cattle and camels and goats coming across because the land on our side was more or less empty.

Turning to the issue of how I was managing the transfer from a Regular British Army battalion to a colonial unit, well, it took time of course but learning a new language when you are young is pretty easy. For me the difference was that in serving with a British Army unit you were just a number and you were one in a line and I mean any sort of manoeuvres and everything you had was all set. There was a company on one side of you and next door there was a company on the other side and all that sort of thing. Well now, you go to East Africa and command African troops. You are mobile, you are open, you are on your own and I mean you are not cornered by British Army regulations and that sort of thing. You become much freer and you become a damn sight better soldier because you learn something on your own instead of being a figure. The people who worked in East Africa were damn sight better soldiers and more what you might call mobile in war than anybody that was trained in England that I know.

As for the cohesion between officer and men: my father was stationed where there was a battalion of Nyasaland soldiers. When I went up country and had my company, I had Nyasaland soldiers that had been with my father in 1902 and this was now 1913. They were soldiers of experience and long soldiering and therefore they knew me and I knew them to some extent. I didn't know them individually but they knew me before I arrived and therefore there was no difficulty here in getting to know them and that sort of thing. They were all trained soldiers with over twelve years' service and therefore there was no difficulty in assimilating yourself with the African soldier.

Their discipline was Guards' discipline. Very strict we were with them, and they liked it. A few of the NCOs would respond to working on their own: as in one case during the war when the company lost all three officers. The sergeant major of the company took command and did damn well. I mean the NCOs were perfectly capable of carrying out what orders they had been given but of course they couldn't command in the same way as a British officer.

Well at the end of July 1914 I came down from where I had been and went to Mombasa and I was there to embark on a Union Castle liner on, I think it was, August 6, 1914. I got orders on August 2 that I was to remain in East Africa and to report to Nairobi and not embark for England. I therefore got onto a train and we went so far to a place where we used to get out and have breakfast. You had eggs on the platform and it was rather fun but there we got news that the war had broken out. That was August 4, 1914. Then I went up to Nairobi.

The first thing which happened was that we were watching the roads and we were told to try and start registering people for the East African Mounted Rifles and the East African Unmounted Regiment. Well, I have never seen such chaos in my life because all the fellows that came in on their ponies and mules, some of them carrying their arms and rifles over their shoulders running about the streets of Nairobi. I mean everybody was in a sort of hubbub for these two days after war broke out. Anyway, I wasn't kept at that for more than about four hours because there was nothing you could usefully do. I then had to do the signals. I was the signals officer as well you see, and therefore I had to try and work the signals. We used to have 10-inch wires in those days; a thing which would carry for 200 miles and I went up into the hills to try and find a station because then I only had four people on mules and I was riding a mule and we went up to find a station. I wasn't very successful on that first journey. Now the interesting thing is that my escort was of Abyssinians; that is, from the Abyssinian company which we had in the 3rd King's African Rifles, and on the way back I went to visit a large coffee plantation and the next thing I knew is that I was on the ground. This mule had suddenly turned round into the coffee and I was shied off onto the floor and there standing looking at me was a male ostrich. The ostriches you see had got into the coffee and I got shied off because the mule didn't like the ostrich. That was my first effort with signalling.

Next I had to go out onto the plains. Here I did it with a telegraph from the railway and then the rest I had to walk but then of course there were giraffes knocking about and there were no poles more than ten-foot long. You had to have a thing at least eighteen to twenty foot for giraffes not to catch their noses in it. Anyway, I laid it on the ground and hoped for the best and it lasted for the necessary time. Then of course, more troops from further north came down to East Africa and they joined up with my company. We got a full-strength company and then we started doing proper soldiering.

After the botched–up landing operation at Tanga, I took my

signals company of the Third King's African Rifles down to Tsavo where we had a consolidated force of Indian troops, the 29th Punjabis, and the rest of the Third King's African Rifles. The first thing that happened was I went down the river on one side and the German company came walking up the river on the other side in thick bush. Well, then they both saw each other. Nobody fired a shot and both ran like hell and that was the first enemy contact that I had, and both sides had been too surprised to do anything. Well, then they came back and we got a company of the 4th King's African Rifles from Uganda who were put out in front of me and the next thing was that I went down with my company in front and the 4th King's African Rifles further down the river and the Punjabis. We lay down and we shot at the Germans. Now whether we hit any I don't know but the 4th King's African Rifles lost their only officer that was near me: he was killed and about four men of the 4th King's African Rifles too.

Now to get round the Germans, we were put in front and the 29th Punjabis sent two officers, Captain Possinger and Lieutenant Bremner, I can remember them well, and a company of their troops to get round behind the Germans. They walked through the bush and when they got to a suitable position, Captain Possinger and Lieutenant Bremner were there with two Punjabis. The rest had all disappeared. They weren't used to bush fighting. They could only fight shoulder to shoulder. So that plan had to be aborted. Anyway that was the end of that little bit of campaigning for the Germans then retired and we had lost an officer and about four men. That was my first effort with the Germans. I lost nobody out of my people. There were a lot of bullets flying all over the place but if they go over your head, they don't hit you.

I came back to Nairobi and we King's African Rifles officers were collected in the mess and the Governor came down and talked to us. His name was Sir Henry Conway-Belfield and he wasn't for fighting at all. He didn't want to fight the Germans. What he wanted to do was say let them fight in Europe and this business out here can be fixed up afterwards which was really quite sensible but the Germans wouldn't have it. They were the ones that were attacking us all the time. That is why we had the fighting in East Africa all the time.

Turning to the German Commander, there is no doubt that von Vorbeck was a first class commander and he always played the game. He never did any sort of monkey tricks as some of his officers did. I mean he was a gentleman but was not invincible. He had damn well-trained soldiers and, of course, he had all the German settlers who were soldiers and the guns of a warship called the *Konigsberg* which took refuge in the Rufiji river. He got the big guns off and the small guns and all the sailors and everybody and turned them all into soldiers. So he had quite a big European element in his African Army.

One encounter, which I remember, was when we were stationed at Voi, which is halfway up from Nairobi to Mombasa, and there you had the road and railway that ran from Voi into German East Africa. And the Germans came into our territory and took up a position on a hill and we were in Voi with quite a large force but the only Africans there were a company of the 3rd King's African Rifles and my company of the 1st King's African Rifles from Nyasaland. We had in that camp at least one battalion of the Punjabis and a battalion of the Rhodesian Rifles, European Rhodesians, and I don't know what else we had. One day the general said we were going to attack the position where the Germans were and turn the Germans out. I was put in an advance guard.

I went there and we camped halfway between Voi and our objective. I suppose we were about twenty miles away. Anyway, we camped that night. I was out in front but the general had put a machine gun section of these Punjabis alongside my picket. A German patrol came along during the night and instead of doing nothing and let them walk straight into my African soldiers, the Indians opened with their machine guns. Well, of course, it gave the whole thing away because all they did was to get out and get back home and tell the Germans that there was a force coming towards them and if those machine guns had not blazed off they wouldn't have known. There was no surprise about it at all. So, anyway we arrived and again I was put in an advance guard and I met patrols and small parties of the Germans all the way along in the bush as I made my way forward.

Anyway our general – he was in the Indian army – got on to me and said, 'Can't you go a little bit faster. We are moving so slowly.' Well, if you are attacking people and trying to get forward, the people behind are always slow because they have got to sit down. I am afraid I was very naughty because I sent back a message, 'If you can do it better than I can. You better come and do it.' I was very angry. Remember I was an independent soldier. I was not used to being told what to do. Anyway, he took no notice but my way of operating in that sort of bush country, where you have got large open spaces and bush, is to do what I used to call 'grading', that is to say you split your soldiers and you went through the bush but you never went through the open because I mean you only got shot at without seeing who was shooting at you. Well, that made this operation slow.

Eventually I got into a line where I was about I suppose 150–200 yards from the German position and we started opening fire at them, and I had all my men in line: the whole damn lot. The general then brought up the Punjabis on my right and extended the line. He had the 3rd King's African Rifles and another force with the Rhodesian battalion to go round and get behind the Germans. Well, you can believe it or not, but the 3rd King's African Rifles were told to carry a Union Jack with their front lot so that the Punjabis could see that they weren't the enemy and were our people. Well, of course, the unfortunate people with the Union Jack, all that happened to them was that they got shot and the flank attack never developed at all.

Out of my people, Jumar, who was number 103 I think in my field message book, got badly wounded and I lost more than half my men, killed or wounded. Out of 100 I must have lost fifty, all that completely for no purpose at all. I lost all my officers. I was by myself and I only had a few men.

When I went back I tried to carry out a corporal of mine who had been wounded in the chest. We carried him out with four men and I was the last to come out but unfortunately the corporal and one of my four men got shot on the way. The corporal got another bullet and it killed him. I got out of it but was extremely lucky. I got one through my hat, one through my haversack, and one hit my rifle.

We achieved nothing but there were one or two interesting things in that, in this plan, my men were partly in the open and so were the Punjabis. The Punjabi CO was killed and several of his officers were wounded and he lost a lot of men. Well when the order came to retire, naturally I had decided to retire in an orderly manner, but the Punjabis all got up as one and ran away. All the fire of the Germans was concentrated on me and my party. That was a thing I certainly didn't like.

Now as to the question of camp followers: when we were in camp at Voi, before this attack took place, we had been sitting there for some time, and the African soldiers that I had were from Nyasaland and they had no women of their own within hundreds of miles. What I did was that I sent up to Nairobi and I got a certain number of women down for my men. I got a message from the general to say that if this was reported to the War Office I would be kicked out of the Army. I took no notice. What I'd done had to be done or the soldiers would have got themselves into trouble, and I kept them fit and well. I mean they understood what I was doing and why I was doing it and of course I had the women checked by a military doctor before they left Nairobi. I was strict about that sort of thing – after all I was fighting a war.

Now when I needed to raise recruits I would go with my sergeant in search of the local headman and say I was looking for recruits, and people used to come along and when I got hold of a certain number I would send them back to Fort Johnson, where the doctor was, and I would have them vetted and passed. They would get a uniform and rifle and pay but no other inducements to enlist, and they would need months of training.

Towards the end of the campaign, chasing the Germans into Portuguese East Africa, when we were ready to advance, I was in command of a column consisting of my battalion and a battalion and a half of Portuguese from Angola. So I had two battalions in my column, part of a strong force following the Germans, and I had them in front of me nearly the whole time, and I fought them or scrapped with their rear guards. They went very fast leaving their rearguard behind about four times. I got right down near the mouth of the Zambezi after them.

The Germans had fought one action there and we knew that they had turned and were coming towards us. The First Kings seem to have got the wind-up so I took up two of my companies to stiffen them. Then I placed my men so that the Germans could not go on the left of the path up the hill.

The Germans came up. I got in to their rearguard. I got a lot of their baggage. I got their notes and things like that but our combined force was just too late into position to trap the Germans and their general escaped again. I caught him later on at another river. Anyway, they were only water holes in it and you had to dig for water and he was on the other bank.

He had a platoon on my side of the river but I neutralized that and he started to move off but I had a fellow called Mason, a gold miner from South Africa, in charge of my mortars. He landed a mortar on them, right in the middle of their table. The four German officers were having tea on the other side of the river, three hundred yards away.

What is the interesting point about this action is that the Germans had a rice plantation there and about two miles down the river they had a big store where they put bags of rice. I hadn't found that on my way up, if I had I should have taken the rice. The Germans on the other hand had found it and we knew they had found it because my flank people saw them coming away and we shot some of their horses and they set fire to the store of rice when they had taken all they wanted. I set at once to put the fire out and got the rice so we both got rice out of the same store. After that I never saw them again. They went right up, up round the top end of Mozambique and ultimately into Northern Rhodesia. When the Armistice took place and details of the whole arrangement was sent across to von Vorbeck and he was told that the war is at an end, he had better surrender. I think it took him twenty-four hours to decide that he wasn't being humbugged.

There is contemporary documentation of much of the above in General Phillips' Field Message Books, which are held in the Liddle Collection in the University of Leeds.

16

FLORENCE FARMBOROUGH FRGS

Nurse for the Russians

By any measure Florence Farmborough was an impressive woman and the use of that adjective must not convey 'forbidding' because her personality was attractive too. What stays particularly in my memory is her beautiful, deep, resonant voice with its precise, slightly accented diction. She lived in Heswall on the Wirral and I recorded her in July 1975. My diary is explicit concerning the impression she made on me: 'Made a marvellous tape. A very fine, lively, kindly, lady.'

I was born in 1887 in the small village of Steeple Claydon in Buckinghamshire. My mother knew the famous Florence Nightingale and I was named after her. My father had a little land and was, I suppose, a farmer. He married my mother when he was fifty and gave up his work soon after we children were born. We were six children, two boys and four girls. With the exception of my elder brother and my eldest sister, we had governesses at home until we reached the teenage years. Then I went, like my second sister Elizabeth, to St Thorolds School in London, a very nice school, very select but very strict. They even taught us how to walk up and down stairs and I was always getting into trouble about rushing down stairs.

I can remember from my very earliest years that I had a longing to travel, and travel far. Not just across the Channel to France or to Belgium, but to go right to the eastern side of Europe and further. Never could I have guessed that my dreams would have come true in so few years time. First of all I persuaded my parents to allow me to go to friends in Austria. I went there straight from school practically and I shall always remember the tremendous thrill that I had when I saw real mountains.

First of all after living two years in Austria, I went to Kiev in 1908, also as a kind of governess/companion to young people. There I lived for two years, a beautiful city and there I was fortunate to witness one of those old rituals, which now can never be seen and are seldom even written about. It was the blessing of the water where in the old days St Vladimir had come, first to Kiev to Christianize the people, the pagans of Russia, and that day that I witnessed it there were hundreds and hundreds of people around the river Dnieper. It was in winter and the Dnieper was of course frozen. I saw the ice broken. There I saw innumerable people, rich and poor, old and young, immerse themselves in the water, in that icy cold water and come out of it drenched, looking terribly blue and miserable but they had done a most marvellous act of worship to their religion, to St Vladimir, their patron saint, and they knew that a blessing remained on them for the rest of that long year.

I saw one carriage come down drawn by two magnificent horses and a man was clothed in an enormous fur. He threw it off, stepped into the water, immersed himself and got up, put the fur around him and drove off home. I saw soldiers with bottles and saucepans taking holy water from the water that has just been blessed.

I went to Moscow in 1910 and I had four glorious years in Moscow travelling with my friends to the Crimea, St Petersburg, on the Volga and widely in Russia. We travelled everywhere and what I most loved and what I really cherish now are the memories of my long months spent in the countryside with the peasants, because in the houses where I was living as a governess/companion all the work was done by peasants. My Russian 'sisters' and I were very friendly with them and they with us. They would give us flowers, they would bring us berries, we would go and chat with then, we would harvest the hay with them and we would all sing together. Russians sang always. They had special songs for cutting down trees in rhythm with the movement of the axe. They had special songs for drawing the great launches and timber rafts down the Volga, there again in keeping with the movement.

The war came to me as a nightmare. I had been in 1914 to see my parents. They made me promise that if I went to Russia I would go home every year if it were at all possible. That year I went home and I had Easter Day in England and I came back in time to have Easter Day thirteen days later in Russia and also my friends wanted me very much to spend the summer with them in their country house. We had tennis, we had horses, we had everything, and I thought it was almost like a paradise. Then at that time I couldn't understand it, but the papers were speaking about extraordinary happenings in Germany, in Austria, England, Belgium and, before really we had time to realize it, there were rumours of war and the war clouds were gathering on all sides.

We were in the country, cut away from the world. We didn't pay much attention to it until nearly the end of July, which would have been at the beginning of August in our English calendar, and then war was declared against Russia by Germany. It came as a great blow to us all. Only the night previously, when I had gone to my room, listening at the window I could hear the peasant boys and girls singing and dancing and laughing, the accordion playing and those happy young people and I was so extremely happy. Then at breakfast the next day the news was broken, Russia is at war with Germany. I can't tell you what a strange feeling it was but it seemed just as though someone had drawn a curtain down on one's happiness. I knew without a shadow of doubt that all our peaceful, lovely, happy moments in the Russian countryside had ceased and could never again come back to us.

We went off to Moscow at once and of course through the head of our household, a famous Moscow heart surgeon, Pavel Yusov (Usov), we were allowed to enter as VADs (Voluntary Aid Detachment 'nurses') in Princess Galitzin's Hospital. We were very lucky. Pavel was of course the heart doctor there and he knew the princess very well and she, knowing that, allowed his two daughters and me to go there as VADs. That was my only training, six months only, and then I took seven exams in Russian, four of them theoretical and the others practical. I could do the practical ones quite easily, they didn't need any speech but the theoretical ones were a little bit different. However I had studied well. Every moment of my free time I spent with many Russian textbooks and skeletons and everything you can imagine. Finally I passed my exams, thanks I still think to the indulgence of the Russian doctors and to the knowledge that I was an Englishwoman and an ally.

Really we were completely untrained. Until the war broke out in Russia and I saw wounded soldiers in bed, I had never seen a sick grown-up person even in bed. Nor had I ever seen death and more than anything else I wanted to see death. It was something I knew I would see and I wanted to see how I could brace myself to see it, to meet it, to challenge it, and the moment came and I saw it and it wasn't so dreadful as I thought. The only thing that hurt me, the only thing that perturbed me, was the fact that it was a human being so far away from me. You could feel he was in a different world but why and where and after death what then? The first dead man I ever saw in my life; he had become shrunken and that was strange to me, that anyone could do that. And then the colour of something that I had never seen before but that was the only one which brought such disturbing introspection. Afterwards I used to see them in their hundreds and afterwards I could touch them, clean them, wash them, put them aside, help to bury them, cover them with sheets, put flowers on them and do everything for them without such disturbing introspection. I saw that first dead man in August 1914 in the hospital sponsored by the Princess.

I saw the Tsar and Tsarina and the four young Grand Duchesses and the Grand Duke Alexei when they came to Moscow after the war broke out to go to the Church of the Assumption and worship there and pray for the success of their troops. The Tsarina was very beautiful. I saw them all very distinctly, Alexei of course being carried by his Cossack nurse and I must add that there were many, many instances of the Empress's kindness and forethought for the wounded. I saw a magnificent train once, all white with great red crosses painted on the roof and walls and that was the train of the Empress and then she sent to us little first aid packets on which was written 'Empress of All The Russias', written in Russian.

Rasputin I never saw, I don't think many people saw him. He was heavily guarded because he was intensely hated. They knew he had this curious kind of influence over the Tsarina on account of her son's illness and people used to say that it was really rather miraculous the way he could quieten the young Grand Duke and the way he could make him forget his pain. Some said that he could do it by hypnotic influence. Others just said that it was through prayer but there is no doubt about the fact that he could help the young Grand Duke. So influential was he in this respect that the Tsarina was ready to do anything and everything to make the life of Rasputin easy and carefree. She would send cars; she would send everything for him and he would come in through private entrances. Very few people saw him, very few.

Now in 1915, after six months in Princess Galitzin's hospital, we took our exams. By that time I was all fire and fury to be sent in a Red Cross Unit to the front. I wasn't content with the hospital or with the town and places where people went when they were injured or in distress or dying by accident. I wanted to go to the front. I had had my training with soldiers and I wanted to continue in a practical way at the front.

It was rather difficult when I first mentioned that to my family. Dr Yusov (Usov) was very much against it and in fact he said, 'Nonsense, Florence, do you not realize that there are hundreds of experienced women in Russia who are at the call of the Red Cross who could present themselves in twenty-four hours, equipment all ready, to be sent to the front into the foremost lines.' And I thought that is true. They have the experience, I have only six months' training but I still persisted and extraordinary though it may seem there was a new unit being recruited in Moscow and I begged Dr Yusov (Usov) to mention my name. He did so and I was enrolled as one of the surgical sisters in this Red Cross unit. I was in the first flying column, four surgical sisters and a housekeeping sister. The second flying column had similar personnel and so we had order-lies and so we had ambulance cars and we had about fifty or more covered ambulances with the Red Cross on, drawn by one or two horses, two or three drivers for each in case one was killed or unable to go. Then an enormous amount of transport and we had every-thing you could imagine because the benefactor of this unit was very rich.

To belong to this unit was a very great honour but the greatest honour of all for me, and a dream of mine that I had scarcely believed could ever be realized, was when they told me that I had been enrolled as a Red Cross nurse to follow the soldiers at the front, to be in a front-line unit and to work night and day with soldiers in the trenches.

When we went out as a unit we had a whole month in East Galicia with just attending to the odd injury. It had been taken by the Russians and we were on Austrian territory and we had no work at all. We went there at the end of March and not until 20 April did the great German offensive begin. Curiously enough, another great thing for which I am very grateful and always shall be was that there were many units at the front but our Red Cross unit was sent to Gorlitz. Now Gorlitz was where the Germans had decided their great offensive with tremendous manpower and their heaviest guns should begin. So you see I, a completely green nurse, found myself in the thick of warfare. Nothing could have escaped. Everything was at its worst. It was disastrous and terrible, I am almost grateful that I was there but within a month I think I had seen all that warfare had to offer.

At first we were just feeding the starving Austrian people who had been left in their huts and their villages in Gorlitz, and there were the people living in their cellars too. At night they would come out and we would send them down bread and soup. Now and then a stray shell fell amongst them especially in the day but at night everything was quiet, and then we heard that the Germans had brought heavy guns and tremendous manpower. The soldiers told us that a great offensive was imminent. We were prepared to some extent but I remember grumbling to our housekeeping sister. She did nothing in the way of bandaging. She only prepared the food for us and saw to it that we, the sisters and doctors, were fed and the transport people too. It was a tremendous job and I remember saying to her, 'If it's going to be as boring as this on the front I might as well have stayed in Moscow because at least there was work with the wounded every day.' I remember her answer, 'You are very anxious to see a massacre aren't you? You are very anxious to have them come crowding in, bloodstained, dying and dead.' I said, 'Good heavens no, not that but just that I want to do work, that is what we have come for.' She said, 'Patience, you will get it.' Within the week we had it.

They came not in their tens or dozens but they came in their hundreds. The offensive had begun and the guns were clamouring, shells landing all round us. All of the Saturday afternoon, all Sunday morning and Sunday afternoon wounded came in; they were creeping and crawling, those who couldn't walk, all round us, beseeching help. We did what we could but there was so many you couldn't cope with them.

We just had our tents there. There was the main house but when they came, they were out in the open and they were all round us, in the fields and paddocks and gardens and everywhere because the retreat had begun. We didn't realize and then someone shouted, 'It's retreat.' Well I had never heard that word before and then they shouted, 'You must go, the Germans are coming in on the other side of Gorlitz,' and even then we had no marching orders. We couldn't go, we were never allowed to move without marching orders, and there we saw the retreating soldiers, torn and miserable, bloodstained, weary, shuffling along. Some of them running, some of them crawling, some of them scarcely moving. For all the dreadful feelings they had experienced in the trenches, and the trenches were level with the ground so they had to get out, and they all shouted to us to go quickly, and then our orders came and they were the most dreadfully difficult orders to obey because they told us leave everything. Leave all equipment, leave the wounded, go, take what you can and go eastwards; and then of course we had to.

Our doctor gave the order and we went mixing with the retreating soldiers. We walked and as we went, the dying and the dead were there and we couldn't attend to them, and they clutched at our skirts. They said, 'You can't leave us, you Sister of Mercy.' But we had to. The retreat went on and on, five and a half months I think in all. During the first weeks, I might almost say the first two or three months of the retreat, there was no time to even think and then we were on the move the whole time, sometimes without bread for a day or more. Our fifty or sixty ambulance vans were often completely inadequate. If the wounded could walk we sent them on, no matter what their wound. If you can walk, go, the base will attend to you. Those who could not go on we had to attend to and, dreadful though it may seem, many of them we had no time to attend to because they were hopeless cases. I shall never, ever, forget the feeling that one had when you came to a hopeless case and he would look at you not able to speak but all his longing was in his eyes. 'Help me, I want to live,' and you just passed him by.

There was no time; we were surrounded by them you see. Hundreds and hundreds and hundreds and they came constantly and then there were the Reserves going up trying to stem the invasion of the enemy but always they came back to us in their hundreds because the shells were going night and day.

It is difficult for me to tell you exactly how much I honour and admire those men and women with whom I worked. When we worked we worked as one man, completely in accord. Everyone helping the other, everyone doing their very best to make life a little bit easier in those tragic, dreadfully difficult times, but when work had ceased and when for some reason there was a lull in the operations then it was that our nerves began to show that they were getting frayed. We would even quarrel sometimes and we would criticize not only ourselves and our neighbours and our workers, but the government, the administration, the high command. Everyone came under our scathing criticism but work was our salvation.

1915 was a year of retreat, the long weary retreat of the thousands of men from the Galician front into Russia. They drove us over the frontier into Russia. The enemy was already in possession of Russian towns and villages. That was a dreadful thing for us but winter came in the guise of an ally. It stopped all operations. We had a few soldiers who would go out dressed in white as snipers but these too suffered many casualties but with the long rest on both sides, our Russian soldiers were replenished. Everything took on a brighter, happier, more hopeful view, when the spring of 1916 came.

The men adored their General, Brusilov, who had led them into Galicia victoriously. We knew he had only to walk over the enemy territory and all his men would follow him to the last man. We knew he had such an aura about him. When our unit took its place in the advance, we were walking on air thankful beyond measure that the tables had been turned and now the Austrians were always retreating. I remember the fields of battle through which we advanced, great wide open places covered with wire entanglements, lined and marked here and there by zigzagging trenches, some of them very deep, the Russian trenches very shallow.

We saw on the entanglements bits of human beings. My

photographs show the bodies strewn over the ground. They were decomposing. There had been no time to bury them. Not only was the ground pitted with great craters, but the forests themselves were mutilated and wounded. Some of them were just as though one had just sliced them down. Others with their heads cut off, others with the branches hanging limply down. Sometimes whole sections of a forest had been destroyed by gunfire.

The Russian soldiers, those wonderful veteran soldiers of the Tsar's army, were true to the core to the Tsar, to their country and to God. Many of them were content to die because they were dying for their country and many of them begged to hold the little icon that was strapped sometimes on a poor bit of string round their neck. One man, he couldn't speak but he was with his eyes and hands beseeching for something and I asked him, 'Is it the icon that you want?' Yes, his shirt had been taken away and the icon had been sewn on to it and I remember nearly a whole morning when there was time with one of the orderlies, we searched through the dirty blood-stained shirts and we couldn't find it and I tried to avoid him to tell him that I couldn't find it but he knew. Had he found it he would have died peacefully.

I have been in the homes of peasants and over the doorway was always the icon, the sacred image. It might be of Christ the Redeemer, it might be of the Madonna, it might be of Christ on the Cross, or the Madonna with Child. Always when the peasants came in they would turn and cross themselves. Always when they went out their last action was to cross themselves and go out to work. In times of great sadness they would go and pray before it. In times of great gladness they would go and offer thanksgiving. So always in the life of the Russian peasant their lives revolved round the icon, the sacred image. For them the Tsar was also a sacred being. They called him Little Father Tsar. They spoke of God as Little Father God. So when the Revolution came and began persecuting the Church and all Christian followers of the Church, there were many who said, 'Well, Little Father Tsar has gone, Little Father God can go.' They were on the same level. Infinite faith and trust in both and to break one was to break the other.

The 1916 offensive was held and then reversed. The following year saw first of all the abdication of the Tsar in the Russian calendar on 2 March 1917. When we heard he had abdicated we were unaware that he was forced to abdicate. Later we heard he was obliged to abdicate. We knew that there was very strong criticism of the Empress but we didn't realize that the Emperor had fallen out of favour. I don't really think he had, but the Empress was of English/German birth. Of course being the daughter of Prince Louis of Hesse and being brought up as a German, all her enemies began calling her the German woman, hand in glove with the Russian enemies, and under the malevolent influence of Rasputin until of course the latter's murder. I knew a little about this because I had caught typhus and been sent back to Moscow the previous year before convalescence in the Crimea.

Kerensky, leading a Provisional Government, made a fatal mistake which completely ruined discipline in the army. He begged officers and soldiers to have a more friendly approach, one to the other. He, as Minister of War, decided it was not necessary for the soldiers to do a standard salute every time they spoke to an officer. Consequently within a month the soldiers were defying their officers and the officers had no power to punish that defiance.

However, I remember Kerensky coming to our sector to try to boost morale and saying to the men that if as loyal soldiers they could go into the trenches and fight against the advancing enemy how much more will they go now as free men to fight for their homeland and their homes, wives and children? So effective was he that they were ready at that moment to do anything he would have commanded. It was a kind of hysteria that swept over them. They carried him to his car. They kissed his car, the ground that he stood on. Some were praying, some were weeping, some were shouting out slogans but all were intent on fighting on to victory.

He promised to send news that the offensive would begin very shortly. They had everything. Morale was high. The only word that was missing was the word go. They waited week after week and it didn't come. Even our own officers looked at each other and wondered what on earth was happening. As time went on, the soldiers began asking themselves what is our freedom to us if we have got to go into the trenches and get killed. At that psychological moment other men came to the front. They were agents. They too scoured the front even as Kerensky had scoured it.

These men aroused a different kind of enthusiasm. They harangued the troops that as free men they need not sacrifice their lives. They could go home, throw their rifles away. The soldiers were totally mystified. Many of them came to our officers and asked what is this thing about freedom? Many of the young soldiers were so illiterate they couldn't even pronounce the word freedom. They were completely cut off as it were from any intellectual bond with the people who could explain to them. They arranged amongst themselves what freedom was and they arranged amongst themselves what they as free men were going to do. They said peace is what we want. We are free. We will not fight, and they began to desert. The officers couldn't do anything. An officer told us that previously he could have taken out his revolver and shot them and that would have stopped many of them going. Now we are in their hands and if we say anything to them they will shoot us and indeed many of our friends were shot.

Our equipment was stolen by the men and, significantly, the methylated spirits. We were frightened of them because we knew what drink would do to them. Always somewhere, not always in the foreground unfortunately, but somewhere in the heart of those mobs, or in the background of those mobs, there were a company of religious, right-minded, public-spirited, noble, faithful men, officers and soldiers amongst them, but they were as nothing surrounded by these thousands of deserters. We were in constant danger, and one must always be grateful, that one got through. There were times when, especially at night, we would hide ourselves. We weren't allowed even to speak in a whisper and we would be surrounded by these deserters, half of them mad with alcohol, absolutely like animals.

I remember going back to Moscow and I felt that everything had gone out of my life and I had been bereft of everything, everything having been in vain. This was in December 1917 when our Red Cross unit was disbanded. I remember that sorrowful meeting. Our doctors told us we shall all meet in Moscow, memorize these two addresses. There we can meet if we ever reach Moscow and we can remember our work together. Now we must separate. The sisters will go to the station. From there they will try and get to Kiev. From Kiev they will try and get to Moscow.

We were at that time in Rumania. There was a Jewish woman doctor. She took my arm and on the other side there was another girl, Anaska, my best friend. We set off and we were with the deserting soldiers and three others came behind us and I remember that the doctor told us whatever you do keep together and I would have been the last person in the world to disobey that order. I would have been too frightened to be amongst all those deserting hordes but there was something wrong with my boot. We had boots and my long dress caught on it and I couldn't walk. I tripped and went down. My friends had gone and I was alone.

I shouted for my friend Anna, and then I heard the voice of the Jewish doctor who had come back for me and she got hold of me and I seized her arm. She said, 'It's alright now, we are together.' I asked where the others were because we were to meet them at the station. We were jostled from all the moving mass and they were shouting at us and they were laughing at us and saying dreadful things about us and I was almost desperate that I had lost Anaska my good friend. We had been all those years together and I shouted her name again. From a long way away came the answer, 'Florence.' She had heard and she had answered and that is all I know of Anaska. I was never to see her again.

We went to the station but there was no sign of the sisters, no sign of anyone. We walked up and down the trains and they were filled or obscured by soldiers. The doctor told me that I must come with her to Odessa to her home as it would be easier to get to Kiev from Odessa. I was willing to go with her. She took me to her home. Her doctor husband was engaged by the Bolsheviks, not because he was a Bolshevik, but because he was a doctor and even Bolsheviks can be ill and require attention. They allowed him one room only of his flat to be his. We shared that room for two days and three nights.

They were so kind to me. He was a Jew and very clever, thin and tired, thankful to have his wife back and it was wonderful to see them so happy to be together, surely the only happy ones in the world at that time. They put a screw in the wall in a corner and put a sheet over it and gave me a blanket to sleep on and a pillow and they had the rest of the room to themselves, and she told the warden that I had been a nurse and they got special food for me for the two days that I was there. He got food only because he served in the hospitals. He got food for his wife because she too was a doctor and could serve in hospitals, and I got food because they spoke for me and one day we had white bread and butter and that I hadn't seen for months and months. Then it was decided that I must go home, so I went to the station and we made enquiries. Many trains were running to Kiev but at very difficult times and no one quite knew when they would go and they were always overcrowded.

On the way to the station we met some friends and they told us of dreadful Bolshevik atrocities in Odessa. The Bolsheviks knew that Army officers, disguised as peasants, were hoping to get away by ship. They knew that they were coming by train and by road and they were seized, weights tied to their feet and thrown into the harbour. However I got away by train. The train was crammed completely and we went to all the carriage doors and then at one place we saw a man and his wife and I asked them if they could possibly find room for me and there was no way to get in except to go through the window, so I went through the window and I found a place and then we went slowly to Kiev. The only difficulty was that the woman was expecting a baby and she was very often sick and then if I got up to help her by holding a bowl to her a soldier would take my seat and then offered me his lap to sit on and still more came in through the window. When Kiev came it was a blessed relief because they all made one fierce plunging rush towards the doors and through the windows and we waited until they had gone. Then we sat for a little while before I went to an address our unit had used in Kiev but without useful result.

I waited for the next train and this too was crammed with soldiers. Somehow I got a seat but I couldn't move and men were on the luggage racks and every time I moved I heard a tremendous groan and I moved again, and again the groan, and then I put my hand down and my foot was on the stomach of a man underneath my seat and every time I pressed my feet down of course it hurt him. We were just a heap of humanity. The train was ambling along towards Moscow and the men began to be rather perturbed about me. I spoke to them. I could speak quite good Russian and I asked them about their work and where they had been and one or two of them seemed to know the fronts where my Red Cross Unit had worked. As time went on the soldiers got more tolerant and friendly towards each other. They began to worry about my not being able to move. They suggested that when we got to the next station that as we were staying there for some minutes that if I liked they would see me out and they promised to keep a seat for me when I came back and that is what happened.

The words above seem to conclude the interview according to helpful staff in the Library at the University of Leeds. This may well be the case and of course I regret it, finding it a puzzle that there is no sign of my invariably proffered thanks. Did the tape run out? Is there an unlisted continuation? Whatever may be the case, Miss Farmborough, in 1974, published a memoir entitled *Nurse at the Russian Front*.

17

COMMANDER N D HOLBROOK VC

Submarine Exploit at the Dardanelles, 1914

In July 1972 I met Commander Holbrook, the first Naval VC of the Great War. His award was earned in the key location of the Dardanelles in 1914. The meeting was for me a particularly exciting prospect. With an ever-increasing academic interest in the Dardanelles in the first two years of the war, listening to Holbrook was to be introduced first-hand to submarine warfare in its British infancy. There was an additional frisson for me but also a potential problem. In fact on that very day in July I was setting off for my first visit to the Gallipoli Peninsula with two veterans accompanying me. Our time schedule had a consequence. The interview had to take place not at Commander Holbrook's home in Midhurst but in a pre-booked unused office in Waterloo Station!

Norman Holbrook was born in 1888 in Portsmouth, his father being a newspaper proprietor. After prep school, Norman was sent to The Royal Naval College's establishment at Dartmouth, the old training ship, *Britannia*.

Britannia was a very old hulk and had been down at Dartmouth for many, many years and trained almost all our Navy since it was a great Navy, and there was another ship to the stern of her called the *Hindustan* and we all lived in her. We were in three terms. The first term, they were known as 'News', the second term as a 'Three' and the third term as a 'Sixer'. Well when you were a New and just arrived there, of course, you were a dogsbody. You weren't allowed to walk across the middle deck. You had to run. You had to keep your coat buttoned up. You had to have your cap on straight, and you mustn't swing your keys on your lanyard. Well when you came back for the next term and you were a Three, you were allowed to walk across the deck, but that was about all. You mustn't do any of the other things I've mentioned. Now when you were a Sixer you were an absolute cat's whisker. You could do nothing wrong. You could wear your cap on the back of your head, have your coat undone, swing your keys, and swank about as if you were Lord of the Manor.

Discipline was very strict, but very fair. I think we had a wonderful upbringing and it was a wonderful ship to get, if you join up to be keen on the Navy. You were only beaten for very, very serious offences, and there was only one boy beaten the whole time I was there. Smoking was forbidden of course and nobody smoked that I know of, and as regards drinking we were always given beer with our food but we never had any other drink. Another rather interesting thing about the *Britannia* was an old lady died, some many years before, and she left some money to supply the cadets with Devonshire cream twice a week, and so twice a week we had all the cream we could eat and it was wonderful.

I have to say that being in the Navy in my opinion we were a very narrow-minded lot of men who really didn't take a lot of interest in what was going on outside the Navy, and as far as I was concerned all I was interested in was my job in the Navy.

After the three terms in *Britannia* we went to sea in the *Isis*. She was a cruiser, and there you have all sorts of sea training, even gunnery there, and those sort of things, and at the end of the *Isis* you have a lot of exams to pass out; and how you pass out in those exams would give you of the *Britannia* a certain amount of seniority before you become a midshipman.

After the training cruise in *Isis* I was appointed as a naval cadet in HMS *Revenge*. *Revenge* was an old battleship, much smaller, lighter, less heavily armed and armoured than the new dreadnoughts. She was in the Home Fleet but I was to be sent out to the China Station. I went out to China from the *Revenge* and I went into a ship called the *Donegal*. Well we started from Plymouth in the *Donegal* and we ran it aground in the Red Sea, and tore the bottom out of the ship, so we came back again to Plymouth, and I went out in the *Monmouth* and I was out in the China station for nearly two years in the *Monmouth*, a county class cruiser.

Now one of the reasons why I chose to move to the relatively new submarines was that I was very keen as an engineer. I'm interested in engines and anything to do with them; that was one thing. And two, of course, you get much more shore time in submarines. You're not at sea so much, and as I was so violently sea-sick all the time we were at sea, it was really one of the reasons I joined submarines, and furthermore we got double pay which was also an inducement. I got ten shillings as a lieutenant, I got six shillings submarine pay, and four shillings command money when you're the captain of a ship, but I had to be captain of a ship first. I got my command and most fellows did within about two years. This would be early in 1912.

The submarine service was very separate really from the rest of the senior service because no one in the Navy knew anything about submarines, and it was very much a different job from any other sort of handling of ships.

When you're training, you're training all the blokes that are there. You go out every day in a submarine, because they are going out to sea every day for practice. Well, you see you're appointed to a ship as a first lieutenant and that's really where you start to learn and get your submarine experience. You've got to learn how a boat is dived. You've got to learn every handle and tap in the boat, which we did in the very small boats we had to begin with. Of course you couldn't in the big ones, and you just watched your captain and saw what he did, and that's about the training you got. I'd say up to the time when I took my command I'd never dived a boat on my own, or looked through the periscope hardly.

As far as space is concerned, in an A-Boat it was about five feet high. You couldn't stand upright, and over the engine it was much less than that, I think about four feet, if that. You had to crawl most of the time on the engine, but the rest of the boat was easier. We had a crew of about nine or ten in an A boat. It was quite extraordinary. The hazards you had were a petrol leak, which you could easily smell, and the worst hazard was this exhaust leak, from which carbon monoxide was emitted. You couldn't smell that in the boat; and fellows would come off the engine and suddenly flop down, out, out to the wide world, mainly from the gas, which you didn't even know was there.

We were petrol driven in these early boats. In trouble, you had to surface and get out through the conning tower of course – no other way possible. We had no escape gear in those boats, anyhow, not in the A-Boats, but we had in the C-Boats. We had I think an inside lavatory in a B-Boat, I'm not quite sure, but we certainly had them in all other boats afterwards. It all went into a tank and then you just blew the tank overboard let out through a hole in the ship's side at any time above or below the surface – no trouble at all. For meals you sat on the floor. I suppose we must have had a table of sorts for the officers. There was of course a chart table.

The atmosphere would get very thick but actually in peacetime you were never under water long enough. But when you are under water as I was in this B-Boat for nine hours at the Dardanelles, the air gets very thick, and if you take these, what we call coastal submarines which we had, like an F-Boat, after about sixteen hours you couldn't light a match, and you couldn't move about very fast, you had to go quite slowly. But when you get into the bigger boats like a J-Boat we used to smoke down below it didn't make any difference at all, she was so big.

You ask about stress in a submarine when she is diving to be submerged. You never think of that sitting in a submarine. When you're diving, it's just the same as sitting in a room with the lights on. There's no difference. I don't think the men worried a bit. You see from a claustrophobia point of view, after all, we've all been trained. You wouldn't have volunteered for a job if you're suffering from claustrophobia. From my point of view, I never was troubled by this at all. For instance, we used to be on the bottom for up to eight hours after we had charged our batteries on the surface. This was when we were doing patrols in the North Sea. Go down on the bottom for about eight hours, happy as a lark. Played the gramophone, played cards.

I must confess sometimes when we were laying mines in the Heligoland Bight I did have a bit of a wind-up now and then, but it didn't really frighten me. However, being depth-charged frightened you. We were depth-charged all one day after we'd laid mines and I must confess I had the wind-up there because we were only in fifty feet of water, and luckily they just got us all wrong. They couldn't find us. Well, we had a signalman there and he said, 'Well if I'm going to be blown to heaven I'm going to lie down here and go to sleep.' And that's what he did. That's the type of man. They were wonderful men you know, a wonderful crew, best in the Navy.

With regard to torpedoes: in a big boat we carried four, two in the tubes and two, loose. Yes they would be expensive with a lot of machinery in them but I can say that a lot of submarines would fire, if they had four, they would fire all four, fanned, and hoping one would hit. If you're going to sink a battleship what's the matter losing two or three torpedoes.

We could recover torpedoes up the fore hatch and re-use them. You have a very big hatch and when you fire a torpedo you've got what they call a sinking valve on it, and at the end of a run the sinking valve opens and the torpedo sinks. For instance, I don't know if you realize that the weight of air in a torpedo is about two hundred and fifty pounds. The air weighs that. Therefore when you fire a torpedo, she'll sink, but not when she's going through the water because her rudder is like a submarine's. It keeps her up, and as she loses this weight of 250lbs, she will float because we fired practice ones and picked them up afterwards. But if you take it her signal is working, she goes her run, and at the end of the run the sinking valve opens and she fills up with water and sinks.

When a target is seen through the periscope, you are at a depth of perhaps twenty-five to thirty feet. The submarine would be about that under water. Depends on which submarine it was and the length of her periscope. We used to try and hit the target about ten feet below the water line. That's good enough for almost any ship or submarine.

When the war broke out I was in command of *B11*, stationed at Malta. The B boats were built later than the As and were bigger and better. I think she'd be about 120 feet long and we had a crew of eleven. She had a periscope in the conning tower, not like a modern boat where you can stand, and walk it around. You had to stoke her up in the conning tower, winding a handle round and when you were looking astern your picture was upside down, so it didn't make things very easy. And to raise and lower the periscope, you didn't do much of that, but you could do it with tackles, that is pulleys. And she had bar hydroplanes and diving rudders the same as any ordinary submarine, and taking them on the whole they were quite good boats for diving, but they're only very short distance boats, with small batteries, and because if you're out in the heat like out in the Mediterranean, the batteries don't last very long. *B11* was far from being a new boat.

Up until the war started you always lived ashore. You didn't have any food in the ship at all. But then when we went out to the Dardanelles, we had a depot ship, and every night we came back to the depot ship and fed in her. I would say I've had my breakfast in the boat and that sort of thing, we had an electric cooking apparatus because we used to go out pretty early on patrol off the Dardanelles and we could cook our own breakfast there, but as regards salt pork and that sort of thing it never happened in submarines, never.

In the first days of the war when the *Goeben* and *Breslau* escaped and went up to the Dardanelles, we were immediately sent out there and we had two boats on patrol from darkness in the morning to dark at night time, always on patrol, waiting if they should come out, and one boat would be alongside the depot ship. She had two days on and one off. *Goeben* and *Breslau* never came out. We saw nothing. We actually used to land on the Peninsula: I've landed at Cape Helles and walked about on the beach. We had a little canvas boat and you could get two in it, and we'd put ashore. There was nobody there. No one took any notice of you. I remember a lighthouse being there, but I don't remember being anywhere near it.

Now as for our attack on the Turkish battleship, *Messudieh*, that was on the thirteenth of December 1914. It was a Sunday. I think all the port turrets were having a jolly good cocktail party on board. I'm not sure because we hit him about midday. I am getting ahead of myself. Off the entrance to the Dardanelles our base was at the back of the island of Tenedos. Concerning actually entering the Dardanelles; our boss, an officer called Parnell, heard that one of the French submarines was out there and was going to try and get into the Sea of Marmora. Well, of course, they could, they were big submarines compared with us, and as I was the only boat that could make a show at all, Parnell suggested what about my having a go. Well, I was young and foolish and I said I'd have a crack at it, certainly I'd like to. Of course it was the daftest thing I've ever done because a B-Boat could never possibly get past the hazards. She hadn't got the battery power, and it's against the tide. Her underwater speed I believe was about eight knots. Well, I've never known a B-Boat do much more than six, and if we were going to boost six knots under water we'd have lasted about half an hour and then you were out. So I worked out, being a fisherman, I knew where the slack water would be, and so I kept right in close to the shore.

This was the north shore, and when I came toward the Narrows, well, I went down to sixty feet, and I waited for about an hour I should think, and when I came up and had a look round, we'd come through the Narrows, and looking through my periscope I saw on my starboard quarter, this warship. So I thought well it's a pity to miss this. I must have a go. It was the Turkish battleship *Messudieh*. So I turned round, altered course to starboard and went down again, because I wasn't sure about these mines and things, and I was under a quarter of an hour or twenty minutes, half an hour perhaps, and when I came up, the tide had got us, and then instead of this ship being on my starboard quarter, she was on the port bow, so I then had to alter course to port, and practically give it full speed to get ahead of her a bit.

When I could get us more or less where I could get a shot at her – a quarter shot – I turned around and fired one torpedo, and it was very shortly after that I just had to slow down because the battery lights were getting low and not much left in the box, and next thing I knew we were aground, stern first. So then I had to give her the works again to get off the beach, and luckily we got off the beach and then I wasn't quite sure which was the way out. And so I was a bit flabbergasted, because we'd been fiddling around, trying to get her off, working the ship backwards and forwards, and, anyhow, she came off with a rush and we got into deep water, thank God, and then, of course, the next thing I had a look round and she was landlocked all round. I didn't know where the sea was, and I examined what I considered as far as I could see through the periscope, the farthest bit of land and I said to the coxswain, 'Well I'll tell you when to steady in a minute,' and then, 'Now steady on there.' And he said, 'Well I can't see the compass.' So I said, 'You can't see anything?' He said, 'No, the whole thing's packed up on me. I can't see anything at all,' and then, 'Well, I think I can see a sort of black spot somewhere.' I said, 'Well, for God's sake keep that in your mind's eye and steer on it,' and begorra we got out.

After about twenty minutes going very fast or as fast as the motors could go then I spotted the sea horizon on the port hand. The men breathed a bigger sigh of relief than I did. So then we turned round in that direction and went down to sixty feet again, and raced along under these mines, which were said to be there, and when we got up the other side we could just limp along with the tide behind us and it just more or less swept us out into the sea.

As for *Messudieh*, all I noticed when I was fiddling around was that she was down by the stern, but of course we had heard a hell of a bang, and I could see an awful lot of fire and smoke coming out from all directions at me. I must say that everywhere I looked there seemed to me that something was firing at me. *Messudieh* didn't go down, you know, she only rolled over. She was on the bottom with her side up for months afterwards, I believe.

We had been nine hours under water and the air was so thick. It was a small boat and I'm sure we had all been breathing hard. Nine hours under water. We got back to Tenedos, I made out a report and Parnell must have forwarded it with his endorsement.

Yes, in course of time I was to be awarded the Victoria Cross but one has got to realize that I could never have done it with a crew that wasn't the crew I had, because they were first class men. I think on that day twelve men because we had a spare coxswain with us. Our hydroplanes were so stiff we had to have two men to work them. One man couldn't work them. They all got Distinguished Service Medals and my first lieutenant got the Distinguished Service Order.

When I went to Buckingham Palace for the investiture, the story I had told at a school where I had been asked to raise a flag had got around through the press. One of the little girls had said, 'Oh, will you tell us how you got your Victoria Cross?' I said, 'Oh yes. That's easy. It wasn't so very long ago I was walking down the road and the King was on the other side of the road and he saw me, and he said, "Well, that's a good looking chap. We'll give him the Victoria Cross," and that's how I got it.' This appeared in the *Daily Mail* and I don't mind telling you, the King had a twinkle in his eye when he pinned the Cross on me.

I recognize that we were very lucky wandering about in the Turkish minefields without striking any thing, not seeing their nets, being entangled with them or being blown up by their associated mines. Others were not so lucky.

Commander Holbrook's later service in the war saw him operating off the North African coast having an unanticipated and dangerous shore encounter with hostile Senussi tribesmen during which he suffered a facial wound. His submarine service then took him into the North Sea and into Heligoland Bight operations; the first included another torpedo success, and the second was for mine-laying work, before becoming involved in the 1919 North Russian Intervention Force campaign in support of White Russian Forces.

18

VICTOR SILVESTER OBE

Soldier in France, Ambulance Service in Italy

Victor Silvester's dance-band music on the radio was enjoyably familiar to me but when I had the opportunity of listening to his distinctive voice with its quiet delivery talking of matters within his immediate experience in 1917–8, it seemed that the well-known aural image of the man and his music had allowed but a limited presentation for the public of a far more extraordinary individual. I could not help recording in my diary with an appreciation of the excellence of the interview overall, the stunning detail that as a soldier in France, underage status now known by the Army, he was detailed for a firing squad.

The interview took place at Mr Silvester's home in St John's Wood, North London.

Victor Silvester was born in Wembley, London, in 1900, the son of the local Church of England vicar. His memories of school, particularly of the boarding school, St John's Leatherhead, were he says 'disastrous' but he made plain that things had, he understood, changed since his time there.

We were treated like, you might say, cattle, and it was schooldays at their worst. There was bullying, there was homosexuality and we had two masters, both of whom were clergymen, who were expelled for immorality. I remember that the first thing I ever learnt about homosexuality was from another schoolboy and he said, 'Do you want to know what it's all about?' and I said, 'Yes.' Well, he took me to the bottom of the football field and showed me how to play with myself. I told another boy about this and he had an older brother whom he passed this on to and the older brother went to the headmaster and I was hauled up in front of him. At that time I might mention that I was only ten years of age and our headmaster, I will not give his name, but I can never remember him ever smiling. He was a clergyman. He said he was going to give me the biggest beating I had ever had in my life. I was taken into his room and he had against the wall a curtain rail with all different sizes of canes hanging up, from the very thin switches to one that was as thick as your middle finger.

He picked out the thickest one and he then made me take my shorts down to see that I hadn't got any padding on and he then gave me twelve which made me scream on every stroke. He drew blood with every stroke but I will say that there was always another master present whenever a boy was caned to make sure they, at least as we understood it, they never took the hand back past the shoulder. I had twelve of those strokes. I couldn't sit down for about two weeks and I also got two hours drill three times a week for the rest of the term where they used to march you round the gymnasium non-stop and that was under the gym instructor. There are so many other incidents that I could tell you about the brutality.

Another thing I was going to mention was that they had a very evil practice that used to exist where boys could get their parents, if they could afford it, to pay for extras and the boys whose parents could afford it they used to get bacon for breakfast. All we used to get was some kind of gruel and my brother and I were so hungry we used to cadge the other boys' bacon rinds to eat to try and make up for it. Another thing I noticed and in some ways it helped with my musical career which followed because I saw that two days a week, at tea time, a few of the boys had jam on their plates. We never got any so on making enquiries I found that they were the choirboys. So I thought well, whatever happens, I'm going to get in the choir, and as I was having piano lessons at the time I managed to make the suggestion to the music master. Eventually, I got into the choir, not to sing but to get the jam.

Going back a bit, prior to these school memories, I had learnt the piano as a boy because all the children in the vicarage had to have some musical accomplishment and I had learnt the piano. Then, later on my brother and I were able to play a little bit, we had to play duets at ladies' working parties and things like that. My lessons used to cost 6d a time. I had a Prussian piano teacher, a very fierce woman, and whenever one didn't sit up straight at the piano, or anything like that, I used to get a backhander from her so probably that helped me to have a straight back as well.

Returning to circumstances at school, the prefects were allowed to cane but I think, again, they were never allowed to give more than six strokes with one of the thin switches. Concerning sport, when the first team were playing, you had, if you were not playing yourself that day, you had to stand on the touch line and cheer and if you didn't the prefects who were walking round at the back used to come and cuff you, and so being little boys you learnt all the tricks that are going, so we used to stand there with our mouths wide open as if we were yawning and no sound coming out at all.

I ran away from school in 1912 and I then went to Lyons School at Harrow, which was a day school, and where I enjoyed every minute of it: however the excitement of the war got into me and despite my age being only fourteen I wanted to be in it. I had never worn a stiff collar before apart from an Eton collar which we wore at boarding school so my father, being a clergyman, I borrowed one of his collars which was much too big for me, turned it round the other way – he wore dog collars of course – and put a tie on and went up and enlisted. When I had my medical examination the medical officer said, 'What do you say your age is?' and so I said, 'Eighteen, Sir.' I was also then well under the acceptable height but a helpful sergeant said I would soon gain the necessary height and I was enlisted in the London Scottish at their Headquarters in Buckingham Gate in London.

In view of Silvester's age it is regrettable that he was not asked for the response of his parents to his enlistment, more particularly because for some weeks, as he relates, he continued to live at home.

We lived at home for the first six weeks and I used to go up every day. We had a railway pass. One did the drill at headquarters and the marches. After, I think, two or two and a half months of that we were stationed at Dorking in Surrey and there we used to go on route marches three times a week of twenty-eight to thirty miles, each one with a heavy pack on our backs and a rifle. Well that, as you will appreciate, was tough enough for a fully-grown man so you can imagine what it was for me. In fact, when we used to come back at the end of the day and sit down I used to fall asleep and one day someone shook me and woke me up and said, 'Oh, go in the next room and find out what the right time is.' When I went in there they all started hooting with laughter because while I was out for the count someone had blacked my face with a piece of coal and I knew nothing about it.

I remember bayonet drill. They had sacks with the Kaiser's face painted on and we had to do our bayonet fighting with that so that every time you lunged you thought that you were sticking it into him. You had to shout, growl or snarl every time you stuck the bayonet in and then twist it and pull it out. You didn't pull it straight out because they said that if it went into bone or flesh or whatever it is that if you tried to pull it straight out it was very diffi-cult . You had to give it a turn and then pull it.

In 1916 I was transferred to the Argyll & Sutherland Highlanders because my age had been reported by one of our sergeants, who happened to come from Wembley, and he had ensured that my name was removed from each draft of men marked for France. As I had joined the Army with the spirit of the times and the idea being to kill Germans, every time my name was taken off the list I resented it, so I applied for a transfer which in due course I got and after further training at Stirling Castle in Scotland I was then put on a draft and sent out to France.

I must say the reality of active service in France was a real shock. The first time I went up the line we were going up a communica-tion trench and there was light shelling going on and one of the shells landed in the communication trench probably about twenty yards ahead of me. It landed at a soldier's feet and it blew one of his legs off below the knee, the other one above the knee and all his body hit by shell fragments. We got him onto a stretcher and he was taken away but died on the way. I can't tell you what that did to one and the only thing that kept me from showing my true reaction was that one was more afraid of letting anyone else know that one was frightened and one daren't show it. Again the spirit of the times, the men around you, everybody being there with you, the drilling that you'd had, the training, this all helped you stick it out. I was fifteen though. Mind you I think that every soldier is scared.

I remember an instance later when the Germans made a raid. We'd had heavy shelling all-night and then at dawn they attacked and there was a fellow standing some distance from me and he said, 'I think we ought to get out, we ought to get out.' He was scared and one of our sergeants told him to shut up. He didn't, he kept saying that we ought to get out and so it was reported to one of our officers who came along the trench to speak to the man but the man didn't seem able to control himself. Well, the officer pulled out his revolver and shot him dead on the spot. Right away it altered everyone's attitude because we had started to think we ought to get out. You only have to have someone saying that to you often enough and strongly enough and you thought that's what we must do. Right away when the officer shot this man dead, although it's a most terrible thing when you think of it, it altered the whole morale of the troops who were there. In fact I think if he hadn't done it we should all perhaps have started thinking about getting out. I don't think it affected our relationship with the officer at all. After all officers have got to be in command, they've got to assert their authority and if he'd shown any sign of weakness we should have been killed or captured in losing that bit of the line. We were under attack and up on the firing step, the Germans coming, dodging down into shell holes and they'd flattened the wire with their bombardment so that it was quite open and we were firing at the time this incident actually happened.

I think it was about April 1917 that the question of my age was raised again, just before the Battle of Arras and I was sent to Etaples, to the camp known as the Bullring.

Silvester should have been questioned here as to whether this were to keep him out of action or as punishment for his deception.

We got pack-drill for any demeanour here, intensive, continuous drill, carrying a heavy pack. One day I was working as a company runner in the orderly room and turning over the Army orders for the day, hanging on the wall, I saw a wad of sheets which gave the names, one man to a sheet, of men being tried by court martial for, for example, being many days absent after leave and then being arrested and, after trial, being sentenced to death and shot.

Well, as it happened, I was detailed for a firing squad and we were taken in a lorry over to part of the main harbour area. You ask about my state of mind before such a duty. To be perfectly honest one never gave it a second thought. Today you wonder how you were ever able to do it, but I would point out that any man who is going to be a good soldier must never question what he is told to do: you are detailed for it and you do it. If you have every soldier turning round and saying in effect I don't agree with that, you can imagine what sort of an army you would have. At the age I was I don't think one queries things, or one didn't at that time, one was imbued with patriotism. The whole of my upbringing, apart from the Army, was that the Britisher was the salt of the earth, that we could do no wrong. Everything we did was right and when it came to it, if a man was sentenced to be shot for desertion; well, you thought he's done something that's very, very wrong and that is the view of the authorities, that he's got to pay the penalty, so you never questioned it. One never thought anything about it. I wasn't an officer. I didn't have to think for other people and through all the training that I'd had, one is taught to obey.

We went off in this lorry. It was early. We left Etaples very early, I suppose it must have been about 5 o'clock. I think there were twelve of us. We had I think it was six or eight deserters to shoot. Now, it was said that some of the rifles were loaded with blanks so you did not know if you yourself were to have killed the man. I did not then know if this were true. We had our own rifles but we were issued with the ammunition. The men to be shot were blindfolded and stood against a post. I can't remember if they tied them. Most of them had their hands behind their backs, probably hooked them on to something and I've tried to think back on this to what actually happened. Then there was an officer standing by the side, with a revolver so that, I assume, if a man wasn't dead, he would go up and fire just one shot and make sure that he was. There was an Army chaplain there as well. Anyway it was something that one just took as being a duty.

We were told to aim for the man's heart. On looking back, you wonder how you could have ever done it but one has to remember that the whole training of a soldier is to do that and, of an infantryman, to kill. When it comes to shooting your own men; if they were deserters you thought well, they were in the wrong anyway. I know I never queried it but I was very young at the time and so one just did what one was told.

The stretcher-bearers came, they put the body on a stretcher and took it away. When it was all over we were given some kind of a breakfast from a canteen, which was standing in Boulogne station, or on the side, and then we were taken back in the lorry to Etaples.

At Etaples, as a result of my age, they told me that I would have to be discharged, but our commanding officer wouldn't agree to that and he got me transferred to the British Red Cross. I was then sent out to the Italian Front. I went really as an orderly with ambulances up on the Italian Front. We had our base in Gorizia but to get there I was sent on my own by train via Paris. I arrived I think in July or August 1917: my first view of Italy having been when I awoke in the morning on the train and saw the sun shining on the Alps as we crossed the frontier. It was so wonderful after the mud and the trenches and the rain in Flanders and on the French Front, everything so lovely by comparison, but then when we got up the line, then, of course, things changed, though the weather remained good.

I had been doing orderly work with the unit for some time when, on September the fourth, I was with an ambulance going up from Gorizia to a place near a very famous mountain on the Italian war front called San Gabriele, and we were bringing the wounded down and we had to do this under very heavy shelling. The ambulances were left under a very large rock where the shells couldn't reach them and we had to go up and bring the wounded down on stretchers and then put them into the ambulance and take them down to the first aid post. On one of these runs a shrapnel shell came over, exploded over the top of us and I got a shrapnel bullet in the leg. I was then taken down to the aid post and there were so many wounded waiting there that I had to wait, I think about eight or nine hours, before I got attention. They wanted to give me preference because I was one of the few Britishers there but there were so many bad Italian wounded cases that I don't think it was any question of heroics or anything but I felt it would be quite wrong to be treated before they were, so I waited my turn. I may add here that I had noticed that no anaesthetic was given before treatment and one man I saw was screaming oaths as he was being held down by two men for metal splinters to be taken from his sliced-open arm with metal tweezers.

In fact Silvester was to be awarded the Italian Bronze Medal for military valour for rescuing wounded under fire.

Having come out of hospital to rejoin my unit, about two weeks before the big Austrian attack at Caporetto in October, we were paraded and I had an Italian medal pinned to my tunic. At this time, with the collapse of Russia and reinforcement of German and Austrian armies, and with clever propaganda too on the lines of the Austrians and Italians all being Catholics – 'why are we fighting each other' – morale in the Italian Army in this sector wasn't particularly good and, of course, a breakthrough was made on our front. We got back with our last load of wounded and the retreat started. Within about three days we had notice to evacuate and everyone got out. We had to leave at four in the morning because they said if anyone stayed longer they'd get taken prisoner. We went back in an ambulance and passed through what was one of the main Italian headquarters at the time – a place called Udine – and all the factories there, which were making munitions, they fired them all at the same time as they were getting out. We went through quite an experience to hear the roar from the explosions and the conflagration. You can imagine blowing up all these munitions factories because with the bullets, they didn't just go off in one explosion, they were just going off intermittently all the time, bombs and shells.

We got through Udine and I think it was the following day we were on a road going south and three planes came over: we were told they were Austrian. They dived on the road and machine-gunned it. The Italian drivers – most of the guns and trucks were pulled either by horses or mules – cleared off, went over the fields and never bothered to come back. Of course, the roads were blocked, nothing could get away, we had to leave the ambulance and from then on everybody had to walk. Then we got to the river Tagliamento, which was in flood. The weather was very bad, raining heavily. On the banks we saw Italian military police, they were on either side of the bridgehead and every Italian who came up had to give an account as to why he was there, why he wasn't with his unit. Anyone who couldn't give a satisfactory answer was taken over to the riverbank and shot on the spot. The bodies were thrown into the river. We saw quite a few of them.

When we went over this river; it was a very terrifying experience because it was absolutely packed with guns and lorries and carts and soldiers, and, as I say, the river was in flood. It was, if my memory serves me rightly, about half a mile across and the flood-water was flowing about six inches from the underside of the bridge. It was a wooden bridge and you could feel it shaking from the weight of all the traffic. We got across all right. We heard afterwards that the bridge was washed away, collapsed with everybody on it, and everything was swept into the river. From then on we went back to Padua, Padova, I think the Italians call it. From Padua we went back to Mantua or Mantova and from there I was told that I was going back to England to a cadet battalion, to get my commission, as I was then nearly eighteen years of age.

Before leaving Italy I would like to refer to just one little incident and that is rather funny when you look back on it and you talk about International Law and the Geneva Convention and things like that. Very often when we used to come down; having brought the wounded down we used to go back empty up to the front again. Often we gave lifts to Italian soldiers carrying boxes of ammunition. They used to load all this into the back of the ambulance and we never gave it a thought, in fact we didn't know anything about the Geneva Convention or anything like that. We thought we were doing a good turn by giving them a lift, to save them having to carry this up there.

In England I went to Worcester College, Oxford, where the cadet battalion was. Most of the troops going for commissions were Australians and New Zealanders, with a minority of British troops of which I was one. That was quite pleasant, of course, having come back from the firing line. Among the training we used to have were the lectures, which were called lust-for-blood lectures, the idea being that it was to make you hate. In other words if you can't hate the enemy you'll never be able to fight him properly, and so these lectures were designed to do that; to make you loathe and detest everything to do with the enemy. One of these lectures was given by a man who was a captain and he told us, 'I want you to realize the type of person you are fighting against. I was wounded, walking wounded, shot in the arm. I was taken prisoner, put on a hospital train, taken to Hamburg. When I got off at the station, or before I got off, I had all my clothes stripped off me and I was made to walk down the platform naked and all the women and children, who were lining the platform or street for the hospital train to come in, had sticks and umbrellas and they hit us and spat at us.' He said, 'I just want you to know that those are the people you are fighting against.' I mention this because I think it was about four years later when I had returned to civilian life and was working as a dancer at a place called the Royal Palace Hotel in Kensington, now called the Royal Garden Hotel, that a man walked in one day and I thought 'I know your face' but I couldn't recollect where I had seen him so I went up and spoke to him. After reminiscing for a bit he said to me, 'Were you a cadet at Worcester College, Oxford, training for a commission?' and I said, 'Yes,' and it suddenly came back to me who this man was. He was the one who had given the lecture about the type of people we were fighting against. He said to me, 'Did you believe what I told you?' I said, 'Of course I did, I never doubted anything about it,' and he said, 'Well, I can tell you now there wasn't a word of truth in it.' So it just brings it home to you what propaganda can do.

Now before I forget, there is one memory I must share with you. It is I think of August 1917 at a place called San Gabriele. One night, another ambulance man named Foster and myself, were unable to get back to our first aid post because of the heavy shelling of the road and we found a ruined house which, although badly blasted, appeared to offer some place to sleep. The roof had gone and we found a large bed in one of the bedrooms exposed to the sky. The tattered bedding was quite dry so we lay on it and were soon fast asleep. A couple of hours later we were suddenly awakened by a bombardment with shells passing, it seemed, only a few feet above the house and exploding on the road. We began to get rather scared and decided we ought to get out as quickly as possible. The stairway had gone so we had to slide down blankets to get to the ground floor. We crossed the road where there was an old barn and getting a couple of stretchers we opened these up and lay down to sleep for the rest of the night.

The first thing next morning, when the sun came up, I looked over the side of the stretcher and saw a mass of congealed blood. On investigating further and looking round I saw the soles of dozens and dozens of pairs of soldiers' boots and the men wearing them were all dead: dead men who had been laid out in rows, one pile on top of the other. They hadn't had time to bury them and we had been sleeping all night with the soles of their boots up against our heads.

To complete the story of the war, I got my commission, served very briefly in Ireland and chose not to stay in the Army. I was demobilized in April 1919.

In 1922 Victor Silvester won the World Professional Ballroom Dancing Championship and was launched into a career which would lead to his having the leading British strict tempo dance-band, broadcasting through the BBC worldwide.

19

BRIGADIER SIR JOHN SMYTHE
1st BARONET, VC MC PC

Indian Army in France, 1915

In 1972 I was beginning to develop a keen interest in the Indian Army and the phenomenon of the remarkably successful working relationship between British Officers, the Viceroy's Commissioned Officers, that is Indian soldiers who had earned a raised status to junior command, and the Indian Army regiments' native troops, the non-commissioned officers and the men in the ranks, that is native-born Sowars in cavalry regiments, and Sepoys in the infantry. This is an interest I still hold with admiration for those on both sides of the ethnic equation, but what an opportunity I had to further my knowledge in meeting Sir John Smythe at his home in London in January 1972!

Sir John was born in Teignmouth, Devon, in 1893, was educated at a grammar school in Oxford and then at Repton Public School before going to The Royal Military College, Sandhurst.

For financial reasons I had to get into the Indian Army or not go into the Army at all. In those days you couldn't live on your pay in the regular British Army and therefore, like Auchinleck and other soldiers that I knew, I had to get Indian Army or nothing. So I had to work very hard at Sandhurst and I passed out ninth and made certain of getting into the Indian Army. But before that, as was normal, I did a year in the Green Howards in India and during that time I paid a very interesting visit to Nepal and that is where I became such an admirer of the Gurkhas. In 1913 I joined the 15th Ludhiana Sikhs in Baluchistan. Somehow, owing I think to the influence of the commanding officer of the regiment, although we were right out in the wilds, on outposts, we were hurried down to Karachi immediately on the outbreak of war and in fact arrived in France in September 1914.

We were supposed to have a period of training before we went into action, so we didn't actually go into action until my twenty-first birthday on the 24th October 1914 and that was in the first Battle of Ypres. This was my first experience under fire.

Well for the first twenty-four hours I didn't realize how dangerous it was and I think for one of the only times in my life I really enjoyed being shot at. I ran from one trench to the other and it was really only when we added up the casualty lists and I found out how many people had been killed that I became a great deal more cautious. In this first battle, for me, everything seemed very confused. Units were shoved in here and there to try and hold our front. There was no barbed wire in front of the trenches at all and therefore you were sort of 'standing to' almost all the time. You might be attacked at any time.

Curiously enough, on the first night in the trenches it is said that the British battalion next door to us was charged in the middle of the night by Germans fuelled with some mixture which included alcohol. I think all nations were trying to find something in the way of a spirit reviver. We had our rum ration in France which was a great heartener after a wet night in the trenches, when the chaps came round with a cup of hot coffee and rum. But on this occasion it was very interesting to me because this mixture of ether and alcohol, I think, made these chaps absolutely fearless and they went right through the British battalion and they were in a wood behind us and we wondered what was going to happen. However at three o'clock in the morning the effect of this spirit on them gave them a tremendous hangover. They were utterly dispirited, just the absolute reverse of what they had been at the beginning and they crawled back, as many of them as could get away, back to their own positions.

We only knew this from one or two of them who were captured and our medical officer was interested and examined some of them and found out what it was that they had taken, but in those early days it was very, very different from the trench warfare that developed with its substantial entrenchments and fields of barbed wire, a different, specialized sort of warfare which we had never contemplated.

In March, the Battle of Neuve Chapelle, in which my battalion was engaged, was the first battle that took place after the continuous line of trenches had extended the whole way across the battlefront, and therefore it was a sort of model in a way for all the other battles which took place afterwards. They only differed in certain particulars, in scale and that sort of thing.

At Neuve Chapelle, and the later battles, you had got to break the German wire and that's why a lot of people denigrate the generalship of the First World War. There was a great deal in this but on the other hand high command was tremendously circumscribed in the sort of tactics which could be adopted because nothing could be achieved in any attack until you had broken through the wire entanglements and the front-line trench system, and therefore just as the machine gun was the defensive queen of the battlefield, as far as the attack was concerned, it was the guns and howitzers of the artillery and then later the tank, that were its weapons of breakthrough. Therefore all these trench warfare battles, and of course the Somme is a particular example, were planned with that first big idea of a breakthrough of the enemy's trench system, and that meant tremendously detailed preparations for gaining surprise by getting your guns in under cover of darkness and by getting them ranged and sighted.

Now Neuve Chapelle was a very good example of this. We achieved absolute surprise. The bombardment was thirty-five minutes long in which 300 guns fired something like 3,000 shells. It was a tremendous bombardment to us at that time. None of us had ever experienced such shattering noise. It didn't seem possible that anything could have lived through it. Also, although the initial attack was successful over two thirds of its length, the attack on Neuve Chapelle and then on towards Aubers Ridge on the left of the attack, there had been one length of German trench that had not been troubled by our artillery bombardment, and that resulted in the almost annihilation of the Middlesex Regiment, which had to attack across uncut barbed wire.

That was one of the great tragedies of all these battles because it was impossible really to ensure that all the way along the front the trench in front of you was shattered and all the barbed wire was cut. And it only wanted one machine-gun nest behind uncut barbed wire to cause the death of thousands of men. That was a very tragic mistake made by the commander of the Royal Artillery because this little bit of the bombardment was left to two siege batteries, which had just come out from home, and they really arrived too late to range and get themselves settled for this bombardment, and that nearly caused the defeat of the whole operation and there were some terrible casualties there.

But the next lesson it brought out really was that even though the barrage generally was a success, when we got into Neuve Chapelle in one or two hours, then came the rub, and this happened in almost every case. The Germans of course were tremendous fighters, tremendously tough, and we were sort of at the end of our advance, running out of ammunition and hadn't yet dug our new trenches or adapted the German trenches to fire the other way round. And then came the German counter-attack and the result was that we lost almost everything that we had gained. Sir Henry Rawlinson, I think he was so wise, he was the Commander of the 4th Corps, and he said his policy would have been bite and hold and he maintained that idea all through the war and I think that was very, very sensible.

Well on the 22nd of April the Germans launched this chlorine gas attack from cylinders on to a French division at Ypres and a most ghastly panic resulted. There was no protection, no gas masks, no warning from captured Germans of what was afoot: absolutely none at all. It was to my mind the one big chance that one side had of winning the war by surprise. If they had only been ready for it themselves, that is the Germans; that was an error on their part. They were really as surprised at how tremendously effective it was, as we were.

At the time that it happened, the Indian Corps was on the extreme right of the British line. Well that was our misfortune because we in the Lahore Division were marched thirty miles. We were taken out of the trenches on the right of the line, and we had a really ghastly march of thirty miles, having been in very wet trenches for a week and all the men's feet were very soft, and we had to make that march up to Ypres. Well when we got there we had no idea of what we were getting into at all. I don't think anyone liked to tell us and when we passed by corps headquarters, along either side of the road were buckets of a certain chemical liquid in which we were all told to dip our handkerchiefs, it happened to be a very warm day. Whether the chemical they provided was any good or not no one knows. Anyway the handkerchief was dry long before we got up there.

When we got up there, fortunately for me and my battalion, we were in reserve. I got on to the roof of a little house, a flat-roofed house. Not that I knew anything about chlorine gas but I couldn't have done anything else really because, of course, chlorine gas is heavier than air and it didn't rise. It didn't, other than the odd whiff of it, actually affect me very much but I had a very good view of the two brigades that were making the counter-attack.

The attack went up to about 100 yards of the German trenches going very well and then from the German trenches came out this great cloud of green-yellow gas which the wind was right for, which it had to be of course, and it just swept over the two brigades and there was utter panic and chaos. Of course later in the war there were gas masks of every sort and anyway the troops, what remained of them, were withdrawn. I actually instinctively didn't swallow any of this gas. That would have been of course certain death. If you did really swallow a mouthful of chlorine it was almost certain death. People did live who had just imbibed a little bit. Actually I got gas in one eye, which affected the eye for about fifteen years. In fact I couldn't really open my eyelid properly for some time.

It was an extraordinary situation. The women of England were at once put on to making these gas masks. The first gas masks that were made, I don't think probably they were very effective, but anyway we just dug in there and spent a very anxious week waiting for the next cloud of gas to come. Fortunately the wind had changed and the reason that they didn't continue to use chlorine was that it could only be used with quite a strong wind behind it and the prevailing wind was really from our side to the German trenches. And of course it was so very visible but from then on of course gas warfare was a great part of the war.

My particular testing time was on the 18th of May 1915, at Richebourg L'Avoue.

(**The London Gazette, as reported later in The Daily Telegraph, has this to say of the award which followed upon the day's events in Smythe's sector: 'His Majesty the King has been graciously pleased to approve of a grant of the Victoria Cross to the under-signed officers, non-commisioned officers and men. Lieutenant John George Smythe 15th Ludhiana Sikhs, Indian Army, for the most conspicuous bravery near Richebourg L'Avoue on May 18th 1915. With a bombing party of ten men, who voluntarily under-took this duty to convey a supply of 96 bombs to within 20 yards of the enemy's positon over exceptionally dangerous ground after the attempts of two other parties had failed, Lieutenant Smythe succeeded in taking the bombs to the desired position with the aid of two of his men, the other eight having been killed or wounded and to effect this purpose he had to swim a stream being exposed the whole time to howitzer , shrapnel , machine gun and rifle fire.'**)

Well, quite simply, I was required to do it. I should never have done it had I not been required to. It was a peculiar action I think. What actually happened was on the 17th of May another division had attacked the German trenches at Richebourg L'Avoue and the attack had been a complete failure and the ground was strewn with dead bodies and wounded. We came up, my brigade, that evening. They had only captured in this attack, 200 yards of the German front-line trench. Now in those days trench warfare was a battle for ground and it was sort of an understood thing that if you won some ground you hung on to it whatever and however many casualties were incurred, which I didn't personally agree with but there it was, and in those 200 yards of German trench which had been captured we were ordered to hold it, a 100 yards of it, with a company of my 15th Sikhs and 100 yards by the Highland Light Infantry.

I was then a first lieutenant. Well in the morning I was back in our front-line trench, which was about 300 yards behind, with the remainder of my battalion and the Highland Light Infantry. With daybreak, the Germans, quite naturally, they set about evicting these obnoxious people who were holding part of their own trench and we had a message back saying that they were running short of ammunition and particularly bombs, that is hand grenades. Now the Highland Light Infantry were a good deal stronger in numbers than we were and during the morning they sent back a party from their front-line trench to try and bring up bombs and ammunition. Now that was a party of about twelve to fifteen men. They, none of them, got more than halfway. They were all killed. Then the Highland Light Infantry from the back, from our front-line trench they sent forward a rather bigger party of about twenty men with bombs and ammunition and they didn't get any further either. They were absolutely slaughtered by machine guns and rifle fire. Well I had been watching this, as had men of my battalion, and watching it with by no means an impersonal eye because I was the bombing officer of the 15th Sikhs and I felt quite sure that I should be asked to do it myself.

Sure enough the CO came on the phone and he was obviously a bit shaky and he said, 'Hello boy,' which he generally referred to me as. He said, 'You know what I'm ringing you up about?' and I said, 'Yes, Sir, I probably do.' And he said, 'Well do you think you can do it?' I said, 'Well quite frankly no. I have just seen two parties try and they have both been completely wiped out and I really can't see why I should be any luckier.' But I said, 'Of course if I'm ordered to do it I will have a go.' So he said, 'Well you don't do anything about it at all. I am going to tell the Brigadier that it's impossible and we can't do it and you stay by the phone.' Well I was quite sure what the answer would be and he came back on the phone and he sounded distressed and he said, 'Well I am terribly sorry but the Brigadier says you must have a shot at it.' He said, 'The Brigadier's got great confidence in you and he thinks you can do it.' Well I went to the company commander, a major, and told him and he said, 'It's murder, you can't possibly do it. You must say so.' He was a very martinet disciplinarian and I was rather shocked and so I said, 'Well you know I can't do that and I'm going to ask for volunteers from your company to go with me,' and he said, 'Well you can do that if you like but no one's going to come with you. They've all seen what happened to those making an attempt.'

I think it was the proudest moment of my life really because when

I asked for ten volunteers, the whole company wanted to come with me. I spoke to them of course in Punjabi. I said to them quite briefly, 'I've been ordered to take up bombs and ammunition to our people who are being very hard pressed in the trench in front and I want ten volunteers to go with me,' and every one, all eighty of them, said they were ready to come with me. That gave me great courage that they were so courageous themselves. So we were loaded up with bombs, forty-six I think to a box, and ammunition, two boxes of bombs carried between two men and ammunition slung around us and at 3 o'clock in the afternoon in broad daylight we dropped over the parapet and set out. Well now the Germans really made one mistake, they knew we were going to try again and instead of leaving it to the machine guns and riflemen they'd laid on an artillery barrage round the trench and as soon as we appeared they put down a big artillery barrage.

We had to go about three hundred yards and the Germans were in the same trench as our men we were trying to assist. Our men had constructed trench blocks and lateral parapets against being cleared out of the trench. Obviously the one thing they needed was hand-grenades. Well the effect of this crash of artillery, it created a lot of smoke and dust and threw up a lot of dead bodies into the air and it acted as a diversion really from us but I think two of the men were killed at once by the shelling.

We were bending as low as we could as we made for the trench, taking whatever cover was available. I was in front leading the party and the others were coming along quite close. Well then we had a bit of luck. I saw just on our right there was a little winding stream going the way we wanted you see, and in the confusion of this shelling we dropped into that and it came up to about one's chest but we were able to get along quite a bit before we were spotted, and then they ran machine guns down the water and we had to get out of that. But anyway, eventually crawling along as best we could we got up quite close behind the trench and then there was the most difficult bit of just the last fifty yards that we had to cover. We had lost one lot of bombs that had been shattered. Fortunately it hadn't exploded but we got the other one and my captain, Hyde Cates, who was commanding the company in front, had no idea what was happening or what the firing was about, so

I yelled to him and he looked over with a face like a white sheet and said, 'Good heavens! What are you doing?' and I said, 'Well I've got to come into the trench with this.' I'd got two chaps left. The others had been either killed or wounded. Anyway I said, 'You fire with everything you've got and under cover of that I'm going to get to you.' He said, 'You'll never make it,' and I replied that I couldn't stay where I was and so I got there with one man. The other chap being hit just as we were getting to the trench. Of course as soon as they knew they had got this other box of bombs they were able to reply to the German bombing and they were alright for the time being. I stayed with them. I couldn't go back until it got dark anyway and I stayed up with them until it got dark. And then under cover of darkness, they could send reinforcements.

The only person who thought I was still alive, they had long given me up for dead, was my orderly, quite an elderly man, and he had sat on the parapet all the afternoon, regardless of bullets or anything, holding my British warm and a flask of hot coffee, and he was the only person who was quite sure I would come back. And when I arrived out of the gloom he just got up to his feet and said, 'Sharbal Sahib,' which means, 'Well done, Sahib,' and then he gave the Sikh war cry: 'Jo Bole So Nihal, Sat Sri Akal' in a chanting voice. It translates as 'He who cries God is Truth is ever Blessed.' Then I went to report to the CO who thought he was seeing a ghost. You see all this had taken several hours.

My two men who had not been killed were taken off to hospital and later invalided out of the service but every man was decorated with the Indian Distinguished Service Order, the senior one got the Indian Order of Merit but that was most unusual, to give a whole party an award.

When I reported to my CO, I was absolutely exhausted not only physically, but mentally. He gave me a tot of rum and wrapped me in a blanket and he put me under the orderly room table and I slept there for about twelve hours.

The first thing I knew about a Victoria Cross award was a telephone message from the 2nd Gurkhas saying many congratulations. That's all it said and I hadn't the faintest idea what it was about.

That was about six weeks later, a month perhaps to six weeks.

Anyway I was sent back home for the investiture and the King pinned the decoration and then he gave me the little plain cardboard box for it. The King drew my attention to the fact that the medal and the box had no more intrinsic value than a penny.

Sir Douglas Haig had recommended me for the award and like a lot of VCs I was given a Russian award, the Order of St George. I remember that at the investiture in Buckingham Palace I was very nervous. I was still wearing my ammunition boots and I found it very difficult to walk across the polished floor to the King. The King was extremely nice to me and talked to me for several moments. It was the biggest investiture that there had been and I think eight or nine other people were getting Victoria Crosses. While we were waiting to go, everyone crowded round us in the Palace and wanted to hear all about it, which we were very loathe to tell them. As regards the press and that sort of thing, of course there was tremendous adulation, and I was entertained to dinner by the dons of Oxford and things like that. You see I had been to school in Oxford.

I went back to France quite soon and there is an incident here that I would like to relate. On one occasion, when we were in the front line where the German trenches were only eighty yards from our trench, we had sent up to us an Indian Prince, small in stature. I was given the task of showing him round. I was commanding a company at the time. He was very smartly dressed and he was carrying a little suitcase and what looked like a gun case in his other hand. Anyway I was very busy and I put him in a little bay or alcove which would be fairly safe and I left him in there and I told him to be very careful not to put his head above the parapet because the German trench was very close. At that time the Germans had adopted the system of steel loopholes, steel plates to guard their loopholes. In a while I heard a tremendous noise from the German trenches, shouting and yelling and I wondered what was the reason for this. I went along to see my little Indian Prince and there he was with a 500 Express Elephant Gun knocking out these steel loopholes one by one. Of course it was strictly against the Hague Conventions to use an Express rifle with a soft nose bullet but they were the very things to deal with the steel plates – our 303s just pinged off the steel. The Germans were absolutely furious and put down a big trench mortar concentration and I hurried my Prince away but it was quite an amusing incident.

Sir John's regiment was later to campaign in the Western Desert of Egypt against the Senussi tribesmen, and then on the North West Frontier of India against the Mohmands, and on the Afghan border against the Mahsuds where he was again to serve with distinction. His account of these experiences is continued in this interview but has not been selected for publication here. However it seems appropriate to conclude with this Indian Army officer's own assessment of his capacity to conquer apprehension before leadership in battle and then some rather unusual encounters with Sir Douglas Haig.

I studied very carefully a book entitled *Right and Wrong Thinking* by A Martin Crane, given to me by a friend in Nepal in 1913. It was a book that had been very highly thought of in America and had gone into a great number of editions and the theme of it was that the thoughts that one has in one's mind at any one time are either discordant thoughts or good thoughts. And if you can train yourself to drop the discordant thoughts such as fear, anxiety, hate, envy, your mind can become filled with the good thoughts of hope and courage and those sort of things, and I did manage to put that into practice in a way that I didn't think I could possibly have done otherwise and perhaps it was that which helped me because I am not naturally a very courageous person, and perhaps that is why I gave people the impression of calmness.

It so happened that what I learned from this book had soon to survive the test of war. I've tried to keep to what I learned since that testing but never quite so satisfactorily as I did in wartime, because I didn't have such a big test perhaps. I know that people did say that I seemed to be wonderfully calm and composed. I remember on one occasion a doctor in the battalion, when some shelling started and we were walking down the road, he said, 'Do you mind if I take your arm because nothing will ever hit you,' and just at that moment a shell splinter whizzed past and cut me across the throat and nearly took his nose off and he dropped me like a hot coal, but anyway it hadn't really injured me very much.

I remember we had an officer in my regiment who was a most splendid games player. He was a wonderful natural athlete, first class at almost any game and he had a wonderful physique but the shelling absolutely got him down. And of course it was tremendously nerve-wracking to be in a trench that was being bombarded. They would range one over and then one nearer and one knew that the next lot were coming almost on top of you and also the trench mortars were very frightening indeed. There was a thing called a *Minenwerfer* and one of them gave me my worst experience. I was buried very deep and my Sikhs just dug me out in time but for this particular officer there was nothing he could do about it. He had a complete nervous collapse and there it was.

There is one thing that I might mention and that is my meeting with Sir Douglas Haig, the Army Commander and afterwards Commander in Chief of our forces in France. It was after Neuve-Chapelle, and I had been lent a car by the corps commander's son, who was a friend of mine, to go into a neighbouring town and have my hair cut and a bit of relaxation. We set off in the car and it was a very wet day. My driver was a young British soldier, very inexperienced. We came to a small town where Douglas Haig and his staff were conducting inspections of Australian troops, I think, who had recently arrived. Well I was sitting in the back of the car almost asleep but anyhow Douglas Haig, who was always very smartly turned-out, highly polished boots and everything, was walking along the pavement and this very silly driver drove past much too fast and a stream of mud flew up all over Sir Douglas Haig's boots. There was a roar of anger and I found the fearsome face of the General looking at me through the window and he said, 'What the hell do you think you are doing driving past like that?' Well of course I said I was very sorry but I had been almost asleep. He responded to this with, 'Well don't do it again.'

So we went into town and I had my hair cut and I had a small bottle of champagne, which was very cheap in a French Hotel. I then told my driver that he wasn't to go anywhere near where we had encountered the general and I gave him a different route out of the town. Well as bad luck would have it we struck another place where Sir Douglas Haig, in the middle of the village, was standing on a sort of raised platform and he was taking the salute of the new brigade, which was going past. Now my driver, who was looking forward to his evening meal saw that the only place he could get past was between Douglas Haig and the brigade that he was inspecting. I really was fast asleep this time and the driver took his chance and went for it. Well there was the most awful row and the military police stopped him and Douglas Haig got down and said, 'By God it's you again.' All I could say was that I was very sorry and that I had instructed the driver not to go near where he, the General, was likely to be. Sir Douglas absolutely glowered at me.

Now a week later I was given a week's leave, a very precious thing. Again my friend at corps headquarters said I must have his car and come to lunch at corps headquarters. I didn't want to do that at all because I was afraid they'd cut it fine and I might miss the boat or something. Well anyway I got off alright but we had two punctures on the way down to Boulogne and I arrived at the quay to find that the leave boat had just cast off the ropes and was just edging out from the quay. Well I was rather a good long jumper in those days and I tucked my kitbag under my arm and I thought well it's either a ducking or missing a day's leave. And I was going to have a go for it but the ship was rather below the quay and so I ran at it and then on the deck of the ship arose the awful figure of Douglas Haig and he shouted, 'Stop you bloody fool!' And he held up his arm and I came to rest on the edge of the quay almost on the edge of the water and I'd lost a day's leave and I was really very sad about this. Well when we came to go back I'd only had six days and Douglas Haig had had seven. He spotted me coming on to the boat and he sent his ADC along to me and I was told, 'Sir Douglas Haig presents his compliments to 2nd Lieutenant Smythe. He's sorry to have done him out of a day's leave but is quite certain he would have fallen in the water.' I replied through the ADC that I would like to thank Sir Douglas for his kind message but that I was quite certain I would have landed on the boat. Curiously enough this happened just before I got my VC so he didn't bear me any grudge.

Some readers will know that Sir John's military career, which took him to senior command in South-East Asia in the Second World War, ended in controversial failure. In 1972 my request for an interview was focussed solely on 1914–18 with a possible extension into his campaigning on India's North-West frontier. There were several reasons why I limited myself to this 1920/2 boundary with all my interviewees – my lack of knowledge and the danger of over-extending what I could cope with, principal among them. Whether this particular 1915 hero, in high command later, arguably to have had feet of clay, lay well outside my remit in 1972.

20

Howard Cruttenden Marten

Conscientious Objector, Death Sentence in France

My first visit to Howard Marten was in February 1973. He appears earlier in this book and I refer to the delight I was to enjoy in his friendship. It was touching that he was later to describe our meeting as 'serendipitous' and it is no accident that serendipity has, since that occasion, remained for me a rather special word. In 1973 Mr Marten was physically frail but mentally sharp. Seated, in conversation, it was hard to credit that he was born in 1884.

My father's family were Quakers for many generations. On my mother's side she was from Huguenot extraction. When they married they were to attend very free non-conformist churches. I followed our family's political sympathies, Liberal.

I remember regarding the gloating after the relief of Mafeking as repugnant and I attended a meeting at the old Queen's Hall where Lloyd George was given a very rough ride. I also remember attending the annual meeting of the Peace Society in my early teens. I never felt I wanted to be part of national celebrations or occasions like Queen Victoria's funeral. We were given a day's holiday for this and I went for a walk in the country, walking from Marble Arch to Uxbridge.

When you ask me about the militancy later, at the time of the call for more dreadnought battleships, I have to say that Quakers, and those who had instinctive aversion from patriotism, lived much more enclosed lives than opponents of war in later times. In my case yes, certainly with the outbreak of war and then the real possibility of the introduction of conscription for military service, I had to consider my position. Of course from my family and friends I had never been under any pressure to change my stance. They would have been astonished at any such a thought. Perhaps I should mention that at some date in the first decade of the new century I had refused compulsory vaccination and my banking – I never dreamt at the time that my employer would tell me with clear disapproval that I was one of three people in London who had not conformed. It was against smallpox and my father had always, through his belief in homeopathy, been against such procedures.

Returning to the question of military service, I was never presented with a white feather and lost but one former school friend and this but temporarily. Though I was not at that time a member of the Society of Friends, the Quakers, I had association with Friends and in 1915 went to a private meeting of thirty or forty men at the Hampstead home of Rowntree Gillett. This gathering discussed the whole conscription matter freely. We faced the question of whether we were prepared to be shot for what we believed in, if it came to that. I never dreamt at the time that I was actually going to be faced with that situation within twelve months but we accepted the view that if it came to it you had to be prepared to be shot. It could be the ultimate outcome.

You ask about second thoughts and considering my benefiting from the potential sacrifice of those putting on uniform. That point of view was put to me but I don't think I ever felt it in that sense because I was strongly of the opinion that the people who took that view were not facing up to, what was for me, reality. The reality to me was a peaceable world. I never had a shadow of doubt that the pacifist position was the right one. I felt intense sorrow for the man who conscientiously felt he must go and fight and very often was probably a better man than I was. I claim no virtue for the pacifist position but for me the pacifist position was the right one. I was much more in sympathy with many men in the services than many of my fellow conscientious objectors.

Regrettably this point was not developed but by inference it may refer to those whose objection was made solely on grounds of obdurate political conviction.

Well in January the Military Service Act was passed allowing for the possibility of conditional or absolute exemption on various grounds, materially from my point of view, on grounds of conscience. The possibility of alternate service was there but the only alternate service offered me was non-combatant service, which meant joining the Army.

I was in fact chairman of a branch of the No Conscription Fellowship set up in the previous year and tremendously supported by the Society of Friends. This organisation led by Fenner Brockway regularly supplied advisory information as the situation developed.

Men taking our stance had to appear before a Local Tribunal to make our case. After the almost certain rejection of our appeal for absolute exemption, we would receive call-up papers and when we refused to comply, we were liable for arrest. After making my views clear to local councillors in an unofficial and unsympathetic advisory body to the Local Tribunal, my original appeal was made to that Tribunal in Harrow School, and on its rejection I made representation to the Middlesex Appeal Tribunal, again unsuccessfully. With my call-up papers received, I was now liable to arrest and I had to resign from my job at the bank. With regard to my arrest, I actually arranged this with the local policeman for it to be at a certain time under the railway arch in Pinner the following day.

I should add here that my answer to the stock questions such as what you would do if a German was attacking your sister, was to say that I was not prepared to say what I would do under a hypothetical situation. I couldn't contemplate fixed action before a circumstance had arisen.

From the police station I was handed over to a military escort from Mill Hill Barracks and with another man in the same circumstance as me we were taken to the barracks. The whole thing was very strange for me. I was thirty and had not been to boarding school and had lived a pretty sheltered life. I am not a person who enjoys a rough house for the sake of it and I spoke reasonably to the escort on the lines of my recognition that he might have orders forcibly to put me in uniform but that under protest I was perfectly prepared to put on uniform but I would not do it under my own free will. Perhaps it was a silly technicality but I hate any undignified procedure and to lie on the floor and kick was stupid knowing that they had the power to put me into uniform.

On being taken from the barracks, we refused to pick up our kitbags and that's when the rough handling started. We passed through a line of NCOs kicking at our heels and pushing us but I cannot say we suffered any real violence. In my experience the NCOs and privates kept an eye on their officers and took the lead from them.

We were taken to the railway station and were left entirely on our own at Finsbury Park in a café while we waited to change trains. We made no attempt to escape. Then we were taken to Felixstowe and a military camp there. Here we were given twenty-eight days' detention at the Harwich Redoubt, an old military prison. Before the completion of this sentence we were hustled out at dead of night and were taken by train from Felixstowe in the morning all the way across London to Southampton and of course we then knew what was in the wind. We were threatened all the way; there will be no one to argue your case where you are going. The threats came from officers and men but some had sympathy like a regimental sergeant major, plainly anxious for us, who said, 'You fellows don't know what you are up against.'

There were seventeen of us in this first batch for France. We were able to write letters and were told on the boat that we were free men, all our previous crimes wiped out, and if we behaved ourselves we would be alright. When we got to Le Havre we were marched out to a camp called Cinder City, a camp largely occupied by men who were unfit and 'old sweats' called up from the Reserve and seething with discontent. We were ordered to parade and divided up among the other companies there and of course as the companies drilled each one now had a man or two left behind as the company marched off.

Disobedience resulted in field punishment. Smaller penalties like loss of leave or pay meant nothing to us. We were subjected to field punishment number one, not tied to gun wheels but roped to a horizontal rope for two hours, three nights out of four. For the shorter men against a uniformly high horizontal rope it must have been particularly uncomfortable. Then the real crime at the punishment barracks was our refusal to drill. We were put in irons as had been the case in Felixstowe, but word must have come down from on high that this was to stop.

All the time we were threatened with the death sentence and we had death sentence cases read to us by an officer as to how they had been dealt with at the front. Finally for disobedience at the punishment barracks we were to be prepared for a field general court martial and I was the first to be picked out. In refusing to drill I must have caught the sergeant's eye as a ringleader but he then found there were three others involved and so he picked them too. They left it at that and they were to try four of us to begin with.

Mine was to be the first case and to make everything more impressive they brought up the base commandant at Boulogne, Colonel Wilberforce. He lectured each of us very severely and this would have impressed the ordinary chap to be brought up in front of the base commandant. I was told to go outside and stand by my marker and come back in five minutes with my decision. Of course it made no difference at all.

We were then told that we were to be put down for field general court martial and we would in due course be given the date of our trial. The advantage of being on this level of court martial was that we went onto full rations instead of prison diet, which was a tin of bully beef and four biscuits a day. Incidentally, during this period we were visited by Dr Myer of the Free Churches. Our situation was known now in England and there was a good deal of concern and the well-respected Free Church Minister, Myer, and Hubert Peat, of the Friends Service Committee, who came over as Myer's secretary, were able to interview us at the field punishment barracks. Perhaps this was allowed to allay public disquiet but of course that is just my speculation.

Each trial was separate. I was led in by a couple of sergeants. I think a colonel presided and there was an officer either side of him. I asked if I could have legal representation and it rather irritated me that the officer who refused it was the chief witness against me. However that court martial was quashed. There was an irregularity and we would have to be tried all over again.

Somehow the second trial seemed to be held in an atmosphere of hostility, which I had not sensed at the first. You have asked me about any doubting among us of our stance, as the peril of our position was so clear. I don't think any one of us veered from our conviction but one or two may have questioned their courage in going through with it. One man, in hospital at the time, may have weakened and got a lesser sentence but when you are absolutely on your own a man could easily imagine all sorts of things.

At the court martial, it was simply a question of examining the evidence against you and your attitude or response to it. Then you were allowed to read your defence. Mine was the same on each occasion, the wrongfulness of war. All the time I based my attitude on Christian teaching. By being placed in a military prison I was compelled to commit the military crimes for which I was being charged.

The base commandant was the principal witness against me but he had had that individual interview with each of us and technically that should have disqualified him as principal witness against us.

Some days later we were called out and paraded to go to Henriville Camp and there we were formed up with perhaps up to two thousand on parade. It seemed to me an enormous square of men but was probably smaller than it seemed. We conscientious objectors were standing to one side. As each man's name was read out he was marched forward under escort.

I was called out first. I walked forward; if I kept in step, it was not by intention. My crimes or misdemeanours were read out, that I had been sentenced for disobedience and then further sentenced for disobedience at the Field Punishment Barracks, and then for these acts of disobedience I was sentenced to suffer death by being shot. Then there was a good pause and it was read out that the sentence was confirmed by the Commander in Chief – I cannot remember whether Sir Douglas Haig's name was given. There was a further long pause, and in my own mind I had the feeling that this was it, and then a final pronouncement was declaimed and this was that the sentence had been commuted by the Commander in Chief to one of penal servitude for ten years. That was the conclusion of the proceedings for me but then in turn the others were sentenced similarly.

I must admit that I had a feeling of sinking in the stomach as I waited for my sentence but you had been threatened with the death sentence for days in and days out so that you almost lost a sense of personality. I have often since felt that on the parade ground I was a different personality. I was part of something much bigger than myself. There was something mystical about it. It was very strange.

The relief to us later was to be in a civil prison and see a blue uniform instead of khaki.

First of all it was back to Boulogne, then after a day or two to a hard labour camp in Rouen in transit. Then by boat direct from Rouen to Southampton. All my belongings had been returned and I had some cash on me to buy a newspaper, June 24, and it contained all the reports of my case and the debates in Parliament. It was the *Daily Mail*. I then did perhaps a stupid thing, parting with my pay book with the death sentence inscribed in red. I posted it by registered post to the No Conscription Fellowship but of course it never got through. However it was all in the papers the following Sunday!

We were taken to Winchester Prison and then to Wormwood Scrubs for a weekend to be interviewed by the Central (Appeal) Tribunal, with a view to being turned over to the Home Office Scheme (that was being engaged in non-war work labour). Practically all of the men from France accepted the scheme and then most recanted. I did not agree with this and was prepared to work on it to the best of my ability for which I made myself very unpopular with my fellow objectors. Indeed, Catherine Marshall, deputizing for Clifford Allen at the No Conscription Fellowship, is said to have judged of those who, like me, made this compromise, that it would have been better if they had been shot; then the cause would have had martyrs.

My experience of the scheme started at a quarry near Aberdeen. Conditions here were so bad that we actually had a death of a man who was in no condition to be engaged in this sort of work. Ramsay MacDonald came to see us here and I was deputed to meet him at the station, three miles from the camp, so I had a good opportunity on the walk back, there being no form of transport, to make his acquaintance. He seemed an ebullient man, so unlike another Labour leader, Snowden, the ice-cold intellectual. I got to know Snowden by correspondence in my role as Secretary of the Settlement at Wakefield and Snowden's concern was the financial side of the running of the Home Office Scheme.

From this quarry at Dyce we went to Wakefield and it was here that a number of men felt they couldn't go on with the scheme. I respected their position as I expected my position to be respected.

Of course there was every different opinion or motivation amongst us. You couldn't have devised such a way of mixing up people of different inspiration. You had Jehovah's Witnesses or, as they were then, International Bible Students, on the one hand, and then the extreme socialists like Guy Aldridge and Thompson on the other. Aldridge was a firebrand from Glasgow, and Thompson until a few years ago was still spouting forth at Speakers' Corner.

In Wakefield I was fortunate. I started in the pay office and then as Secretary of the Camp or Settlement. The Settlement then had about 1,200 men and although I was nominally in the pay office most of my time was spent writing letters and conducting the affairs of the Men's Committee. All the talents were represented among the men and I remember painting, music and drama in particular. I made a good chum there, George Benson, and we went to a number of pantomimes together. It was Benson who told me of the seriously rough treatment two objectors, Beardsworth and Dukes, had been subjected to.

We were not locked in our cells or rooms I should call them. The locks were taken off. Each hall or wing had had dining tables put down in it, but despite the relaxed regime there were men who were determined to smash the scheme. Men like C H Norman. He was a clever man himself but he could not accept the point of view of those who judged the scheme workable.

In February 1917 we were told that numbers of us in Wakefield were to be sent to Dartmoor. A previous party had gone from Warwick and seventy-five of us followed. Of the men from Warwick, we were pretty sure in time that one, a man called Beale, was an agent provocateur. I heard this confirmed later by Government officials but whatever may be the case he joined or re-joined the Army.

In Dartmoor we were not under a regime of warders. The only officials there as far as we men on the scheme were concerned were the governor, re-christened the agent, and the principal warder, his secretary. Our morale here varied. I think morale was much higher in the early stages when we were really up against things from the military authorities, because at Dartmoor there was just bickering about whether the marmalade was right and stupid things like that. Yes there were quarrels and an extraordinary incident of one man shooting another! How he got a revolver into his possession and what the circumstances were we did not know. It was kept very quiet. The shot man did not die.

On happier matters, we had accomplished artists and musicians amongst us, and experts who could give us talks on, for example, medical matters. We were well provided for in that sense.

We were hammering away to get men to be able to take up normal employment and I was one of the first out of Dartmoor about a year before the Armistice. I got permission to join the Friends War Victims' Relief Committee and I went first of all to the accounts department. I knew a number of people in the organization and of course my case was notorious. The committee on which I served had talented established business and professional people on it, chairmen of well-known companies and the secretary was Ruth Fry. After a short time I was asked to be assistant secretary but I was keen to establish my right to go back to the bank.

I applied to the Home Office and got permission to go back. However, the bank did everything possible to humiliate and downgrade me. I had lost pay for three years and yet I was put on the same grade as that on which I left. And I was put at a branch which had been known as the convict settlement for anyone who blotted his copybook. Furthermore I was put down as second cashier to a man I had trained.

Fortunately a man in the War Victims' Relief Committee accounts department had a brother who had just been appointed secretary to one of the Lever Companies in Bristol. He needed an assistant and I was invited to accept the appointment. Even though I was about to be married, after discussion with my wife-to-be, I accepted the invitation and within a couple of weeks we were in Bristol.

As far as any discrimination in Bristol was concerned, we always moved in very tolerant circles and I never suffered socially for my wartime stance apart from in my bank and in any case the manager's position there was understandable because he had lost a son in the war.

21

THE RT HON HAROLD MACMILLAN,
1st Earl of Stockton, OM PC

Grenadier Guards Officer in France

In September 1979 when I went to Birch Grove, Chelwood Gate, in Sussex, to interview Harold Macmillan, I was much less interested in politics beyond 1945 than I am now. Of course I regret that today but it remains a fact that my focus was sharply on 1914–18 and because the former Prime Minister had himself written extensively on his life and there were biographical works too, I judged that to get a response to my Great War questions might contribute most usefully to a pretty well-known story. Within the narrow framework of our meeting, he was graciously welcoming, easy and pleasant to work with, and I thought I picked up a sort of wistful loneliness. This however could be explained by the fact that to my surprise, as is recorded in my diary, 'I was shown round the house and its many treasures and then he walked me round the grounds and I saw no one else whatsoever.'

He was born in 1894, was educated at Summerfields, then Eton, where pneumonia affected his progress. Private tutors helped him secure a place at Balliol College, Oxford. When war broke out he was on vacation from college but also recovering from an operation for appendicitis.

I joined The Artists Rifles or something of that kind which was, as it were, an equivalent of an Officer Training Corps which I had not belonged to before the war. We drilled and eventually after a few weeks or so I got a commission in a Kitchener's Army battalion of The King's Royal Rifles and was told to go to Southend. The men were in billets. The weather was very bad. We had no arms, some, but insufficient uniforms, and then there came along a dear old colonel called Colonel Sir Thomas Pilkington, a great family, who was of course, a retired officer of the regiment. I should say what young men call old – I suppose fifty. Anyway he had a white moustache and a straight mouth.

All we young officers studied two great manuals, one was King's Regulations and one was Infantry Training. There were very good passages in King's Regulations that interested us as scholars. For instance, a splendid passage on embarkation followed by this wonderfully crisp line on disembarkation, which runs as follows: 'disembarkation is carried on in a similar manner to embarkation.' There is another very good passage which we delighted in which runs: 'Field Officers on entering balloons are not expected to wear spurs.'

I shudder to think about it now but I wanted to get a transfer to where all my friends were. I mean that in those happy days such things could be arranged and my mother arranged it. She happened to know the lieutenant colonel of the regiment and so I got a transfer to the Grenadier Guards, much to my delight. I went some-where about mid-February I think it was. Well, very few of my friends had got out to France by then. When everybody first joined, the great idea was to get out. Everybody said the war would be over by Christmas. There were a few lucky people who got out but very few of my Oxford friends. They had all joined similar regiments. They had been in the pre-war territorials of course, and they were mobilized and probably sent overseas. If they weren't, they were in similar forms of training, Kitchener's Army, as I had been in. Anyway, my transfer to the Grenadier Guards got me started again and of course, it was very amusing for me. We took the Army slightly as a joke. I mean all the comical sides of it amused us as rather cynical young men from Oxford and then suddenly you arrived at Chelsea Barracks.

Well, then of course, the first thing they told you was to forget everything you had possibly learnt for the last six months. You were to start all again. Turning to the right by numbers, saluting by numbers, and all the rest of it, in plain clothes, carrying an umbrella and a bowler hat. Lots of my friends were there. Then you began; you got your uniform at last and then you got drill and then the adjutant was in charge of what were called 'young officers'. Young officers was an expression which meant anyone between the age of eighteen and forty whom they had accepted as a second lieutenant and that always remained in my mind, the drill sergeants, and we also found a new thing in the regiment which didn't exist in the regiments of the line. Not only a battalion sergeant major but two drill sergeants and, of course, the standards were very impressive and I can't tell you the relief you feel if you find you can cope. To do the job at all you had to do it properly.

People aren't really, I feel, going to be brave men in the war which they had to go through when they had been poorly trained. It was what might be called a very good show but the adjutant asked the drill sergeant how the young officers were going on. He said, well Mr X, he does try, and Mr Y, well he's a bit dozy, but as for that Mr J, he doesn't seem to have any idea at all. But the art of forming platoon on the left is somewhat different to the art of higher mathematics.

However it was all very enjoyable. So then we soldiered on there. We learnt our job and then eventually somewhere in the summer of 1915, I think it was, the command decided to form a division of guards; a most formidable thing, as in the days of the great legions. That meant that there were to be four companies in each regiment, a thousand fighting men. It was later brought down to three because of the losses, so that three brigades of four battalions each made twelve thousand fighting men, plus extras. Well, it was a tremendous instrument. In order to achieve this, the Grenadiers had to produce one more battalion. They had three, the Coldstream, two more, and so on. We had to produce a fourth battalion and that was formed, and I as a young officer was put into it. It consisted partly of officers who had been wounded or brought back from France and it was formed at Marlow where we camped in the summer of 1915. In due course our battalion, the 4th Battalion Grenadier Guards, sailed from Southampton to France.

Of course, when we got on board our transport, as we had been properly taught, and after everybody had been settled down and the men had got their suppers, we went into the saloon where we suddenly found an enormous dinner laid on. The Ritz Hotel, I think, had seen to it. It was through Major Morrison, a retired officer and a millionaire, and he had produced this, together with the famous waiter, Charles I think it was, from The Ritz and so we sailed.

We had a very friendly reception in France. Women threw flowers and gave the men wine. It was all very amusing. Then we were settled in billets. The men in camp, or in barns I suppose, all sorts of buildings, and we waited. In fact we were waiting for the start of the late September Battle of Loos. Then we set off, I don't know how far but the whole division got itself moving. And all I remember about it is that we were stuck somewhere at a place called Bully-Les-Mines, and not very far then from the battlefield where an attempt was being made by Sir John French, the Commander in Chief, and Douglas Haig, the Corps Commander, to break through the lines there in that mining area. We stood a long time waiting, much to our annoyance, on the road at night while the cavalry were going through. Such was the concept apparently of the high command that you would be able to use cavalry in this battle and all they did was to get most frightfully in the way.

The next night we were put in. By that time the battle had begun and we spent the night before we attacked in some reserve trenches from which the original attack had been made. Although they did very well when they started they had been rather knocked about and driven back and so we sat there. I remember we slept, and it interested me very much that the reserve trenches in that chalk there were built through the churchyard, and there were corpses and skeletons and things were grimly exposed, and I was struck by the humour of the men who thought this was very funny. We just sat there.

Then the next day we got an order and advanced towards Hill 70, I suppose it was, across what must have been a slightly undulating plain going towards what you called a hill, which was hardly discernible, and we advanced in what was called artillery formation: a thing we had practised for the right moment, when the guns were in action I suppose, and artillery formation meant each platoon not being in a fixed formation. As if you had taken a dice and thrown them on the ground and they were supposed to be blocks so as to prevent so much damage from the shrapnel and the shelling and we marched, I suppose, about two miles across. It certainly seemed about that. It was a little bit disturbing because the trenches, it is horrid to say, the trenches through which we passed and the country which we passed, were full of wounded and dying men who had been repulsed and I am sorry to say were broken men, which I had never seen before.

A broken battalion, from officers downwards, is a very unpleasant sight and this did upset one. Fortunately, we were on the top and they were all crouching in the trenches. We marched along. One was a little bit wondering whether it upset our chaps but it didn't at all. The only thing that broke our formation was when a hare got up and everybody in my platoon said, 'There she goes,' and everybody started to run after the hare. I saw this.

We got into some town, and when we made the attack, the battalion afterwards got somehow divided into two. The commanding officer was killed, gassed, the second in command was killed, and I found myself with Colonel Morrison with two companies and the other two companies had been joined up to the next battalion. So we made a so-called attack on the hill, which wasn't very successful. I think we took it and then we were somewhere near the top and we began to dig ourselves in and that was that. By bad luck I was shot through the arm and hand the next morning I think. Well, we were relieved then. So, my officer made me go back. It was a great bore because I wasn't really badly wounded but it became bad because it swelled up and so on. It is very painful being hit in the fingers. Well, a bit like being stood on your toes. If you ever suffered from gout you will know what that means. So, my war experience is really quite absurd. That is all that happened and then I went back and was put in some dressing station and that was that. Then I went home. Not bad but my arm in a sling and all that.

Eventually I got back in the spring of 1916. I got back then to the 2nd Battalion, not to my own, the 4th. You were posted as you were needed of course. The 2nd was commanded by Colonel de Crespigny; a very splendid officer, a tremendous character, and it was a very good battalion. The de Crespigny's were a great family, frightfully supporting people. They were Huguenots, I suppose, by origin, but they were steeple- chasing, hunting, shooting and fishing people. And the Colonel, I don't think he read and wrote much, and was quite uneducated, but he was a very charming and a very intelligent man. He was very nice to me.

Well, then we had the ordinary life of trench warfare, which didn't go on for me very long, but of course, it is so easy to criticize the high command now. I think, concerning morale, the folly was keeping men in the line too long. A wounded man or a man out of the line, sick, had probably recovered by the time he got back, but an unwounded officer could be out in France for a year or more under the strain of command at his level and it could prove too much. I remember a particular captain of the company to which I was attached who really ought to have gone home. He had not been wounded. He had started at Mons as an ensign, commanded a company all through the winter, and by the summer of this terribly boring but also rather risky routine, he had had more than should have been required of him. Up four days in the line and four days in reserve, backwards and forwards, up and down the line, up and down the communication trenches. Then the night you had to set off as it was your turn to go up to the front line again.

He really wasn't fit. He ought to have been sent home on leave for six weeks and then he would have been all right. I blame the staff very much for that. Anyway, we had our routine in the reserve. I wasn't bothered about the ordinary routine of trench life. There is lots of exaggeration of the horrors of trench life I think by the people who produce films and things: not half as bad as all that. We didn't sit permanently in the front line shooting or being shot at and starving and covered with water.

However there were problems related to the routine. You were probably in the front line for four days, then you would probably go into brigade reserve for four days and then perhaps the whole brigade would go out for eight days and somebody else would come in. The tiresome part of it was the most alarming, if that were the right word, and it was the communication trenches, which were very bad. And then the front line whenever we got into it we alleged was always extremely badly kept by lazy troops as we thought. They ought to have been properly dug and so we had to work and work and work.

It was work the whole time for your own protection and to get the wire out and so on. Then the trouble of working in that spot, as we had to, was that if you build a house at least you hope to live in it but we never went to the same place. You went somewhere else but we always complained. Perhaps we were wrong. Our men were rather tall you see too, and it could be dangerous from exposure as well as backbreaking. There were the usual quiet periods and then there would be a day pretty quiet as long as you didn't show your head but you couldn't really work except at night. Night was all work: little dugouts, but not proper dugouts, and so you worked away. Then you were taken out and then you came back and so that was the normal routine. I was very fortunate because I only had that routine from, would it be, that April to the Somme in September. Some chaps had had a year of it and it was very hard work.

I think going up a communication trench if it was a bad one, not very deep, was alarming because the Germans had machine guns trained on to the corners and I developed what was thought to be a very odd system but at least a system. Occasionally you have charge of a company because your company commander had gone back or something on a course. My system was of making them walk outside the communication trenches on those occasions. It was thought foolhardy but I took the view that it was better to be shot through the ankle than through the head, which was shared by my men. It gave me an unusual reputation for courage but it was really timidity.

I know it sounds awfully impertinent to say so but the Brigade of Guards was quite a unique system and the Grenadiers of course, was the best regiment in the Brigade. We thought the Coldstream, quite good, we thought the Scot Guards, a little indisciplined, and the Irish Guards fought well but were quite mad, but in fact, the Brigade of Guards was a similar organization to the Greek phalanx; a complete system of discipline unique of its kind. It is difficult to describe it at length and many people must have done it. Naturally being a scholar, and if you follow soldiering as I did, it has amused me, that the contrast from leaving this more or less undisciplined group of people at Southend and entering a properly organized machine was very great.

The commanding officer hardly appeared. The adjutant ran the show except in battle or training, under him the sergeant major and two drill sergeants. In your own company you depended on your company sergeant major and your company quartermaster sergeant who were probably men of seven or eight years' service. The general routine was a very high discipline inwards but not externally imposed. Indeed the discipline might not have satisfied the barracks at home but good discipline combined with a great sense of comradeship was the thing. For instance, in the mess, you called everybody by their Christian name. You weren't allowed to call the commanding officer Sir or anything like that. You wouldn't call him Colonel. It was a great sort of comradeship between the officers and downwards. In your own platoon you depended on your platoon sergeant. You got to know the chaps when you were out for a bit which we were when we were forming up for the Somme. After all, you censored all their letters. You read them, a knowledge which gave me a first insight into working-class life which I had never seen and was very interesting. It held me in great stead when I became a Member of Parliament for Stockton. They would come to you with their troubles. His wife had gone off with a man. What was he to do, and that kind of thing. You had a very friendly relationship.

Then there were the great jokes. Of course, every battalion had its jokes. To the young officer, the biggest man, balloon-sized, was the battalion sergeant major, in our case a man called Wood, known as 'Timber' Wood of course. When we had a rather good line of trenches, he would come up. He hardly ever appeared in the general run of things but if he did it would be in the daytime to everybody's annoyance and to do what he called a bit of 'sniping' through a loophole. And he would come up with the drill sergeant and a batman and after a long interval he would shoot off a shot and the drill sergeant looking over the top with a periscope would say, 'Got him, Sir,' and everybody would say, 'Yes, got him Sir.' Of course, he hadn't hit a thing and then that went on a bit and then he solemnly marched off. All the amusements and jollities of life and the traditions, which had formed themselves already. There was a very high standard I think of friendship between the officers and men because after all we asked them to do quite hard things but under discipline. It is difficult to describe. Not a bit like Naval discipline. It was nothing like the difference in those days between the lower deck and the officers: not at all. After all we lived together in the trench so it was rather different. Everybody had a nickname. I was just known as Mac but I had a ridiculously high reputation for courage I see in some letters. It is not true at all.

At this stage of the recording there is a short loss of Mr Macmillan's voice. He was describing taking out a patrol, being wounded, and being unable to write the subsequent report. It was therefore given under interrogation by the platoon sergeant who, asked what he had done when his officer was wounded, replied that he had hit the German who had thrown the grenade at Mr Macmillan, on the head with his club and his hat or helmet had come off. Asked what he had done then, the sergeant's response was: 'I hit him again with my club and the back of his head came off.'

Mr Macmillan resumes his story with an account of his experience in the September 1916 Guards Division assault on the German positions on the Somme.

We didn't arrive at the battle until about the beginning of September and then the order came to move up and we marched up. Of course, in those days they marched and they sang. I always remember that there was a lot of singing. We marched up and we eventually came to a place called Mailly Maillet and there there was a great mass of troops. I remember where we were very well because we went up past it on a Sunday. There was a great mass of the Highland Division all singing songs. It was an impressive sight of them having church on Sunday in the square and singing the old Scottish songs which rather touched me. Then we went up and lay somewhere and there it was. We had heard about the battle but not much. You don't get much news as a private soldier in the ranks. We knew of course that something big was going on but in fact we got very little news or bothered about it very much.

The only thing that I remember was that the night before we had to go up or day before – why they asked me I don't know, I suppose it was our company, I was still belonging to a platoon not a company – I was told to go up and just make sure of the way. It was very dark and a very difficult way to get our battalion into the front line, from which we were to make the attack, so I went up with an orderly. I was rather good at map-making. It amused me. I got it very clear into his mind and mine and I always remember as well there was a particular point where it was difficult to turn and there was a dead German soldier on the ground with his hand out like that and I noticed that as a sort of helpful mark. I hoped it would be there the next day when we came up to our trenches the evening before the battle.

Attacking the next morning – I think we were the leading company but mine was not the leading platoon – I could see the company and I watched with interest and amusement and great confidence that practically every man shook the dead German by the hand and said something of the order of, 'Goodbye, Fritz, meet you soon.' That meant they were in good heart. Wonderful, they would be all right then.

So, my experience was very small. Well then, we had this show and at 4 o'clock in the morning we all got up. Colonel de Crespigny, who never kept any order of any kind, the Grenadier Guards were very undisciplined upwards, very well disciplined downwards, he walked in front. I can see him now. A gold peak hat and gold spurs, which he always wore contrary to rules. Never touched through the whole war. In the darkness we formed-up. Now the forming-up is an awkward moment. Say you were to attack at five in the morning and you had to be there like every team about two hours before. Even if it is lining the streets for royalty, it is always two hours that you wait and then of course, it is a bit touchy (nerve-wracking). The men separated and people go off a bit. I remember one officer who was an awfully brave chap. He knew he would be killed, and indeed he was, and you have to help the men out. I remember a Corporal Newton coming and saying to me, we were just walking along and he said, 'Can you give me anything of yours, Sir?' and I gave him a silk handkerchief which his mother sent to me fifty years later.

Well, then you start, but that is an awkward period you have been through, that I admit. And then you advance without seeing much or knowing much and we took what is called the first objective. We formed-up and there had been many casualties: a certain amount of shelling. I was hit in the knee with a fragment of shell. It wasn't enough to put me out of the show although it became extremely tiresome afterwards: much worse than my big wound. We had done what was required of us and then we got back into our trench and we were told to hold it. We were not to take the second objective because the people on our right weren't up. We were going to make an attack later in the afternoon on to the second objective. Between us and the second objective was a very tiresome machine-gunner fellow shooting at us. Somebody said to me, I think the commanding officer or my Captain, 'We must take him out.' So I collected three or four men and we went off to go for him and unfortunately he got me and that was the end of me. My men got him I learned later but he got me through the pelvis and destroyed my back and pelvis. Our chaps had gone on ahead, on to the next objective I suppose. I could do nothing except roll myself down into the bottom of a shell hole.

Unfortunately the attack on the second objective failed and our chaps were driven back to the first objective. So I was in a very curious position all day, which I was quite conscious enough to know, between the two positions after our attack was driven back. I would have said it was towards evening when they were driven back over me and I knew that I was in between the two lines. How far was the distance between the lines? I should think perhaps 150 yards, 200 yards perhaps, but I was in the middle. Then each side started shelling each other and, except for shorts or overs, I was in a rather good position.

I remember the Germans making a couple of counter-attacks which were driven back by our people and looking out of the corner of my eye I could just see them running round the shell hole. They didn't bother to come down because they were trying to make an attack and then, when they were pushed off, they were driven back again. Then somewhere when night fell, I think somewhere about nine or ten perhaps because they had to look for people who were wounded in no-man's-land, and they knew where I was more or less because the other man with me had come back, or perhaps there was another man too somewhere of my little team, a man came out and it turned out to be Sergeant Major Lawton. It was in the darkness then and he took me away, and that was about the middle of the night I suppose. I was there all day and had been reading a book in Greek, which happily I had in a pocket. My wounds were not awfully painful then.

I got to the trench and the commanding officer said, 'You must go back,' and I was carried back. There was supposed to be a dressing station at Ginchy. The two stretcher-bearers carried me back and there was another fellow called Ritchie who was also badly wounded. He was hit in the arm. He could really have walked.

When we got to Ginchy it was quite clear there was no dressing station. It was being shelled so I said, 'This is ridiculous to take four unwounded men through this place. Tell the stretcher-bearers to put us down short of the little village and go home.' That is back to their aid post.

The men did as they were ordered. They could see the sense of it. I said there can be no dressing station there because it was finished. It had disappeared. It hardly existed. It was just burning. We were outside of it. So, then I crawled along. I couldn't walk really but somehow I got myself along to I think the far side of the little village. By this stage I was separated from the other wounded man. It was very alarming. I got very frightened. Well, you know, no responsibility to exercise then. Courage is chiefly a matter of vanity I think, or pride at any rate. I don't remember any more except rolling down into a ditch. I was picked up I think the next day by some artillery carriers or something and taken down. I don't remember much more except being in a dressing station. Then moved much further back.

I was in and out of hospital for about two years, yes, over two years. They kept trying to take bits out and then my mother got another surgeon and then he said, 'He is young and healthy, has lived a good and honourable life, let nature do it.' So, after many operations to try and take out these bits of bullets and bits of water bottle that had got in, they stopped doing that and eventually they did heal over, but I still had a tube in when I went as an ADC in 1919 and I had to see to this every day.

As for my time in and out of hospital, I don't remember very much. The coming of the Lloyd George government was well received by us in our room. That I remember. The fall of Asquith was thought by the officers to be a good thing. We all thought it was a good thing. Lloyd George would be more energetic. At any rate something new. That was in December 1916. It made quite a big impact. Then I would come out of hospital for a bit and then go back again you know. In fact, I had a little job at Chelsea in the drill room to help you know, and then I would go back into hospital.

As a final word, my war service and then seeing the same people unemployed on the Tees had a tremendous influence upon me. You see, my first political experience was among the same boys in the bad times when half the population was unemployed and I lived with that. That is why I wrote so much about it but I think the war service was one's first experience of seeing ordinary people, except at home, a few gardeners and foresters. Unless you have a very great estate with a large number of employees you aren't likely to meet working men much. It was the war that threw us all together and then I found them again in my twenty-five years on Teesside. Not twenty-five years in Brighton or Bexley or some suburb, but ordinary working men who were in the war. They were mostly Durham Light Infantry, a lot of Grenadiers, a lot of Guardsmen.

Of course I had read about the 'Two Nations' before that. I had read Disraeli before that; I had read *Sybil* before that, a wonderful book. I was fully conscious of the 'Two Nations' and the need to bring them together.

Index